AUTOMOTIVE
AIR CONDITIONING
HANDBOOK—
INSTALLATION, MAINTENANCE & REPAIR

AUTOMOTIVE
AIR CONDITIONING
HANDBOOK—
INSTALLATION, MAINTENANCE & REPAIR

JOHN E. TRAISTER

TAB BOOKS Inc.
BLUE RIDGE SUMMIT, PA. 17214

FIRST EDITION

FIRST PRINTING—MARCH 1978
SECOND PRINTING—APRIL 1979
THIRD PRINTING—APRIL 1981

Traister, John E.
     Automotive air-conditioning handbook.

     Includes index.
          1. Automobiles—Air conditioning—Maintenance and repair.I.
Title.
TL271.5.T7   629.2'77   77-18948
ISBN 0-8306-9980-5
ISBN 0-8306-1020-0 pbk.

Cover art courtesy of Chrysler Corporation.

Preface

Before 1971, only a small percentage of the passenger cars manufactured in the United States were equipped with factory-installed air conditioners; it was thought to be a luxury reserved only for the wealthy and installed mostly on the more expensive cars. Today, however, the percentage of installations has increased tenfold—close to 80% of all cars manufactured in this country have air conditioning installed.

But what do these figures mean to the average car owner? They mean there are over 60,000,000 cars on the road with air conditioners that are going to need servicing several times during their lives—including the unit on your own car! With all of these units to service, air-conditioning mechanics can demand top dollar and still turn away work—just as TV repairmen. Therefore, the average car owner is going to have to pay through his nose each time his unit needs servicing.

Another factor to consider is the time element. You have paid dearly for the option of having air conditioning installed in your car. When the unit becomes inoperative, you want the problem solved immediately; you don't want to wait until cool weather for a serviceman to get to your car when you need it during the hot summer months.

In reality, the most common problems occurring in automotive air-conditioning units are within the capabilities of the average handyman—the do-it-yourselfer who wants to save both time and money by doing jobs within his or her capabilities right at home.

This book, therefore, is meant to fill a need for those who are looking for a practical text on automotive air-conditioning maintenance and repair—one that takes the guesswork out of most servicing problems and tells you the *what, how,* and *why* of automotive air-conditioning servicing.

The chapters are designed in a logical sequence so that you learn first things first: how automotive air conditioners work, the most common problems that occur, the basic principles of servicing and maintaining your air conditioners. As you read from chapter to chapter, you will be continually expanding your knowledge of air conditioning fundamentals and servicing techniques. When you have finished the book, you will be able to solve most any servicing problem that you are likely to encounter with your own system—regardless of the make of air conditioner you have in your car. You can then stay ahead of the game by saving money on your own air-conditioning repairs, and performing the repair immediately without waiting for a repairman. Finally, you may even be able to pick up a few extra dollars by helping out your friends and neighbors with their air-conditioning systems in your spare time.

While this book is aimed primarily at the handyman or do-it-yourselfer, its contents would also be of interest to the pros—especially those who are beginning a career as automotive air-conditioning mechanics.

I am indebted to the many manufacturers who supplied some of the illustrations in this book and up-to-date reference material on the modern techniques of servicing air conditioners on the later-model passenger cars.

John E. Traister

Contents

Chapter 1

Operating Principles Of
Automotive Air Conditioners

Comfort air conditioning—as we know it today—has been growing rapidly since the early 1940s. At first, it was installed only in commercial buildings where the added customer traffic (and consequently more sales) would offset the added cost of installing and operating the system. Businesses were also discovering that office and factory workers were able to produce more in a comfortable air-conditioned area.

The inclusion of air conditioning in new and existing homes, however, was then considered to be a prohibitive luxury—reserved only for the wealthy. But it didn't take long for our society to appreciate the comfort of air conditioning so much that many people were willing to pay the cost so that they could be as comfortable at home as they were at work. This desire started the residential air-conditioning boom of the 1950s, which has been on the increase ever since. In fact, nearly every new home under construction today includes central air conditioning in its budget. Many of the older homes have also been updated with central air conditioning, or individual room or window units.

By the 1960s many people were enjoying air conditioning at work and in their homes...enjoying it so much that the next logical step was to include the same comfort in their automobiles. When they finished a day's work in a comfortable air-conditioned office, all they had to do in order to ride home in comfort was to roll down the window of their car for a brief moment to let out the blistering hot air, and crank their car engine. By the time the car was underway and the window rolled up, the air-conditioning system was putting forth cool air which rapidly lowered the interior temperature of the car as well as dehumidified the air.

It was soon learned that air conditioning also worked wonders in rainy weather, clearing a windshield fogged so badly that driving was difficult—if not impossible. In mild or cold weather, the car's defroster working with the car's heating system would take care of the job. In hot weather, however, the use of this defrosting system was highly uncomfortable to the occupants in the car. This is where the air-conditioning system comes in. Since these units dehumidify the air, they defrost (and defog) any glass on the car. The air-conditioning controls or thermostat will maintain a temperature that is not too cold while using it as a defroster.

BASIC OPERATING PRINCIPLES

A diagram of a conventional air-conditioning system is shown in Fig. 1-1. This diagram is typical of all refrigeration units regardless of whether they're for use in residential, automotive, or other applications. In general, heat is picked up by the boiling refrigerant at the evaporator and then rejected at the condenser; this heat must then be carried away by air, water, the evaporation of water, or some other means. The compressor provides the energy for the system's operation, while the function of the controls or expansion valve is to permit the compressor to maintain a pressure difference. A more detailed study of this system will be covered later on in this chapter.

Although both residential and automotive air-conditioning systems operate on the same basic principle, the two units operate in entirely different environments. For example, a residential air conditioner operates on a steady source of electrical power (120–240 volts, 60 cycles) and is never exposed to extremes in operating conditions.

The automotive system, however, is belt-driven by the car's engine which operates anywhere from a slow idle in city traffic to high speed on the highway. The automotive air-conditioning system must properly cool the interior of the car regardless of the speed the engine happens to be running. Then too, the unit is subjected to extremely high (300°) temperatures under the hood as well as continuous vibration from the engine and road shocks. From these statements, we can fully understand why the automotive air-conditioning system is going to need certain repairs from time to time.

THEORY OF REFRIGERATION

In order for the car owner to approach the job of maintenance and repair on his air-conditioning system more intelligently, a brief

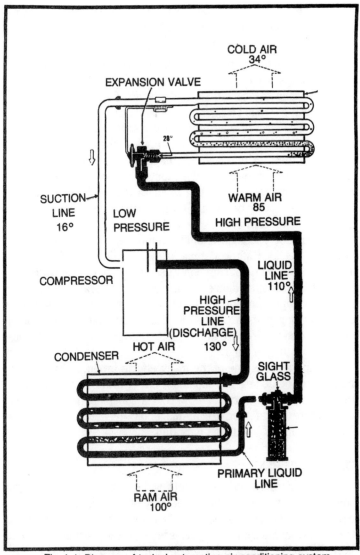

Fig. 1-1. Diagram of typical automotive air-conditioning system.

explanation of the theory of refrigeration is in order. With this foundation, you will be in a much better position to troubleshoot your automotive air-conditioning system, and correct the problem in the shortest period of time.

Refrigeration is a process which involves the transfer of heat from any given article or space. In the mechanical air-conditioning system this transfer of heat is accomplished by means of a refrigerant, which is conditioned so that it will absorb heat from the space to be cooled, and after this absorption, conditioned so it will give up this heat to an outside air supply.

To understand the operation of a mechanical refrigerating system, it is necessary to understand a few of the fundamental laws of heat, especially the conditions under which liquid refrigerant will vaporize and gaseous refrigerant will liquefy.

Heat is a form of energy which will cause certain changes in substances; that is, heat may cause the substance to become warmer, to melt, or to evaporate, depending upon the quantity of heat absorbed and the state of the substance. For example, at room temperature water is a liquid. But when water is made hot enough, it becomes a gas known as steam. If water is made cold enough, we all know that it will turn into a solid called ice.

Heat is not a substance and therefore cannot be measured by volume or weight. Rather, it must be measured by the effect that it produces. The unit most commonly used to measure heat is the Btu (British thermal unit), defined as the amount of heat necessary to raise the temperature of one pound of water by 1°F. Automotive air-conditioning units are rated in Btus. The unit in your car is probably rated somewhere around 20,000 Btuh—capable of producing 20,000 Btus per hour.

Temperature is one of the many effects produced by heat—a measure not of the heat in a substance but of its intensity. Temperature indicates how warm or how cold a substance is. Whenever temperature is referred to in this book, it will be in degrees Fahrenheit unless otherwise indicated.

TRANSFER OF HEAT

The basic law in the transfer of heat is that it can flow only from a body of a higher temperature to a body of a lower temperature—never in the reverse direction. Therefore, the result of such a transfer is that the colder body gains heat and the warmer body loses heat. When the colder body receives heat, two changes can take place: (1) its temperature may rise or (2) its state may change from solid to liquid or liquid to gas. When a warmer body loses heat, two changes can also take place: (1) its temperature may lower or (2) its state may change. This change will be from a gas to a liquid or from a liquid to a solid.

When the state of a body is changed, either from a solid to a liquid, a liquid to a gas, or vice versa, the temperature of the body remains constant during the time the change is taking place. For example, assume that a glass jar is filled with a solid piece of ice. The temperature of the ice will have to be less than 32°F to remain as a solid. However, if heat is applied to the jar, the ice will warm up to 32°F and then begin to melt. Although heat continues to be added, the temperature of the ice will not rise above 32°F until all the ice has melted. After the ice has melted entirely, the temperature of the water will continue to rise (as long as the heat is applied) until the water reaches 212°F. At this temperature, the water will start to boil but the water temperature will remain at 212°F even though heat is still applied to the jar. Continued heating of the boiling water will result in vaporizing the water into steam. Figure 1-2 shows the temperature changes resulting from heating ice.

Water, however, does not always boil at 212°F; the boiling point varies according to the pressure to which it is subjected. To illustrate, water in a boiler under 100 psi pressure boils at approximately 338°F, while water under reduced pressure (less than atmospheric) can be made to boil at below its freezing point!

The boiling points of different liquids vary a great deal. Under normal atmospheric pressure, water will boil at 212°F, alcohol at 173°F, mercury at 674 1/2°F, methyl chloride at −11°F, ammonia at −29°F, and Freon −12 at −22°F. The latter two liquids have been used extensively in refrigeration units. Like water, if the pressure of these liquids is increased, the temperature at which they boil is raised, and if the pressure is decreased, the boiling point will be lowered.

To boil, a liquid must receive heat from a substance of a higher temperature. To boil water at normal atmospheric pressure, for example, the source of heat must have a temperature higher than 212°F. However, Freon-12 will boil at atmospheric pressure if the source of heat is only slightly higher than −22°F. In fact, melting ice at 32°F is really warm when compared with the boiling point of Freon-12 at −22°F. For this reason, Freon-12 at atmospheric pressure can be easily boiled and vaporized at the temperature of melting ice. Heat will flow to the Freon-12, causing it to vaporize into a gas.

THE REFRIGERATING PROCESS

By placing the refrigerant in a suitable container and then placing the container in contact with a warmer substance, the liquid refrigerant will be vaporized by the warmer substance. Although the liquid refrigerant is receiving heat from the warmer substance, the temperature of the refrigerant will not increase as long as the pressure remains constant. This is due to the fact that heating a boiling liquid does not increase its temperature but instead vaporizes

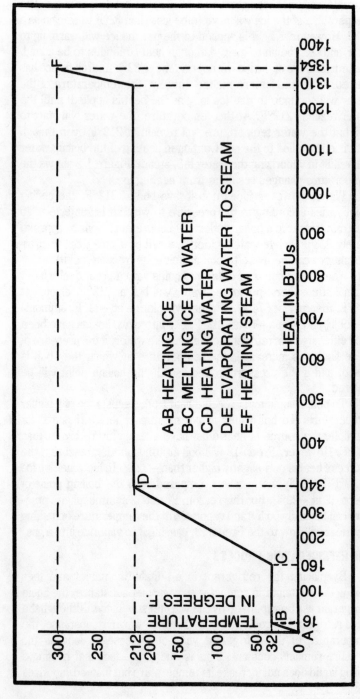

Fig. 1-2. Temperature changes resulting from the addition or subtraction of heat from water.

A-B HEATING ICE
B-C MELTING ICE TO WATER
C-D HEATING WATER
D-E EVAPORATING WATER TO STEAM
E-F HEATING STEAM

HEAT IN BTUs

TEMPERATURE IN DEGREES F.

the liquid more quickly. With the pressure remaining constant, the liquid refrigerant will continue to boil at a constant temperature as long as it receives heat from the warmer substance.

The warmer substance, in giving up its heat to the refrigerant, must naturally undergo some change. Unless it freezes in the process, loss of heat will result in a lowering of its temperature until it is equal to that of the refrigerant. Heat can then no longer flow from the warmer substance to the refrigerant and the boiling or vaporizing process will stop.

OPERATION OF A REFRIGERATION SYSTEM

The illustration in Fig. 1-3 shows a simplified diagram of a complete refrigeration system. This is basically the same system used in all types of cooling units like your home refrigerator, home air conditioners, and, of course, the air-conditioning system used in cars. The basic components consist of a compressor, a condenser, an expansion valve, and an evaporator.

Compressor

The purpose of the compressor in Fig. 1-3 is threefold. First, it pumps or withdraws heat-laden gas from the cooling unit through the suction line; second, it compresses this gas to a high pressure and discharges it into the condenser; and third, its discharge valve acts as the dividing point between the low- and high-pressure sides of the refrigerating system.

Condenser

The function of the condenser is to reject the heat in the refrigerant to the surrounding air or to a water supply, condensing it to a liquid. One type of air-cooled condenser is the fin-and-tube, or radiator, type. With this type, comparatively cool air is passed through a compact, finned radiator by a fan on the motor pulley; your car's engine cooling system is a good example of such a unit.

Expansion Valve

As the compressor pumps the refrigerant from the cooling unit it must be replenished with low-pressure, low-temperature liquid capable of absorbing heat. This is accomplished by a liquid control valve, which is known as an expansion valve. This valve has three functions. First, it acts as a pressure-reducing valve, reducing the pressure of the high-pressure liquid that was condensed by the condenser to a low-pressure, low-temperature liquid capable of

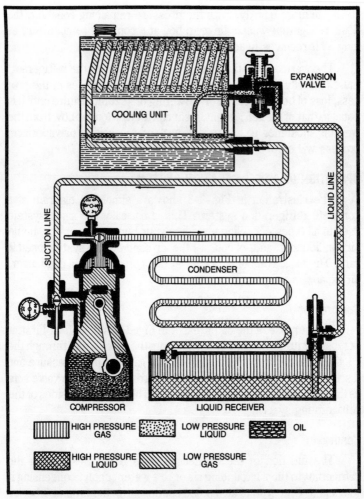

Fig. 1-3. Simplified diagram of a complete refrigeration system.

absorbing heat; second, it maintains a constant refrigerant pressure in the evaporator; and third, the valve acts as a dividing point between the high- and low-pressure sides of the refrigerating system.

Evaporator

The evaporator is that part of the refrigerating system directly connected with the refrigerating process. The refrigerant in the cooling unit absorbs heat from the space or air to be refrigerated and so cools it. As the evaporator absorbs heat from the space or material to be refrigerated, the low-pressure, low-temperature liquid refrigerant in the vaporizing tubes (or coils) is vaporized.

The evaporators found in most automotive air-conditioning systems are of the type known as *headered* type, like the one shown in Fig. 1-4. The refrigerant in this type of evaporator—after passing through the expansion valve—flows into a reservoir which connects all of the evaporator tubes. The refrigerant makes a single pass through a single tube, evaporating as it does so. The refrigerant then flows through a suction throttling valve (described later) on its way to the condenser.

DESCRIPTION OF AN AUTOMOTIVE AIR-CONDITIONING SYSTEM

Figure 1-5 shows a pictorial diagram of an automotive air-conditioning system. Note that the condenser is mounted just behind the grille and in front of the radiator. Air flow through the condenser is dependent upon the speed of the car as well as wind velocities. To illustrate, a car travelling at 55 mph on a calm day has a net air flow through the condenser of approximately 55 mph. However, if the same car runs into a 20-mph headwind, the net velocity of air over the condenser will then increase to 75 mph. From this, we can see that the amount of heat removed from the condenser is not constant, but will vary as the air velocity changes with the speed and direction of the car.

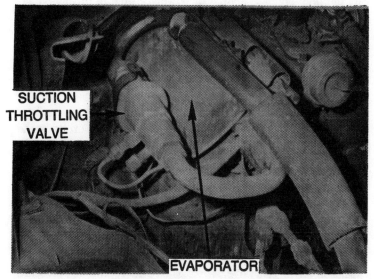

Fig. 1-4. View of evaporator from engine side of car; Note the suction throttling valve.

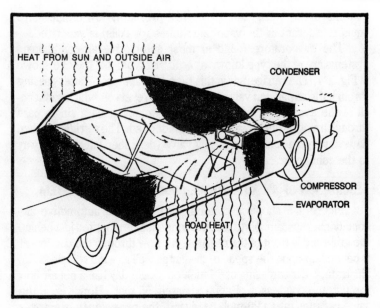

Fig. 1-5. Pictorial diagram of an automotive air conditioning system.

Because of its large electrical requirements, the popular totally enclosed hermetic compressor—used in refrigerators and residential air-conditioners—cannot be used in automotive systems. In a car, the only practical source of power capable of driving an air-conditioning compressor is the car engine. Therefore, an open compressor must be used—one that has a shaft extending through the compressor body. The compressor is driven by the engine shaft through pulleys, belts, and a magnetic clutch. The type of compressor is not entirely free of leaks; however, a properly installed shaft seal permits only a small amount of refrigerant loss.

The location of the compressor in Fig. 1-5 is behind the radiator and just above the motor. Note that the compressor is driven by the fan belt.

In general, the compressor increases the temperature and pressure of the refrigerant vapor—just as in any refrigeration system—and routes this high-pressure vapor through a rubber discharge line to the condenser (Fig. 1-6). The condenser removes heat from the vapor, causing it to condense to a liquid before it enters the receiver-drier through the condenser outlet tubes.

From the receiver-drier, the liquid refrigerant flows to the expansion valve. This valve, as explained earlier, permits a pressure drop in the liquid circuit. The low-pressure liquid is sprayed into the evaporator and changes to a vapor. When it emerges from the

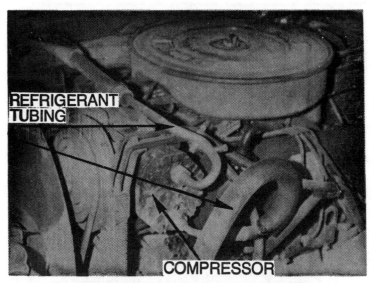

REFRIGERANT TUBING

COMPRESSOR

Fig. 1-6. Air-conditioning compressor with related tubing.

evaporator coil, the low-pressure gas returns through the suction line to the compressor where its pressure and temperature are again raised.

A typical automotive air-conditioning air-flow pattern is shown in Fig. 1-7. In most factory-installed systems like this one, the air within the passenger compartment can be recirculated, or fresh air can be brought in from the outside. When the inside air is being recirculated, it passes through the evaporator and is routed by ducts

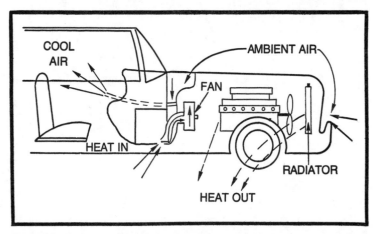

COOL AIR

AMBIENT AIR

FAN

HEAT IN

RADIATOR

HEAT OUT

Fig. 1-7. Path of air flow in an automobile; the air to which the heat is transferred exhausts through the engine compartment and under the car.

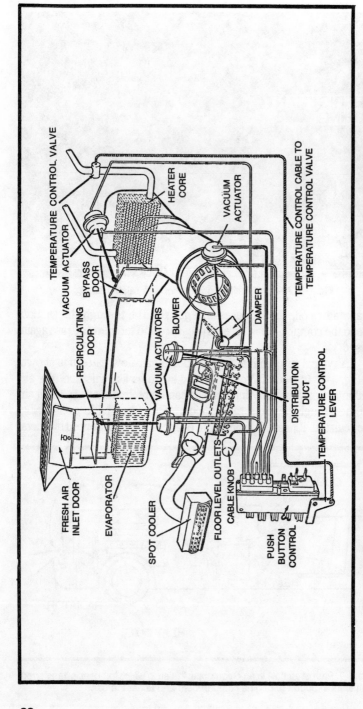

Fig. 1-8. Air flow system showing blower, ductwork, dampers, and vacuum controls. Courtesy of General Motors Corp.

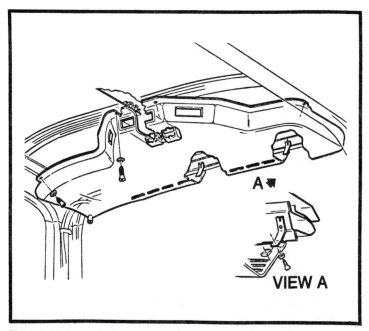

Fig. 1-9. View of rear duct in an overhead air-conditioning system—utilized mostly in vans and other light trucks. Courtesy of General Motors Corp.

to pass through the heater core or to bypass the heater core. The air then passes through a duct system under the dash and enters the passenger compartment through various directional outlet grilles (Figs. 1-8 and 1-9).

The heat absorbed by the refrigerant in the evaporator is carried to the compressor, raised to a higher pressure and temperature, and then routed to the condenser. The condenser transfers the heat to the outside air flowing over the condenser tubes and fins. The car's radiator fan also serves as a condenser fan to help remove heat when the car is stationary or traveling at speeds up to approximately 40 mph. At higher speeds, the radiator fan becomes unimportant as the forward motion of the car provides a greater air flow than the fan. The air passes through the engine compartment and under the car as shown in Fig. 1-7.

From the preceding paragraphs, you should know that automotive air-conditioning systems consist of two subsystems: the refrigeration system and the air-handling system. All of the parts of both subsystems must be integrated in order to provide cooling to the car's interior. The following chapters show how to keep all these parts working properly.

Chapter 2

Maintaining Your

Car's Cooling System

The primary desire of any car owner is to keep his car in top running condition at all times, and at the lowest possible cost. Several manuals on the market amply cover automotive troubleshooting; because this book deals with automotive air conditioning, this chapter will be devoted only to maintenance procedures for the air-conditioning and related systems.

An air conditioner will always cause the engine to work harder and have some effect on the normal operation of the car in general, especially the car's cooling system. Therefore, it would be logical to begin with the maintenance porcedures for these affected items.

THE CAR'S COOLING SYSTEM

Begin the inspection of the car's cooling system by checking the condition of all water hoses, especially at the ends (Fig. 2-1). With the engine idling, closely examine all hoses for leaks. Be careful not to get your hands near the fan blade while the engine is running (see Fig. 2-2).

Leaks at the hoses ends can often be repaired by loosening the hose clamp, removing and trimming the end of the hose, and then replacing. Leaks between ends, of course, mean replacing the entire hose.

Sometimes, although there are no leaks, your car's cooling system still gives you trouble. For example, perhaps your engine runs cool enough at low speeds, but the temperature rises when you hit higher speeds on the open road. Perhaps the lower hose from the

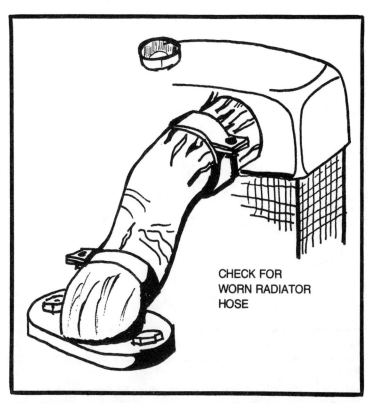

CHECK FOR
WORN RADIATOR
HOSE

Fig. 2-1. Begin the inspection of the car's cooling system by checking the condition of all water hoses.

CAUTION-FAN

Fig. 2-2. Heed this caution when the engine is running; never place the hands near the fan blade.

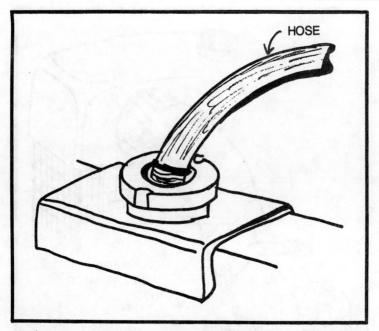

Fig. 2-3. Reverse-flushing the car's radiator and engine block—especially when done with a good de-clogging solution—should solve the problem of slight clogging.

radiator to the engine block is collapsing. Slight clogging of the radiator core could also be causing the trouble; that is, the water is not able to pass through the system fast enough.

If a collapsing hose seems to be the trouble, replace it with a new heavy-duty type. Reverse-flushing (Fig. 2-3) the car's radiator and engine block—especially when done with a good solvent solution—should solve the problem of slight clogging.

Other conditions that may cause your engine to overheat include: a slipping fan belt, insufficient oil, overloading, and not enough water in the cooling system. You can also cause temperature problems by overfilling! Keep the water level not higher than two inches below the top of the overflow pipe. Make sure that the pressure cap is working properly (Fig. 2-4). Pressure permits a rise in coolant temperature without boiling; therefore, if the pressure cap is not operating properly, the water is likely to boil at too low a temperature and run out the overflow pipe. As this water continues to boil, the water level becomes too low in the cooling system and causes the engine to overheat.

Another common cause of engine overheating is a stuck exhaust manifold heat-control valve—stuck in the position which

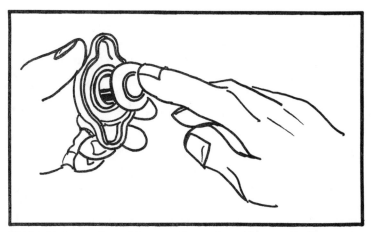

Fig. 2-4. Make sure the radiator pressure cap is working properly if your car is overheating.

results in constant preheating of the gas mixture. Keep this important valve free by spraying it frequently with some type of gum solvent.

One of the most common causes of engine overheating is a faulty thermostat. For this reason, every car owner should have his radiator thermostat checked annually—replacing it if found defective. Another common cause is the restriction of air flow through the condenser and radiator caused by the accumulation of bugs, dirt, paper, leaves, and the like (Fig. 2-5). Clean both of these units

Fig. 2-5. The accumulation of bugs and leaves in the car's grille can cause the engine to overheat as the debris blocks air passage to both the radiator and the condenser.

regularly, but be extremely careful not to bend or otherwise damage the delicate radiator or condenser fins and cores. A garden hose equipped with a nozzle will do wonders in removing this trash.

Now let's take a look at the various problems that occur with the actual automotive air-conditioning system, those that can be corrected by the average car owner. These problems are solved—as with any other type of troubleshooting—by first diagnosing the cause, and then correcting the problem by proven methods.

The diagnosis and correction of the problems covered in this chapter requires only a basic knowledge of mechanics and the use of common hand tools. Furthermore, this chapter has purposely avoided covering service problems which require you to come into direct contact with the refrigerant. Still, some safety precautions must be taken. For example, the R-12 refrigerant normally used in automotive air-conditioning systems is considered to be about the safest type available commercially, but it can still seriously hurt a person if handled carelessly. For this reason, wear safety goggles—or at least a pair of glasses—when checking or servicing any part of the air-conditioning system. If you're not going to be working with the refrigerant, disconnecting any of the refrigerant line, or taking apart any of the components through which the refrigerant circulates, why bother with the goggles? There are many reasons, but one of them is due to worn refrigerant lines. One of the lines may be worn to the point that only a slight pressure (by hand) could cause the line to break—allowing the refrigerant to escape. As R12 refrigerant escapes into the air, it evaporates so rapidly that it tends to freeze anything that it touches, including your flesh and eyes. R-12 in the eyes can cause blindness!

In addition, when refrigerant R-12 evaporates in the open air, it will displace all air in the immediate vicinity. If this area is enclosed and without adequate ventilation, the action could cause suffocation. Therefore, always maintain good ventilation in the area of the car and, as mentioned previously, always wear glasses or safety goggles.

THE ELECTRICAL SYSTEM

The electrical system has numerous duties to perform, from starting the engine to powering all the electrical necessities and luxury items including lights, radios, tape decks, windshield wipers, power windows, and parts of the air-conditioning system. Although the system runs throughout the car and is relatively complex, our concern for the moment is with its use in automotive air-conditioning systems.

There are two basic sources of energy for the electrical system: the battery and the alternator. The battery receives and stores electricity for starting the engine and operating lights and similar electrical items. This stored energy, however, is limited and must be replenished as the current is drained.

After the engine is started, electrical power is generated by the alternator (often called the generator), which meets all the electrical needs of the engine and other electrically powered devices. It also returns electricity to the battery (recharging) where it will be stored for the next starting.

The electrical current flowing from the battery or the alternator goes to the coil, which acts as a transformer to boost the 12 volts supplied by the battery or alternator to over 20,000 volts at very low amperage. The increased voltage is needed for the engine spark that ignites the mixture of gasoline and air in the cylinder.

This increased voltage goes only to the spark plugs; 12 volts goes from the battery to accessories such as the evaporator blower motor. The low voltage is normally referred to as the primary electrical circuit while the high voltage from the coil is called the secondary electrical circuit.

When electrically-operated air-conditioning controls, blowers, and the like begin to give trouble, most of the problems can be traced to a defective electrical system—for example, a blown fuse or a dead battery. While the battery certainly can be a weak link in an automobile's electrical system, the original trouble probably began with some external reason. Dirt on the battery terminals, for example, can cause poor contact so that the alternator cannot properly recharge the battery. The failure of other components directly related to the car's electrical generation system can also cause a dead battery, such as the voltage regulator, alternator, or defective wiring.

If your battery seems to be giving trouble, begin the diagnosis by checking the tension of the alternator drive belt (Fig. 2-6). Unlike the generators found on older cars—which didn't require a particularly tight drive belt—the newer alternators require a relatively tight belt to drive them properly. If your belt seems loose (you can depress it more than 1/2 inch when you press down halfway between the drive pulleys) adjust the tension. If the drive belt tension seems OK, check the battery cables and connections. Defective cables should be replaced and corroded terminals should be cleaned with a brush and soda compound. Also, make sure that the connections are tight at the battery terminals.

Fig. 2-6. Always check fan belts for proper tightness when your car shows any signs of overheating.

Connect a dc voltmeter between the positive battery cable and the battery post while all electrical equipment is turned off, including your electric clock. If you get no reading on the meter dial, test your battery with a hydrometer according to the meter's instructions. If the hydrometer test shows bad cells, replace the battery. If your battery checks out all right, the problem is probably in the car's voltage regulator or alternator.

During the voltmeter test, if the meter shows a reading, remove fuses from the car's fuse panel, one at a time, until the circuit drawing current is found. Repair the circuit; it probably has a short in the components or the wiring.

From the previous paragraphs, it would be safe to say that a frequently discharged battery would probably be caused by (1) alternator belt slipping, (2) faulty voltage regulator, (3) faulty alternator, (4) low voltage regulator setting, or (5) a worn-out battery.

CONTROLS

Most electrical controls are switches that operate electrical devices such as fans (blowers), magnetic clutches, solenoid valves, and relays. Once you get into troubleshooting your own automotive air-conditioning system, you will more than likely find that most of your troubles will be in these controls. Therefore, if you have a basic knowledge of how the controls work, you will find it easier to diagnose the problem.

Switches in your car function just as those that control the lights in your home—to open and close the circuits to electrical load devices. In both cases, the switch is connected between the power source and the load device, so that when the switch is ON (closed), the circuit is completed and the electrical device connected to the circuit is energized. When the switch is OFF (open), the load device is de-energized and it ceases to function.

There are several types of switches used in the typical automotive air-conditioning system. For example, there is usually a manual slide or pushbutton switch used to turn the air conditioner on and off, and a manual blower-speed selector to control the rate of air flow through the system. This selector switch may be combined with a control cable or vacuum control system that also operates the heater.

A thermostatic switch is one that responds to changes in temperature and is usually made up of two parts: a temperature sensor and an electrical switch. Most thermostats respond to the temperature inside the passenger compartment and regulate the air-conditioning system to maintain the desired temperature. Two types are normally used in automotive air-conditioning systems, the bimetal thermostat and the bellows type. The bimetal thermostat is the simplest of the two and its basic operaiton is shown in Fig. 2-7. The two essential parts are a bimetal strip and a stationary contact. As the name implies, the bimetal strip consists of strips of two different metals that are fused together. One of the metals is a

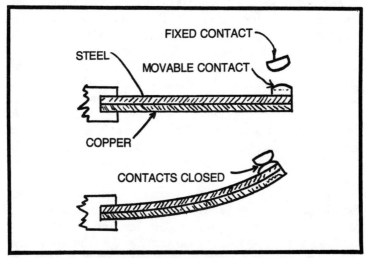

Fig. 2-7. Basic operation of a bimetal thermostat.

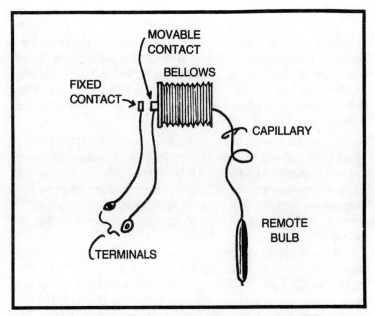

Fig. 2-8. Basic components of a bellows-type thermostat.

fast-expanding type such as copper, and the other is a relatively slow-expanding type such as steel. When the temperature rises, the copper will expand faster than the steel, causing the strip to bend in the direction of the steel. If one contact point is attached to the strip and another is fixed to the insulated base of the thermostat, the rise in temperature will cause the strip to bend and close the contacts, completing the electrical circuit. The flowing current will activate the magnetic clutch on the compressor, the blower, and other devices to start the air conditioner operating. When the car's interior is lowered to the desired temperature, the strip will straighten or bend in the other direction and open the contacts. This breaks the circuit, causing all electrically operated devices to stop functioning.

The operating temperature of the bimetal strip thermostat can be adjusted by moving the fixed contact, usually done with a set screw and a sliding band, on which the contact is mounted. This establishes the distance that the bimetal strip must bend to make or break contact.

A bellows-type thermostat is more sensitive than a bimetal thermostat and is generally used where close temperature control is required. This thermostat has a bellows unit with a capillary tube extending from the bellows, as shown in Fig. 2-8. The bellows and capillary tube contain a substance which expands with an increase in temperature and contracts with a decrease in temperature. The free end of the bellows operates a switch which normally consists of a pair of contacts similar to the ones used on the bimetal thermostat. When the bellows expand, closing the contacts, the circuit is completed and allows current to flow to the electrically operated devices operating the air-conditioning system.

A relay is another type of electrically operated switch. Essential parts include those shown in Fig. 2-9. Current flowing through the electromagnet produces a magnetic field. This field attracts the armature, a hinged strip of iron, pulling it down against the spring tension. The relay has one stationary contact and one contact on the armature. When the electromagnet is energized, the contacts are closed, completing an electrical circuit. When the electromagnet is de-energized, the magnetic field weakens and the spring pulls the contacts open, breaking the circuit. Relays of this type are normally used for remote control in an automotive air-conditioning system, and usually operate on very low current. They can, however, control a much greater current.

Safety controls are a part of every air-conditioning system. Fuses, for example, open a faulty or overloaded electrical circuit. A safety control device protects the compressor from mechanical seizure and complete failure by disengaging the compressor clutch when the refrigerant charge is low or lost. Safety controls are also incorporated to prevent the air-conditioning system from operating when the outside air temperature is too low.

Blowers used with air-conditioning systems usually have several speeds controlled by switches which route the current through various resistors connected in series with the motor windings. If you

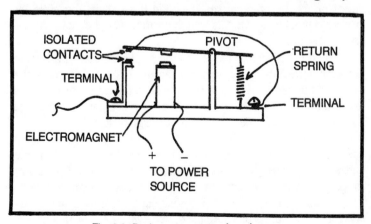

Fig. 2-9. Basic components of a relay.

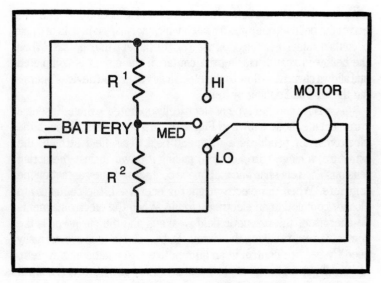

Fig. 2-10. A three-speed motor control circuit.

add resistance to a circuit, the current flow will decrease, while reducing resistance will cause the current flow to increase. The lower the resistance (or the greater the current), the faster the motor will run.

Figure 2-10 shows a three-speed system where voltage is applied to the motor through two resistors and a three-position switch. The switch is shown in the LO position in the illustration. By tracing the circuit, we find that current flows from the battery through resistors R_1 and R_2 and then to the motor. Two resistors in series offers the greatest resistance in this circuit; therefore the current is most limited in this switch position, and the motor runs at its slowest speed.

When the switch is moved to the MED position, the current flows from the battery through one resistor (R_1), then through the switch to the motor. With only one resistor, the circuit resistance is less than through the LO position and more current flows through the circuit—making the motor run at a higher speed.

Now assume that the switch is set in the HI position. If you trace the circuit in Fig. 2-10, you will see that the current from the battery flows directly to the fan motor—bypassing the resistors altogether—which permits the motor to run at its highest speed.

Rather than the "set" positions just described, some air-conditioning systems use variable speed switches. For this type of operation, the individual resistors as previously described are replaced by a variable resistor, or rheostat. In this arrangement, the resistor is made up of coiled wire with a semicircular resistance element. When the manual control knob is rotated, a sliding contact moves over the surface of the resistance wire. The farther the contact is rotated in a clockwise direction, the less resistance there is between the sliding contact and the battery terminal. As the resistance varies, so does the motor speed.

A cycling clutch-control system which turns the compressor on and off to maintain the desired discharge air temperature is incorporated in most automotive air-conditioning systems. A thermostat— connected in series with the magnetic clutch of the compressor— controls the compressor operation (see Fig. 2-11). In general, power from the car's electrical system is supplied to a terminal of the blower switch. When the blower is switched on, power is available at the air-conditioning terminal of the blower switch and also the thermostat. The circuit is completed through the closed contacts on the thermostat (if the thermostat calls for cooling) to the magnetic clutch on the compressor. With the clutch engaged, the compressor pumps refrigerant to cool the system.

TRACING CIRCUITS

You should now have a good idea of how switches work and, to some degree, how they are used in automotive air-conditioning systems. With this knowledge—and a little practice—you should be able to trace and troubleshoot most of the electrical problems that

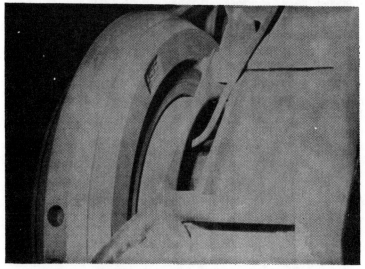

Fig. 2-11. Magnetic clutch showing control wire connection.

occur in your air-conditioning system. However, before you begin, you should try to obtain a circuit diagram of your car's electrical system. This diagram will show how the wiring, switches, relays, etc., are arranged and, most importantly, how the wires are color-coded. You should also have a voltmeter suitable for 12 volts dc or a neon test lamp. When using the latter, be careful not to short out wiring with the long exposed metal point of the tester. You can help prevent this by wrapping the point with insulating tape, leaving the tip exposed.

A simple test routine may go as follows: with your voltmeter or test lamp, test the fuse panel for current; then, with the ignition switch in accessory position, trace the "hot" wire (usually blue in color) from the fuse box to the blower switch. The terminal where the blue wire attaches should read hot on your meter or test lamp. If not, check for a blown fuse.

From here on out, you will want to refer to your wiring diagram, similar to the one shown in Fig. 2-12. Switch the blower switch to LO. The LO terminal on the blower switch (usually a dark green wire) should be hot. Trace this wire to the resistors in the switch and then to the air-conditioning relay. The LO or No. 2 terminal on the relay should indicate a voltage reading. Also check the hot side of the blower (usually a white wire); this terminal should also be hot and the blower should run at low speed. If the terminal at the fan reads hot but the fan does not operate, check the other fan terminal to see that it is properly grounded and then see if you get a voltage reading between the two terminals on the blower motor. If you do but the fan doesn't run, then the winding in the fan is probably bad and needs to be replaced.

Go back to the A/C switch and move it to MED (an orange wire should be connected to this terminal). Repeat the test procedures for this circuit as described for the circuit in LO position.

Continue by placing the blower switch in the HI position. The terminal with the white wire attached to the blower switch should now be hot, as well as terminal No. 4 (white wire) on the A/C relay. Check the fan terminals as described previously.

Next trace the brown wire (in most cases) from the blower switch to the line side of the A/C thermostat. The thermostat terminal should be hot when the blower switch is in any position except OFF. If the system calls for cooling, the other thermostat terminal should also show a voltage reading. Continue tracing this brown wire from the thermostat, through the dash panel grommet, to the engine compartment where the compressor and the magnetic

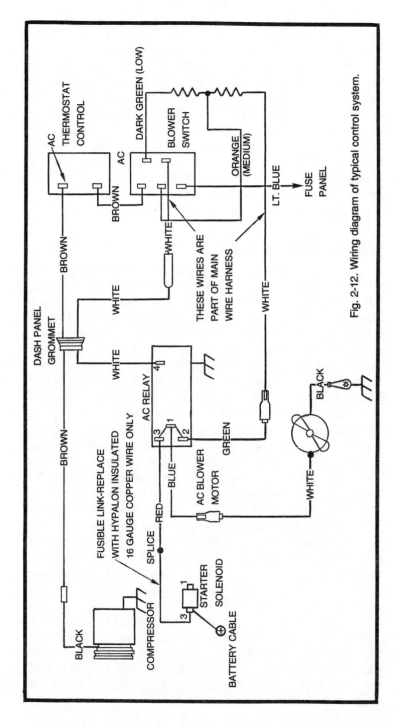

Fig. 2-12. Wiring diagram of typical control system.

clutch are located. When the thermostat calls for heating, the brown wire at the compressor clutch should be energized.

To summarize, start at the fuse panel at the sign of any malfunction of the electrical system, and check for a blown fuse. If one is blown, however, continue checking out the system before replacing it. Something caused the fuse to blow—a short circuit, an overload, a jammed motor blade, etc. Try to find and correct the trouble before replacing the fuse. Then check out the switches. If you get a reading on one side of the switch but none on the other when the switch is turned on, chances are you have a defective switch. For other problems not mentioned here, you can check the chapter on troubleshooting found later in the book.

CHECKING THE REFRIGERANT CHARGE

Instructions will be given in a later chapter for a complete test of your refrigerant, as well as how to recharge the system. However, due to the potential hazards involved, you may not want to tackle a complete inspection at this time. Still, there are simple ways that you can check for low refrigerant, some of which will be discussed here.

Locate the receiver-drier, mounted on the side of the condenser, and clean its sight glass. See Fig. 2-13. The unit will resemble a small cylinder, like the ones used for propane torches. It is basically a storage tank for liquid refrigerant, but also incorporates filter pads or a strainer to trap dirt.

Crank up the engine and while it idles, adjust the air-conditioning controls for maximum cooling. With the air conditioner operating, observe the sight glass. If a lot of bubbles appear in the glass, the air conditioner has an insufficient refrigerant charge. No bubbles indicate either an ample supply of refrigerant or no refrigerant at all. To determine which condition, have someone turn the air-conditioning controls on and off while you observe the sight glass; keep the engine running. If no bubbles appear during this cycling of the controls, no refrigerant is in the system, and you should have it charged at once. If no refrigerant is present, there is a good chance that you have a leak in the system. This should be checked and repaired at the same time.

You can easily test the receiver-drier to see if it is performing properly. After the system has been operating for five minutes or so, move your hand slowly over the receiver-drier from one end to the other. The temperature should be the same all over. If there are cold spots, the receiver-drier is restricting refrigerant flow and the unit should be replaced.

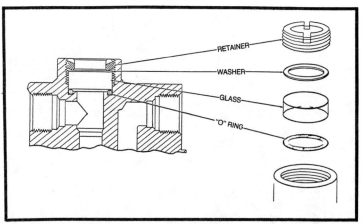

Fig. 2-13. Illustration showing sequence of typical sight glass replacement.

During ice-ups in the evaporator core, a thermostatic de-icing switch shuts down the air-conditioning system until the problem is corrected. To test this switch, fill a container with crushed ice, some water, and rock salt. The salt will cause the solution to drop below freezing just as in home ice cream freezers. Connect an ohmmeter to the switch (with the car's ignition switch *OFF*) and put the sensing tube in the ice-water-salt solution. There should be an infinite reading on the ohmmeter when the bulb is placed in the solution because the contacts should open. When the tube is taken out of the solution and warmed up, the contacts should close and a zero-resistance reading should appear on your ohmmeter. If the test doesn't work this way, the switch is defective and should be replaced.

BLOWER TROUBLES

If your blower motor seems to work but the air output is low, chances are that the trouble is a clogged air distribution system. Maybe some matchbooks were knocked off the top of your dash into the defrost vents, or perhaps you forgot to open the air-output dampers. The problem could be an obstruction caught between the blower fan and the housing. Check 'em all out.

Other reasons for poor air circulation could be a low charge in the battery, a loose wire connection, a short circuit, loose switch contacts, or a binding shaft or blower blades. However, most air circulation problems can be traced to a blown fuse, bad switch, loose connection, or a bad motor.

Don't overlook debris in your outside air intake vents. These are almost perfect for catching leaves, twigs, and similar trash,

Fig. 2-14. Don't overlook the trash that gathers in the car's outside air vents. Clean these regularly.

particularly on newer cars (Fig. 2-14). Clean these vents regularly as well as the grille screen, condenser, and radiator. These latter items can easily be cleaned with a garden hose or an air hose. It is best to blow from the engine side.

COMPRESSOR DRIVE BELT ADJUSTMENT

Satisfactory performance of the air-conditioning system is dependent upon drive belt condition and tension. If the proper tension is not maintained, belt slippage will greatly reduce air-conditioning performance and drive belt life. To avoid such adverse effects, use the following service procedure.

Any belt that has operated for a minimum of one hour is considered to be a "used" belt. Adjust the air-conditioning drive belts at the time of installation and then readjust after they have been used for one hour. Measure the drive belt tension regular service intervals, using the torque method, and readjust as needed.

On all new-belt installations, new-belt tension specifications should be used when the belt is first installed. Thereafter, these replacement belts should be serviced according to the above procedure. Always replace belts in pairs if so equipped; otherwise the old belt will have insufficient tension and the load will be primarily on the new belt.

Chapter 3

Install Your Own

Air-Conditioning System

Most experts will agree with the statement that it is best to have an automotive air-conditioning system installed at the factory when the car is built, rather than adding a unit later. The reasons for this statement are too numerous to mention in this chapter—but let's look at a few of the more important reasons.

First, factory-installed units are designed to fit a specific make and model of automobile and space is provided in the car for this particular unit. This makes a neat installation with very few—if any—of the components protruding into the passenger compartment. Appearance is further improved by building all controls into the instrument panel of the car. The heater and air-conditioning system are combined into one package which allows the system to be used as a dehumidifer. They are also built to operate with either recirculated air or all fresh air. Cars with factory-installed air-conditioning units also have larger engine radiators and fans which help to keep the engine from overheating.

Add-on air-conditioning units, while they do an excellent job of cooling, have none of the features mentioned in the paragraph above, with the exception of the dehumidification feature. Even this does not operate as well as the factory-installed units because the cooled, dehumidified air must be recirculated through a separate heater in the add-on systems. The factory-installed units pass air first through an evaporator and then through the heater in one passage.

The add-on units do have their advantages. They are less costly than the factory-installed units and are also available for some cars for which factory units are not manufactured. They will often provide faster cooling than factory-installed units and are much easier to service because their components are not built into the car like a factory-installed unit.

For those of you without factory-installed air conditioning in your car, kits are available for less than $200 that will allow you to install your own air-conditioning system in your car in just one weekend—and you'll still have time to watch the game on TV or play 18 holes at the club.

Before you rush out and purchase one of these add-on units, however, let's read through a typical installation of an automotive add-on air-conditioning unit.

While most of the kits on the market today are supplied with adapter kits to fit practically any make, model, and year of car as well as complete step-by-step instructions and drawings for installing the kit, you will still need some mechanical skills to properly install the unit. To illustrate, it will be necessary to remove the radiator, air cleaner, fan, pulleys, and perhaps the automatic transmission oil-cooler connections in order to fit the various air-conditioner components into the allotted space. The power steering apparatus may have to be removed in order to install the compressor. So don't think that the installation of an add-on unit is a breeze, even though it does come in "kit" form.

Fig. 3-1. Raise the hood of your car, look at the various items mentioned in the text, and decide how much time and how many tools are going to be required to remove the radiator, pulleys, etc.

Raise the hood of your car and look at the various items mentioned previously (Fig. 3-1). How much time and how many tools are going to be required to remove the radiator? How about the pulleys? If there's any doubt about your capability to remove these items (and put them back on the way they came off), you may be better off purchasing the kit and having a local garage make the installation for you. Or perhaps you can recruit the services of a neighbor who happens to have the tools and skills of an automobile mechanic. But if you have made minor repairs on your car already—such as tuning the engine—then you shouldn't have any problems installing an add-on air-conditioning unit yourself.

In general, an adapter kit comes with the unit to enable it to be installed in your make and model of car. It contains brackets and braces for mounting the compressor on top of the engine block, a fan and pulley, an idler pulley for adjusting the belt tension to the compressor, a crankshaft pulley, a V-belt, various fasteners and other hardware, as well as step-by-step instructions with illustrations.

To select an add-on unit from the many makes available, obtain sales literature and installation instructions from several manufacturers. After studying this literature closely, choose a unit that provides maximum clearance between the components and the existing parts of the car. This unit will be the easiest system to install, and experience has proven that the unit easiest to install normally gives the least mechanical trouble.

Once you have selected the unit, purchased it, and are ready to begin the installation, plan the job very carefully before you lift one wrench. The first step would be to read through the installation instructions completely to get an overall picture of the entire job. If this is one of your first projects of this type, it might be well to read these instructions over a second time. The instructions should tell you if any additional parts not included in the kit must be obtained. If so, purchase these parts before starting the installation. Then check over all items for defects or missing parts, using the parts list as a guide. Continue by listing the tools recommended in the instructions and make certain you have all that you will need. Often a special tool needed for the installation may be rented from a local hardware store, garage, or similar establishment for the short time that you need it and for very little money.

Assuming that you now have all the tools and components necessary for the complete installation of the add-on unit, raise the hood of your car and check the installation area to be sure there is

Fig. 3-2. Before getting too involved with the installation, check the area under your hood, and lay out the routing of all refrigerant lines as well as deciding where you will mount the other components.

room for all the parts. Lay out the routing of the refrigerant lines and decide where you will mount the other components; mark these spots clearly (Fig. 3-2). Where drilling is necessary, always check for obstructions on both sides of the surface. These obstructions could require you to relocate some of the parts—either add-on unit components or existing items found under the hood.

Another important step in preparing your car for the add-on air-conditioning unit is an evaluation of your car's cooling system. An add-on air conditioner will always have some effect on the normal operation of the car, and especially the car's cooling system. For example, placing the condenser in front of the radiator (just behind the grille) to allow for air movement to remove heat will also impede the flow of air to the radiator, decreasing its cooling efficiency. In some cases, it may be necessary to install an oversized radiator to prevent the engine from overheating.

Begin the inspection of the car's cooling system by checking the condition of the water hoses, connections, and similar items; repair or replace any defective items. Continue by following the suggestions given in Chapter 2, including reverse-flushing the car's radiator and engine block. Then follow the step-by-step procedures for installing the add-on unit which follows.

STEP NO. 1: REMOVE THE RADIATOR

Chances are your antifreeze is worth saving, so provide some container to catch it as you're draining the cooling system. When the

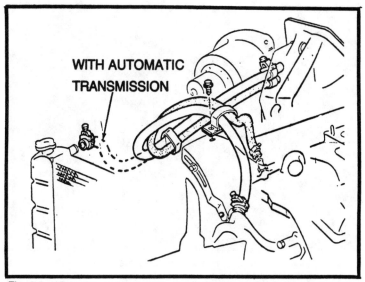

WITH AUTOMATIC
TRANSMISSION

Fig. 3-3. When the cooling system is completely drained, loosen the hose clamps, and remove the radiator inlet and outlet hoses. Courtesy of Chrysler Motor Co.

cooling system is completely drained, loosen the hose clamps and remove the radiator inlet and outlet hoses (Fig. 3-3). If your car has an automatic transmission, the transmission oil lines may be connected to the radiator. If so, provide some container under the connection to catch the oil, and carefully disconnect the oil lines (Fig. 3-4). Before continuing any further, tape the ends of these lines with electrical tape to prevent any foreign matter from entering the lines.

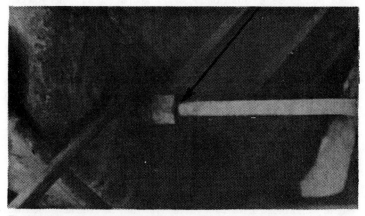

Fig. 3-4. If your car has an automatic transmission, the transmission oil lines will probably connect to the radiator also.

Fig. 3-5. Check the clearance between the fan blade and the radiator core in case an adjustment is necessary.

You should also check the clearance between the fan blade and the radiator core in case an adjustment is necessary to fit the condenser or other component of the add-on air conditioner (Fig. 3-5).

Next remove the radiator mounting bolts and store them in a safe place so you don't lose them. Carefully remove the radiator and set it in a safe place, where the fins and tubing will be protected until the unit is replaced in the car. The fins are easily bent, so extreme care should be taken when handling or storing the radiator. This would also be a good time to give the radiator a thorough check for leaks, punctures, or other damage. If it is in need of repair, you can probably send it to a radiator repair shop and have it fixed while you're installing the add-on air-conditioning system.

STEP NO. 2: REMOVE THE FAN PULLEY

Most add-on air-conditioning kits contain a five-blade fan to provide extra cooling air while the car is idling or running at speeds under 40 mph. The exact procedure at this point will vary according to the make, model, and year of the car, so check the installation instructions for your particular car; they will come with the kit. Some cars will require a spacer on the fan pulley in order to line it up properly with the new pulley on the crankshaft. In other cars, an additional pulley will be required to accommodate the compressor V-belt. Regardless of the exact details for your car, the fan should be removed by loosening the machine screws. The removal of the fan—whether absolutely necessary or not—will give your more working room, and you're going to need it.

STEP NO. 3: MOUNTING THE COMPRESSOR

The compressor mounting bracket shown in Fig. 3-6, is typical of those furnished with add-on air-conditioning kits. Most compressor mounting brackets are designed to secure directly to the engine block which means that certain machine screws will have to be removed. To remove them, you're going to need a wrench with plenty of leverage and perhaps a rust-cutting solution to saturate the threads if they are very rusty.

When you remove any screws or bolts from the engine block, make certain you are able to identify each one and to which hole it belongs; the holes may be of different depths. However, if you do get them mixed up, you can find the correct hole by trial-and-error—one or more bolts will not tighten up flush with the engine block if any are out of place.

Once the required bolts and screws have been removed from the engine block, put the mounting bracket in place, line up the holes, and insert the bolts finger-tight. In some cases, the manufacturer of the add-on kit will furnish replacement bolts for certain holes, but such replacements will be pointed out in the installation instructions. Remember to tighten the bolts only finger-tight because the bracket will probably have to be adjusted slightly in order to permit the compressor to be moved into correct alignment with the crankshaft pulley. The bracket will also be provided with an adjustment screw for adjusting the tension of the belt later on.

Next mount the compressor itself on the bracket according to the manufacturer's instructions, using the hardware provided with the kit. The compressor itself can be secured firmly to the bracket, but the bracket should remain loose until the compressor is aligned with the crankshaft pulley.

STEP NO. 4: MOUNTING THE PULLEYS

The number and types of pulleys necessary for the installation of the add-on air-conditioning kit will vary with the make, model, and year of the car in which the system is installed. However, in most cases, the kit will include a crankshaft pulley which secures to the existing pulleys. Before mounting, thoroughly clean the machined mounting surfaces of the original pulley hub, as well as the compressor pulley. Then remove the bolts and fit the new pulley in place. Tighten the center bolt on the crankshaft pulley solidly, using a

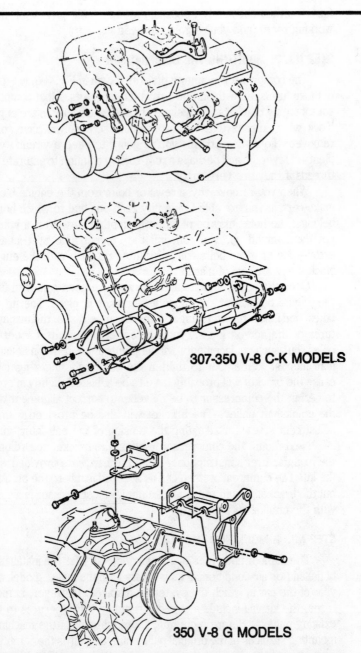

307-350 V-8 C-K MODELS

350 V-8 G MODELS

Fig. 3-6. The compressor mounting brackets, shown here, are typical of those furnished with add-on air-conditioning kits. Courtesy of General Motors Corp.

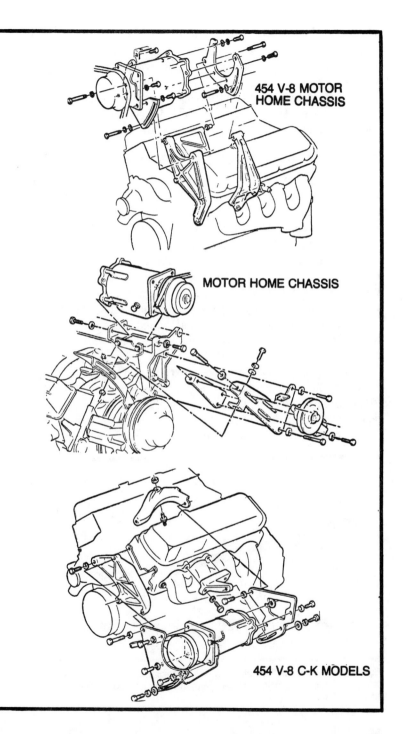

454 V-8 MOTOR
HOME CHASSIS

MOTOR HOME CHASSIS

454 V-8 C-K MODELS

49

long-handled wrench for plenty of leverage. Use a rubber mallet to pound against the wrench handle to make the bolt even tighter.

You can check the installed pulley for wobble by removing the distributor cap from your ignition system, and then having someone bump the starter several times while you observe the revolving movement of the pulley. Hold a straightedge across the pulley while the car is being cranked for a more accurate check.

STEP NO. 5: ALIGNING THE COMPRESSOR PULLEY

When the crankshaft pulley is properly installed, the compressor pulley can then be aligned. The simplest way is to hold a long metal straightedge (such as one of the metal yardsticks available at hardware stores) against the machined edge of the crankshaft pulley while you move the compressor mounting bracket until the machined surface of the compressor pulley comes into contact with the straightedge (see Fig. 3-7). Then tighten the bolts holding the bracket. Recheck the pulley alignment, however, before fully tightening the bolts. Finish tightening with a torque wrench. The torque is critical on the engine head bolts and the exact specifications will usually be given in the kit instructions. If not, check with a local car dealer or mechanic.

Mount the idler pulley bracket next, but don't forget any spacers which may be necessary for the car you're working on. Again, a torque wrench should be used to tighten the bolts to the specifications included with the instructions. This pulley is used to adjust the belt tension and pivots on an eccentric for this purpose. Loosen the

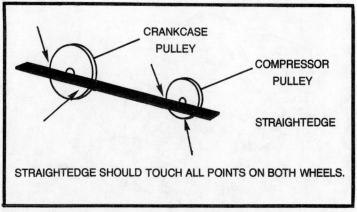

Fig. 3-7. You can check the installed pulley by holding a straightedge across the pulley while the car is being cranked (with the distributor cap removed) for an accurate check.

adjusting bolt and position the pulley all the way toward the center so that it will be easier to attach the V-belt later on. Check the alignment of this pulley with a metal straightedge in the same manner as given for checking the alignment of the crankshaft pulley with the compressor pulley.

The method of installing the fan pulley will vary with the make, model, and year of your car. Some fans come complete with the pulley for installation on the car's water-pump shaft, while on other cars the old fan has to be removed from the fan pulley and the new heavy-duty blade attached in its place. In yet other kits, an additional pulley must be installed next to the existing pulley. In any event, once the fan is installed according to the instructions, align the pulley as described before.

Depending upon your type of car, this may be all the pulleys necessary for the installation. Therefore, the next step could be to install the V-belts. The original belt that drives your car's fan and alternator should be installed first, on the pulley nearest the engine. Slip the belt over the fan and crankshaft pulleys, loosen the alternator bolt, swinging it in toward the engine block, and then slip the V-belt over the alternator pulley. If your car is equipped with power steering, next install the V-belt required to power the hydraulic oil pump.

Now comes the air-conditioning V-belt. Install this belt similarly to the other belts; that is, slip the belt over the edge of the pulley grooves, but do not force it so hard as to damage the belt. Loosen the idler pulley mounting bracket if necessary, so that you can get the belt in the proper groove without undue side pressure. If subjected to side pressure, the steel cord in the belt (in steel-cable belts) will separate from the rubber and the belt will wear faster and fail much sooner. Fiber cord belts will wear in the same way, but perhaps not as quickly should undue side pressure by applied to the V-belt.

The tightness of all the belts is very important for proper operation of the equipment they drive. Normally you can judge the correct belt tension by pressing down on the belt with your forefinger in the middle of the belt's longest span. If the belt depresses no more than 1/2 inch, the tension should be just about right. After this tension is achieved, securely tighten all bolts, locknuts, etc.

Since all new belts will stretch somewhat during the first few minutes of operation, you should again test the belt tension and make any adjustments necessary after the unit has been in operation for about 30 minutes. It wouldn't hurt to check this belt tension fre-

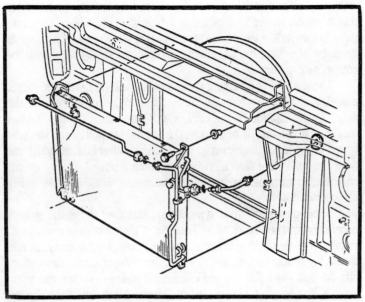

Fig. 3-8. Typical condenser installation for an add-on air-conditioning system. Courtesy of General Motors Corp.

quently the first week the air-conditioning system is in operation—just to be sure.

STEP NO. 6: MOUNTING THE CONDENSER

A line drawing of a typical condenser installation for an add-on air-conditioning system is shown in Fig. 3-8. Note that the unit mounts in front of the radiator and behind the car's grille, usually on the same mounting channels used by the radiator. If you're lucky, your kit will have condenser brackets that are made to fit the mounting yoke channels on your car exactly. If you're not this lucky, your kit will contain universal brackets—ones having many holes in them to fit a variety of cars. In this case, if the holes in the mounting bracket don't line up with the existing holes in the radiator yoke, drill more holes to secure the condenser bracket. In other kits, it may be necessary to bend the condenser bracket to fit the surface properly.

Begin the installation of the condenser by securing the brackets to the condenser. Holding the condenser in place, mark the point where the brackets will fit on the mounting surface of the radiator yoke. Remove the condenser and, if the marks don't line up with the existing holes in the radiator yoke, either drill holes at the marked points or bend the brackets to fit; the former of these two solutions is preferred.

Now position the condenser back in its mounting position and bolt the brackets to the mounting surface on the radiator mounting yoke channel. Two bolts for each of the condenser brackets will usually be required. Securely tighten these bolts when you are certain that the condenser is positioned properly.

After you complete the installation of the condenser, you're more than halfway finished. In fact, the hardest part of the installation is over. Soon you'll be riding in comfort that will more than pay for your efforts on this project.

STEP NO. 7: RUNNING THE REFRIGERANT LINES

In preparing your car for the installation of the add-on air-conditioning system, you should have laid out the routing of the refrigeration lines to the various components. Look over your original layout before attempting to run the refrigerant lines. Make certain that the lines themselves will not interfere with the normal operation of your car or the air-conditioning system. Then check to make sure that any holes that need drilling will not meet with any obstructions on either side of the material in which the holes are to be drilled.

The condenser and the hoses contain a factory-sealed charge of refrigerant at low pressure to keep out moisture and air until the unit is installed and permanently charged. The fittings are also sealed and these seals should not be removed until immediately before the connection. Further precautions should be taken to avoid crushing or kinking the refrigeration tubing, as this will restrict the flow of refrigerant, which in turn reduces the cooling action of the entire system.

At least two holes will have to be drilled through the partition separating the engine compartment from the passenger compartment; this is commonly called the firewall. One hole is needed in this partition for the liquid refrigerant line, and another hole is needed for the refrigerant suction line. There will also be some electrical wires running from the control panel on the evaporator housing to the compressor clutch, but since the diameter of these wires is small, you'll probably be able to use one of the existing holes in the partition.

Check the rough-in drawings provided with the kit to locate the connections of these refrigerant lines on the evaporator unit. Again check both sides of the firewall for clearance, and then drill the required holes. Normally, a 7/8-inch-diameter hole will allow you to pass the hose fitting through the hole and leave room for a soft rubber grommet. Rubber grommets not only protect the refrigerant

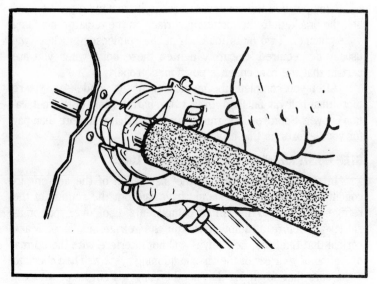

Fig. 3-9. With two wrenches tighten the fitting as shown.

hoses from cuts on sharp edges, but also provide a tight seal between the engine and passenger compartments.

For a neat hole, first drill a pilot hole and follow with a metal-cutting bit or hole saw of the proper size. The hole saw should be equipped with a pilot drill to guide the saw for a perfect cut. After the holes are cut through the firewall, inspect the routing of the refrigerant lines from the compressor to the condenser. You may have to route the lines under, over, or around the radiator yoke mounting channels. If any drilling is required, you might as well do it while you have the drill handy.

Install the refrigerant lines loosely along your proposed route—following any suggestions given in the instructions accompanying the kit. Continue running the lines through the holes previously drilled for them, making sure all rubber grommets are in place to protect the lines. Even with the grommets in place, be extremely careful not to link or otherwise damage the tubing. After all the lines are run, try to plan your work so that the end fittings of these lines will be open for a minimum length of time.

To begin the connections, remove the seal from one end of a refrigerant line and also from the corresponding fitting on the condenser. Apply a few drops of refrigerant oil to the threads to help maintain a tight connection, and quickly make the connection running the threads up hand-tight. Then, with two wrenches, tighten the fittings as shown in Fig. 3-9. This procedure should be done as quickly as possible, but don't rush and end up cross-threading the fittings.

The other refrigerant hose to the condenser is connected in the same manner as the first. The instructions accompanying the kit will show exactly to which openings these lines attach.

Assuming that the work on the crankcase and the condensing unit is complete, you can go ahead and put the original radiator back in place. Remember, if it needs repairs, now is the time to have it done in order to save money—even if it means doing without your car for a day or two.

When you reinstall the radiator, again be extremely careful not to damage the core or fins (Fig. 3-10). Either can be damaged by striking against the fan blades or other sharp objects in this area of your engine compartment. It is also easy to scrape the radiator against the new condensing unit and damage them both. Bolt the radiator mounting bracket in place, reconnect the radiator hoses and the transmission cooling lines if present. Check to make sure you have at least 1/2-inch clearance between the fan blade and the radiator. This can be done by turning the fan blade by hand while you hold a ruler or gauge between the two items.

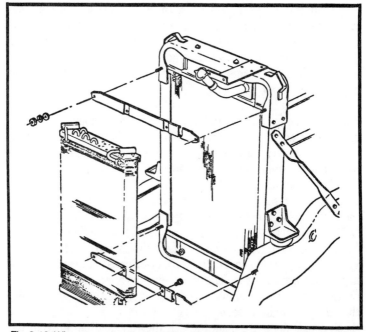

Fig. 3-10. When removing or reinstalling the radiator, be extremely careful not to damage the core or fins. Courtesy of General Motors Corp.

TOO CLOSE!

Fig. 3-11. Check to see that all refrigerant hoses are at least 3 inches away from the hot exhaust manifold.

STEP NO. 8: MOUNTING THE EVAPORATOR

Mounting brackets are used to secure the evaporator unit under the dash or on the floor of the passenger compartment of your car. Place the unit in its proper mounting position and check to see if you have enough clearance to reach the accelerator pedal. Also make sure the unit is lined up and parallel to the dash. Will the glove compartment door open properly?

When you have the unit lined up properly and some means of holding the unit in position (a block of wood on the floor works fine), mark the holes for the mounting screws and a hole in the floor for the drain hose. Now remove the unit and tighten the bolts that hold the mounting brackets to the evaporator.

Once the small pilot holes are drilled for the 1/4-inch sheet-metal pan-head screws, run the screws in and out of the holes so that they will screw in easily when the unit is positioned back in place. Drill a 1/2-inch hole in the floor of the car after removing the carpet. Install the evaporator according to the instructions provided with the kit. You may have to connect the refrigerant lines to the unit before it is permanently mounted. These connections are made as described previously; that is, remove the seals, apply refrigerant oil to the threads, and tighten each connection with two wrenches. After these connections are made, attach the rubber drain hose to the evaporator drain nipple and insert the end of the hose through the hole you cut in the floor. Route this hose so that the carpet can be replaced on the floor board.

Raise the unit into position and start one screw through each mounting plate into the dash holes you drilled. Do not tighten these until all screws are in place. Insert the remaining screws and then firmly tighten them all. If there is excess refrigerant hose on the passenger's side of the firewall, push the excess through the hole into the engine compartment, making sure that it doesn't interfere with any of the operations in this area. Also see that the hoses are run as directly as possible throughout the entire system. If bends are necessary, try to make them as smooth as possible and definitely without any kinks.

STEP NO. 9: FINAL CONNECTIONS OF THE REFRIGERANT LINES

Connect the refrigerant hose from the suction side of the evaporator to the suction side of the compressor. Then connect the liquid refrigerant hose from the evaporator to the outlet fitting on the receiver-drier. Check to see that all refrigerant hoses are at least 3 inches away from the hot exhaust manifold (see Fig. 3-11). Also recheck to make sure these same hoses do not interfere with any of the operations of other parts of the car such as the choke control, throttle levers, etc. Also protect the hoses from sharp edges that may cause damage due to vibration (Fig. 3-12).

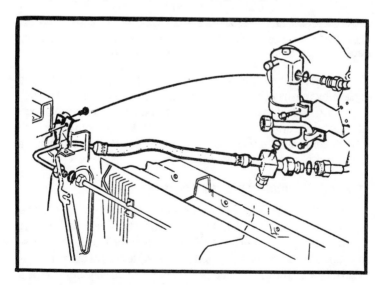

Fig. 3-12. Protect the hoses from sharp edges that may cause damage or vibration. Courtesy of General Motors Corp.

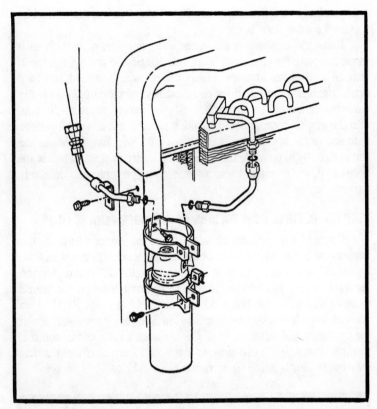

Fig. 3-13. To firmly secure the refrigerant lines, they should be clamped into place by means of hose clamps. Courtesy of General Motors Corp.

To secure the refrigerant lines firmly, they should be clamped in place by means of hose clamps usually provided with the kit (Fig. 3-13). If not included, such clamps may be purchased from a local auto parts dealer. Attach the clamps, after placing them along each hose at convenient places, using No. 10 sheet-metal screws and a 1/8-inch drill to start the holes.

STEP NO. 10: CONNECTING THE CONTROL WIRING

Just like your home air-conditioning system, an automotive system has to be controlled to work properly. Connect the short electrical wire from the blower in the evaporator unit to the accessory terminal on the ignition and then fuse it according to recommendations in your instructions. The wire is usually fitted with a connector that can be attached to the terminal with existing accessory wires.

The longer wire is then run to the terminal block at the clutch by routing it through an existing hole in the firewall and connecting it according to directions given in the kit's instructions. This just about completes the basic installation of the add-on air-conditioning system, but it's not quite ready for use.

Before operating the system, it will have to be evacuated as described in Chapter 8, charged with refrigerant as described in Chapter 10, and checked for leaks, which is covered in Chapter 6. When these steps are completed (and you may want to have these done at a local automotive air-conditioning shop with the proper tools) you're ready for riding in comfort.

The maintenance and troubleshooting procedures given in Chapters 2 and 5 apply to the add-on units as well as the factory-installed systems.

Chapter 4

Automotive

Air-Conditioning Controls

In order for an automotive air-conditioning system to function properly, some means of regulating the system is necessary. This is accomplished by a combination of manual, automatic, and remote controls which consist of electrical and mechanical devices. For example, electrical switches and relays control the operation of the blower fan, the magnetic clutch, and the solenoid valve, to name a few.

Since the most frequently encountered air-conditioning problems occur in the controls, a good knowledge of the function of these controls is essential for troubleshooting automotive air-conditioning systems. This chapter, therefore, is designed to acquaint you with the basic controls, both electrical and mechanical, common to all automotive air-conditioning systems. Furthermore, it will cover the individual controls that differ from each other in several of the more popular makes of cars.

Troubleshooting air-conditioning controls is well within the reach of nearly every car owner. With only an inexpensive volt-ohmmeter, a few hand tools, and a knowledge of the contents of this chapter, you should be able to detect and correct any control problem that may occur with your own automotive air-conditioning system. Besides requiring few tools, work on the controls also has the advantage of being relatively safe since in most cases you will not be required to work with any refrigerants or other potentially dangerous parts of the system.

PRACTICAL SYSTEMS

A schematic drawing of the electrical switches and other control devices that make up the control circuit in a typical air-conditioning system is shown in Figs. 4-1 and 4-2.

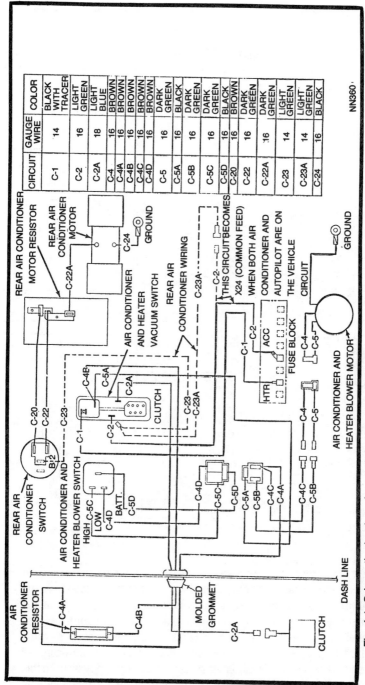

CIRCUIT	GAUGE WIRE	COLOR
C-1	14	BLACK WITH TRACER
C-2	16	LIGHT GREEN
C-2A	18	LIGHT BLUE
C-4	16	BROWN
C-4A	16	BROWN
C-4B	16	BROWN
C-4C	16	BROWN
C-4D	16	BROWN
C-5	16	DARK GREEN
C-5A	16	BLACK
C-5B	16	DARK GREEN
C-5C	16	DARK GREEN
C-5D	16	BLACK
C-20	16	BROWN
C-22	16	DARK GREEN
C-22A	16	DARK GREEN
C-23	14	LIGHT GREEN
C-23A	14	LIGHT GREEN
C-24	16	BLACK

NN360

Fig. 4-1. Schematic drawing of control devices incorporated in a typical air-conditioning circuit. Courtesy of Ford Motor Co.

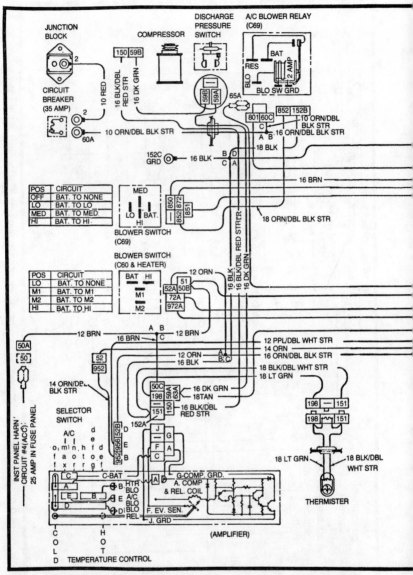

In these diagrams, note that 12-volt power is obtained from the car's electrical fuse panel, usually located under the dash in the passenger compartment. The light blue wire runs from the fuse panel and connects to a terminal on the multi-speed blower switch which is usually located in the instrument panel on the dash. All functions of the air-conditioning system obtain their power from this switch. For example, power from this switch runs through various

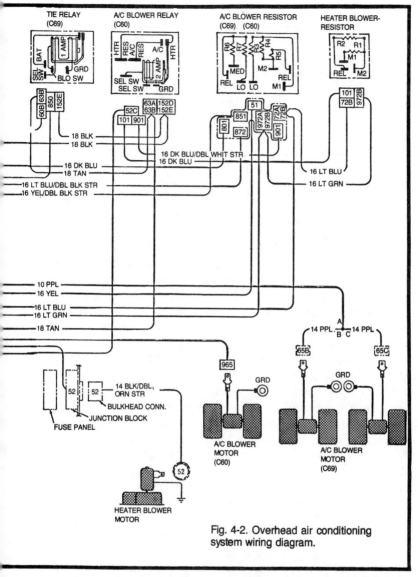

Fig. 4-2. Overhead air conditioning system wiring diagram.

resistors to obtain the different fan speeds (low, medium, and high) of the blower. Another wire runs from this panel to a thermostat and then continues to the magnetic clutch of the compressor which controls the compressor operation.

Like residential or commercial air-conditioning systems, automotive air-conditioning systems are composed of four basic systems: the refrigeration system, the ductwork, the air-moving system, and the control system. The basic components of the refrigeration system are: the compressor, the discharge line, the condenser, the receiver-drier, the liquid lines, the expansion valve, the evaporator coil, the suction line, and the flow-control valve. The duct system—as the name implies—consists of the evaporator-heater duct system. The air-moving system consists of the evaporator blower and motor, the condenser that is positioned ahead of the radiator, and the radiator fan. This chapter will cover the remaining system—controls.

The simplest control system for automotive air-conditioning systems permits heating, defrosting, and air conditioning on the same system, while the more complex controls besides offering these three previously-mentioned modes will automatically maintain the desired temperature inside the car by introducing fresh air that has been appropriately heated or cooled.

In order to operate all of these modes in the various individual or combined situations, a control assembly consisting of either a pushbutton or slide-type switch is provided. This switch operates a series of vacuum motors which operate the various dampers or doors within the air system. Vacuum motors provide the power to move or change the damper doors to the required positions and are sometimes called actuators, vacuum actuators, power units, or vacuum power units. A cross section of a typical vacuum motor is shown in Fig. 4-3a.

The usual vacuum motor consists of a metal can or housing which has a rubber diaphragm across its center. A shaft connected in the center of the diaphragm moves when a vacuum is applied. Note the port in Fig. 4-3; this is where the vacuum is applied to the motor. A built-in spring is also provided to move the shaft in the opposite direction when the vacuum is released. This particular type of vacuum motor is known as the single-action type.

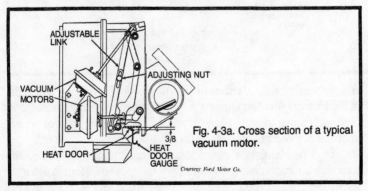

ADJUSTABLE LINK

ADJUSTING NUT

VACUUM MOTORS

HEAT DOOR

HEAT DOOR GAUGE

3/8

Fig. 4-3a. Cross section of a typical vacuum motor.

Courtesy Ford Motor Co.

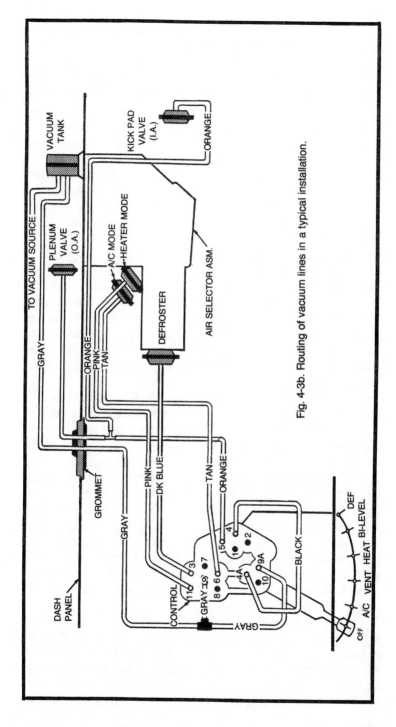

Fig. 4-3b. Routing of vacuum lines in a typical installation.

65

Vacuum lines attached to the ports of vacuum motors are fed by engine vacuum, which is routed through a reservoir tank in the engine compartment, and a switch on the instrument panel (Fig. 4-3b). If any of the damper doors are thought to be defective, the vacuum motor can be checked as follows. Refer to the operator's manual supplied by the manufacturer of the system and then make certain that the vacuum control switch on the instrument panel is set to supply vacuum to the particular vacuum motor being tested. Pull the vacuum hose off the motor and connect a vacuum gauge in the hose before starting the engine and running it at idling speed. With the vacuum gauge attached, check the vacuum reading at the hose. If the reading indicates more than 18 inches of mercury, the vacuum motor should operate. Replace the hose. If the vacuum motor does not move it is either defective or the mechanism to which it is attached is stuck. The later problem can be checked by removing the linkage from the vacuum motor. If the motor still does not operate, replace the motor.

A vacuum motor operating sluggishly may mean that the system has a vacuum leak. This is especially true if all the motors operate in a sluggish manner. Begin checking for a leak at the vacuum source, the intake manifold, while the engine is idling. The vacuum will normally measure 15 to 20 inches of mercury on a vacuum gauge.

Continue the check by installing the vacuum gauge in a "T" connector with a short piece of hose at the outer hose of the vacuum reservoir tank as shown in Fig. 4-4. This is the main supply hose for the car's heating and cooling system. Set the instrument panel control on defrost and start the engine. The vacuum gauge should read between 15 to 20 inches of mercury. Leave the defrost control in position and turn the engine off. If the vacuum indication on the gauge does not decrease for the next 25 seconds or so, the tank and the side of the vacuum motor to which the vacuum is being applied are working. However, if the vacuum decreases during that time, leave the gauge attached at the tank, remove the unit supply hose, and plug the open end of the "T" while checking the vacuum with the engine on and off as before. If the vacuum decreases, the reservoir tank is defective and must be replaced.

If a vacuum motor is defective, it is usually best to replace the whole motor as they are difficult to repair. However, the linkages can usually be adjusted so that the damper doors will seal properly. When either adjusting or replacing vacuum motors or the linkages attached to them, always refer to the manufacturer's service manuals. By doing so, you will save a lot of time and also ensure that the

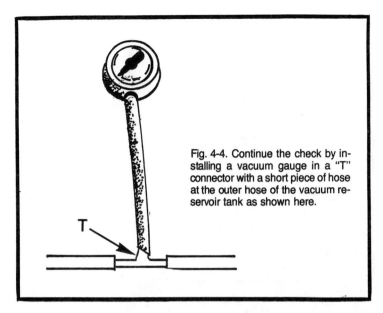

Fig. 4-4. Continue the check by installing a vacuum gauge in a "T" connector with a short piece of hose at the outer hose of the vacuum reservoir tank as shown here.

adjustments are done properly—as recommended by the manufacturer.

The manufacturer's service manuals must be referred to for each particular model because manual-control assemblies are specially made and therefore differ for each make and model of automobile. A typical assembly consists of a frame to which various individual controls are assembled and interconnected by levers, cams, vacuum hoses, and electrical wiring. While it would take volumes to describe each of the different controls, a few typical examples are in order.

The control used on a 1973 Ford automobile with factory-installed air conditioning is a manual control assembly and controls three basic functions: the temperature control, the function control, and the blower control. The operation is as follows.

Ventilation

The temperature control (upper) lever is moved to the COOL position while the heater selector (lower) lever is moved to the OFF position. The air vent knobs may then be pulled as desired for outside ventilation (Fig. 4-5). This is known as the cowl vent system.

To operate the power vent system of the car, move the temperature control lever to the COOL position, then move the heater selector lever to the VENT position. The fan switch may then be

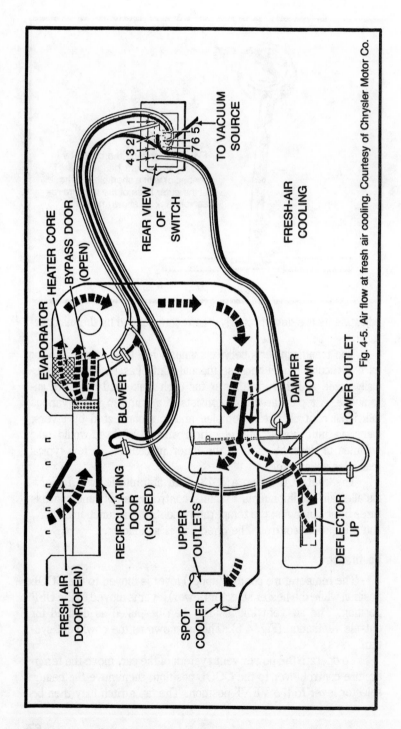

Fig. 4-5. Air flow at fresh air cooling. Courtesy of Chrysler Motor Co.

moved to the desired fan speed. The air vents or registers at either end of the instrument panel may then be adjusted to direct the air in practically any direction (Fig. 4-6).

Heating and Defrosting

To heat the car, move the temperature control lever toward the WARM position. The temperature of the air may be warm when the lever is approximately midway between COOL and WARM and hot when the lever is moved all the way to the right. This control allows for several different combinations of heat; when the lever is moved to HEAT, the operator will obtain floor heat only. When moved between HEAT and DEFROST, floor heat will be provided along with windshield defrost at the same time (Fig. 4-7); the lever moved to HI LO will distribute air to both panel registers and floor. At any of these positions, the fan switch may be adjusted to any of the fan speeds. High speed is the fan setting to use for keeping the car windows from fogging.

Defrosting the Windshield

Move the temperature control lever toward WARM and the heater selector to the DEFROST position. Move the fan switch to the desired fan speed to obtain air flow toward the windshield. The distribution of air between the defroster and the heater (Fig. 4-8) can be regulated by positioning the air control lever between HEAT and DEFROST.

To defog the windshield, it is usually best to set the heater control in the DEFROST position and operate the fan at high speed while the temperature control lever is positioned in its highest position. When the windshield starts to clear, the lever is usually changed to a more comfortable position and the fan speed is then reduced.

Air Conditioning (Cooling)

Cooled air is directed throughout the car by means of registers located in the instrument panel. The register louvers are adjusted by a control located in the center of each register. By rotating the register, air may be deflected in the desired direction. This same control can also limit or shut off the cold air flow from these registers.

To cool the car, the lower control lever is moved to the A/C position while the upper temperature lever is moved towards the COOL position. This operation recirculates air in the car to more

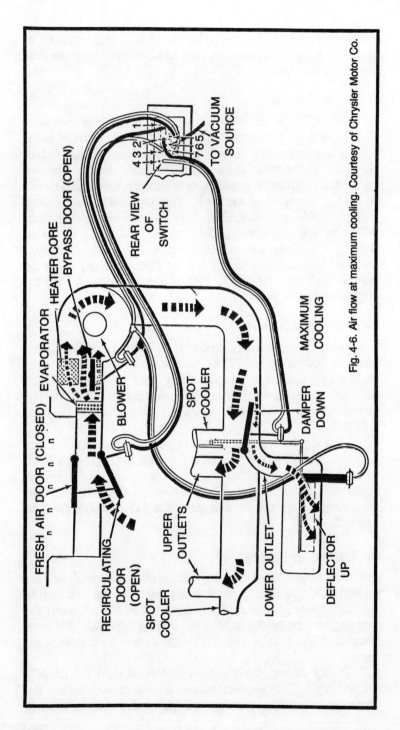

FRESH AIR DOOR (CLOSED)

EVAPORATOR

HEATER CORE

BYPASS DOOR (OPEN)

REAR VIEW
OF
SWITCH

4 3 2 1

7 6 5

TO VACUUM
SOURCE

BLOWER

RECIRCULATING
DOOR
(OPEN)

SPOT
COOLER

UPPER
OUTLETS

SPOT
COOLER

LOWER OUTLET

MAXIMUM
COOLING

DAMPER
DOWN

DEFLECTOR
UP

Fig. 4-6. Air flow at maximum cooling. Courtesy of Chrysler Motor Co.

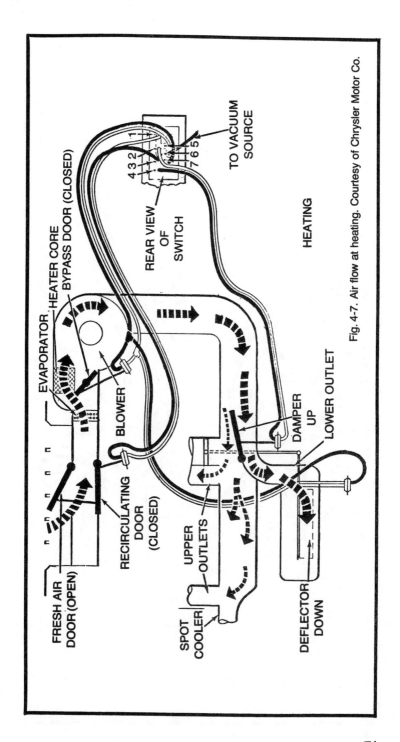

Fig. 4-7. Air flow at heating. Courtesy of Chrysler Motor Co.

71

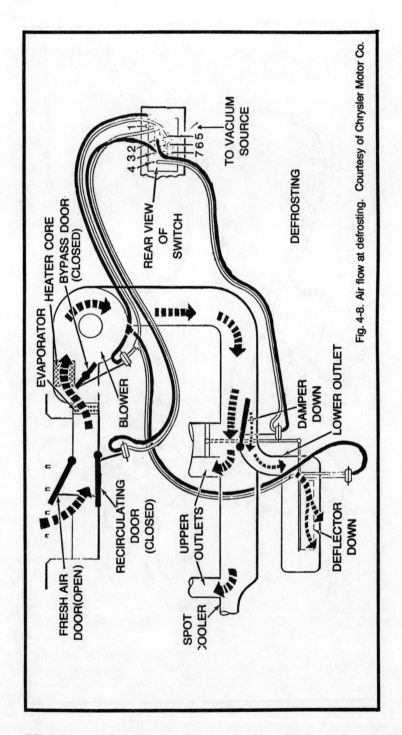

EVAPORATOR

HEATER CORE

BYPASS DOOR
(CLOSED)

BLOWER

REAR VIEW
OF
SWITCH

4 3 2 1

7 6 5

TO VACUUM
SOURCE

FRESH AIR
DOOR (OPEN)

RECIRCULATING
DOOR
(CLOSED)

UPPER
OUTLETS

SPOT
COOLER

DAMPER
DOWN

LOWER OUTLET

DEFLECTOR
DOWN

DEFROSTING

Fig. 4-8. Air flow at defrosting. Courtesy of Chrysler Motor Co.

72

quickly cool the vehicle. The fan switch is then moved to the highest of the four speeds and operated until the desired temperature is reached. Then the fan control lever is adjusted for the desired air flow and the temperature lever adjusted for the most satisfactory temperature. Moving the temperature lever approximately one inch from COOL will allow outside air to be introduced into the system.

All of the functions just described are made possible by the use of controls. This 1973 Ford manual control also regulates the vacuum mode selector switch, the water-valve switch, and the compressor clutch switch. Vacuum hoses from the control panel connect to the various vacuum motors for proper operation.

Now that we know what the controls can do on this particular make and model of automobile, let's take a closer look at the system to see how all of these functions are accomplished. Refer to Fig. 4-9 for the location of the various items about to be described.

When the temperature-control lever is set to the COOL setting, it depresses the pin in the water-valve vacuum switch. This switch connects the supply vacuum and the heater water-valve motor and shuts off the water flow as well as the air flow to the heater core—therefore, water and air bypass the heater core unheated. If the lever is moved away from the COOL position towards the WARM setting, the vacuum switch disconnects the vacuum from the water-valve vacuum motor and opens the water valve to allow hot water to flow through the core. Adjusting the lever further to the right (towards WARM) moves the blend-air damper door which mixes the hot and cool air for temperature control. In the warmest setting (completely to the right), the bypass is shut completely off so that all air flows through the core, providing maximum heat.

Next comes the mode selector lever which selects the desired function to be performed. It is connected to a vacuum selector valve which receives its vacuum from the supply tank mounted in the engine compartment and distributes the vacuum to all vacuum motors corresponding to the control lever setting. They are the outside air door, the recirculating air door, the restrictor air door, the heater water valve, the air-conditioning heat door, and the heat-defrost door.

The air-conditioner clutch switch is closed by a cam on the selector valve when the lever is in the A/C position. This switch is wired in series with the blower switch so that the blower switch must be on in order to operate the clutch which in turn operates the compressor. With the selector switch set for the air-conditioning mode and the temperature control lever set on COOL, the restrictor air door checks the air flow through the heater core. In this situation,

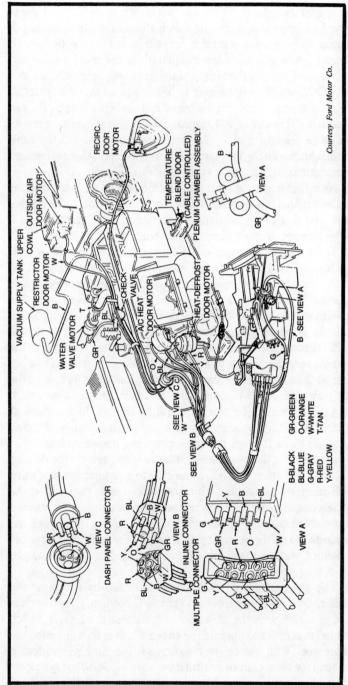

Fig. 4-9. Diagram showing the location of items described in the text.

Courtesy Ford Motor Co.

VACUUM SUPPLY TANK UPPER
COWL OUTSIDE AIR
DOOR MOTOR
RESTRICTOR
DOOR MOTOR
W
B
WATER
VALVE MOTOR
T
GR
BL
RECIRC.
DOOR
MOTOR
TEMPERATURE
BLEND DOOR
(CABLE CONTROLLED)
PLENUM CHAMBER ASSEMBLY
CHECK
VALVE
A/C HEAT
DOOR MOTOR
HEAT-DEFROST
DOOR MOTOR
B
GR
VIEW A
B
B SEE VIEW A
G
O
BL
Y
Y R
SEE VIEW C C
W SEE VIEW B

B-BLACK   GR-GREEN
BL-BLUE   O-ORANGE
G-GRAY   W-WHITE
R-RED   T-TAN
Y-YELLOW

VIEW C
DASH PANEL CONNECTOR
GR B
T

VIEW B
INLINE CONNECTOR
R BL
B W
R O
BL B
W GR
MULTIPLE CONNECTOR
G

VIEW A
Y B
G BL
GR R O W

the water valve is closed, and all air flows through the evaporator coil and bypasses the heater core. On a warm temperature-control setting in the A/C position, cool evaporator air cannot go through the heater core because the restrictor door is closed. Instead, air will flow across the face of the core to temper or warm cool air slightly, keeping humidity low.

When the blower-motor control lever is in the OFF position in the A/C mode, the water valve is closed regardless of the temperature-control lever setting (Fig. 4-10). The cam on the vacuum selector is not engaged with the compressor clutch switch, and the system is completely off. In the VENT, HI LO, or DEFROST (Fig. 4-11) modes, the air-conditioning clutch switch is disengaged and the water valve is open—allowing full hot-water flow through the heater core. The temperature-control lever modulates the air from no heat to full heat in these modes.

If trouble is suspected in this type of air-conditioning control system, the vacuum mode-control should be tested first by checking the supply-tank vacuum and the vacuum motor performance. This is accomplished by visual inspection and with a vacuum gauge; the reading should be from 15 to 20 inches of mercury. If no vacuum motor leaks or vacuum hose leaks are found, the vacuum selector switch on the control is probably defective and must be replaced.

When checking the compressor switch, examine all of the other electrical parts also. These include the wiring in general, connections, fuses, and the electrically operated clutch. If the fuse is intact and voltage is not present at the various connections, the compressor switch is defective and should be replaced.

Should the blower motor fail to operate, first check for a blown fuse in the fuse panel. If the fuse is satisfactory, check for a defective blower motor, bad speed control resistors, loose connections in the wiring, and proper voltage at the terminals. If your voltmeter indicates no voltage at the first terminal away from the speed control switch, either the switch is defective or some of the wires are loose. First tighten all wires and test the system again. In order to get at all necessary terminals and other parts of the switch for testing, the control assembly will have to be removed. Follow the instructions in the manufacturer's service manual. A typical control assembly might be removed according to the following instructions.

Remove the courtesy light and all control knobs. Then remove the various mounting screws on the control panel and pry the trim off. Disconnect the temperature control cable from the lever and the parking-brake release cable from the instrument panel, if necessary.

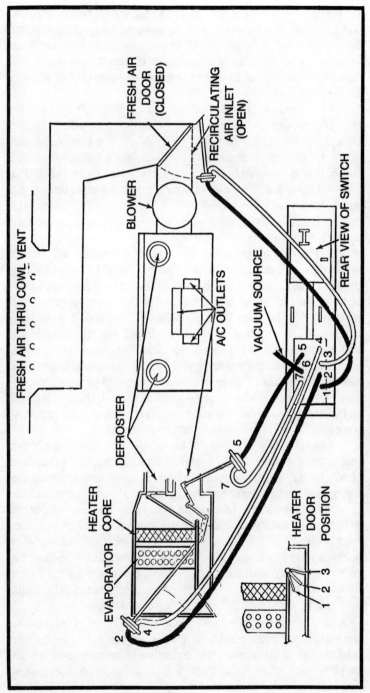

FRESH AIR THRU COWL VENT

FRESH AIR DOOR (CLOSED)

RECIRCULATING AIR INLET (OPEN)

BLOWER

REAR VIEW OF SWITCH

A/C OUTLETS

VACUUM SOURCE

DEFROSTER

HEATER CORE

EVAPORATOR CORE

HEATER DOOR POSITION

Fig. 4-10. Air-conditioning controls in off position. Courtesy of Chrysler Motor Co.

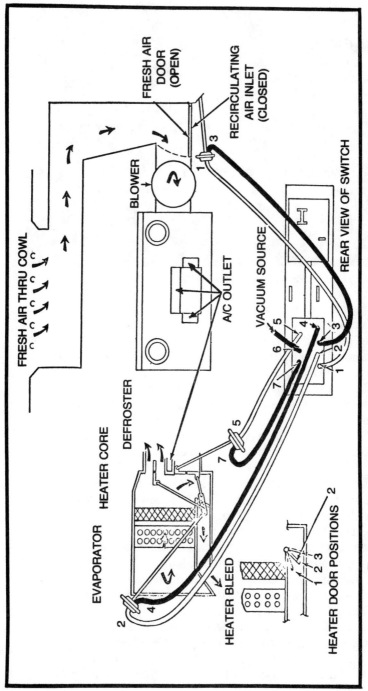

FRESH AIR THRU COWL

FRESH AIR DOOR (OPEN)

RECIRCULATING AIR INLET (CLOSED)

BLOWER

A/C OUTLET

VACUUM SOURCE

REAR VIEW OF SWITCH

EVAPORATOR   HEATER CORE   DEFROSTER

HEATER BLEED

HEATER DOOR POSITIONS

Fig. 4-11. Air flow diagram when system is on defrosting cycle. Courtesy of Chrysler Motor Co.

Fig. 4-12. Control panel for a 1970 Pontiac.

Continue by removing the rear support bracket from the control and then slide the control assembly out from under the instrument panel and remove it from below. Next remove the vacuum harness from the vacuum selector valve, disconnect all electrical terminals, and finally remove the screws anchoring both switches and lift them off. The procedure will vary slightly from car to car, but any home mechanic should be able to detect these variations with little difficulty.

After testing, if your voltmeter does not indicate the proper voltage reading, the switch should be replaced.

Figure 4-12 shows the control panel for a 1970 Pontiac manufactured by General Motors. Figure 4-13 shows the control cable and vacuum hose routing, and Fig. 4-14 shows the wiring. When any of the various modes are put into operation, a vacuum valve is actuated to distribute vacuum to the various vacuum motors for the particular function selected—as in the Ford air-conditioning controls covered previously. The General Motors system, however, has a 3-position fresh-recirculate damper door which recirculates inside air, recirculates all outside air, or a combination of the two. Other controls are essentially the same.

A secondary vacuum switch in the General Motors controls actuates the heater water valve by applying vacuum to the valve vacuum motor when the control lever is moved away from the COLD position—again like the action performed in the previously

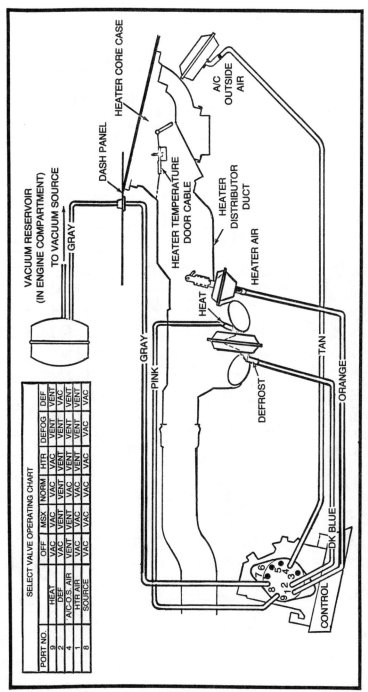

SELECT VALVE OPERATING CHART

PORT NO.		OFF	MSX	NORM	DEFOG	HTR	DEF	VENT
9	HEAT	VAC	VAC	VAC	VENT	VAC	VENT	VENT
2	DEF	VAC	VAC	VENT	VENT	VENT	VAC	VAC
4	A/C-O.S. AIR	VENT	VENT	VAC	VENT	VENT	VENT	VENT
1	HTR AIR	VAC	VAC	VAC	VENT	VENT	VENT	VENT
8	SOURCE	VAC	VAC	VAC	VAC	VAC	VAC	VAC

Fig. 4-13. Simplified diagram of the control cable and vacuum hose routing. Courtesy of Chrysler Motor Co.

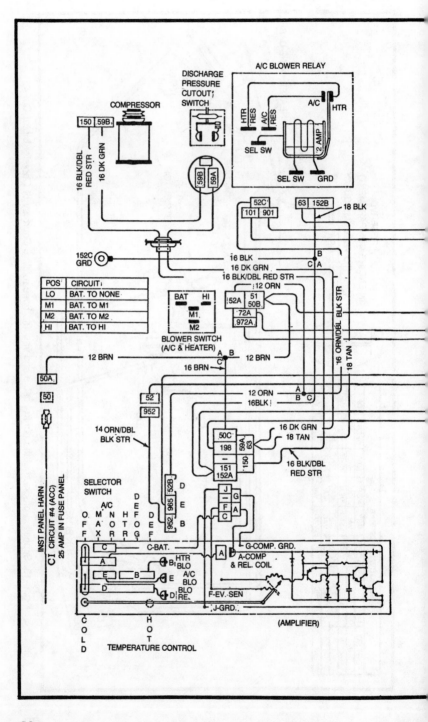

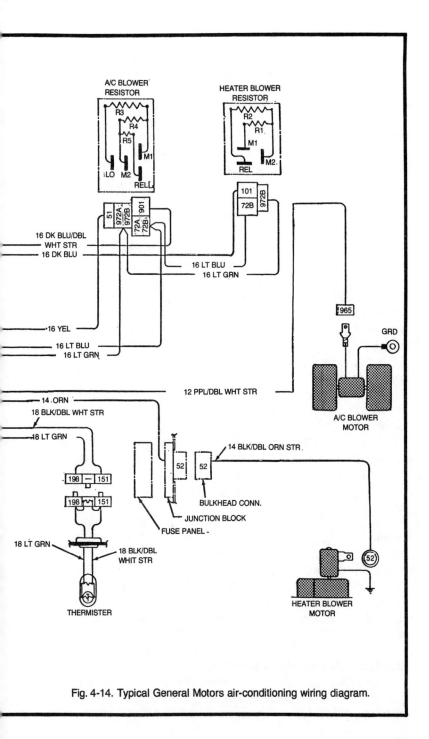

Fig. 4-14. Typical General Motors air-conditioning wiring diagram.

described Ford control. The basic operating principles of the General Motors control are as follows.

In winter months, heated air may be introduced into the car at foot level or directed toward the windshield to remove sleet and snow. In warm weather, refrigerated and dehumidified air enters the interior of the car through five outlets to provide passenger cooling. Air outlets are provided at the ends of the instrument panel, with individual passenger-controlled shut-off valves that can direct cooled air to suit the occupant's desires. Another outlet located high in the center of the instrument panel contains a rotary vaned valve that can be vertically adjusted to direct air flow to the rear seat area. The other two outlets are located lower on the panel to cool the driver and front passenger.

A combination of heating and cooling may be selected wherein warm air is supplied through the heater floor outlet while cooler air is supplied through the upper instrument panel outlets. Operation in this BI LEVEL mode results in the upper level of the vehicle being cooler than the lower level to give a pleasant sensation to the upper body and face of the occupant, particularly on cool days with bright sunshine.

Refer to Fig. 4-12 and the chart in Fig. 4-15 as the following explanation of the controls is given.

Air Control Lever: The system may be operated in any of the five positions or OFF. In the OFF position, the entire system is turned off.

Inside: When the lever is moved to INSIDE, the passenger compartment air is recirculated, blended with a small amount of outside air and then conditioned before returning to the air outlets.

A/C: In this position, fresh outside air is conditioned and directed out of the five upper air outlets.

Bi Level: The BI LEVEL position provides fresh conditioned outside air through the five upper air outlets as well as the lower heater outlet. Air from the upper outlets is slightly cooler than air from the lower outlets.

Heat: In this position, fresh outside air is conditioned and directed out the lower heater duct. A small amount of the air is also directed to the windshield. This provides clear vision under normal operating conditions.

De Ice: The DE ICE position directs maximum air flow to the windshield. This quickly clears the windshield of fog or frost.

Norm-Vent Lever: In the normal position, the refrigeration system is on. This cools and dehumidifies fresh outside air before it enters the passenger compartment. In the VENT position the re-

AIR CONDITIONING CONTROLS FOR 1970 PONTIAC

	NORM-VENT LEVER		AIR CONTROL LEVER						BLOWER LEVER	TEMP. LEVER
	NORM	VENT	OFF	INSIDE	A/C	BI-LEVEL	HEAT	DE-ICE		
FAST COOL DOWN (HOT WEATHER)	X			•••					HI	FULL COOL
HOT WEATHER DRIVING	X				X				2 OR 3	AS DESIRED
MILD OR DAMP WEATHER	X				•	•			2 OR 3	AS DESIRED
HEATING (STANDARD)	X	••					X		2 OR 3	AS DESIRED
MAXIMUM HEAT	X	••					X		HI	FULL WARM
WINDSHEILD DE-ICING	X							X	HI	AS DESIRED
REFRIGERATION OFF		X			•	•	•		AS DESIRED	AS DESIRED
TO AVOID OBJECTIONABLE ODOR OR DUST	X		•	•••					AS DESIRED	AS DESIRED
TO TURN SYSTEM OFF			X							

• MODE OF OPERATION IS OPTIONAL AT DIS-
CRETION OF OPERATOR.

•• OPTIONAL TO TURN REFRIGERATION OFF.

••• DO NOT USE INSIDE POSITION EXCEPT IN
EXTREMELY HOT WEATHER OR BRIEFLY WHEN
UNPLEASANT ODORS EXIST. AS IN A TUNNEL.

Fig. 4-15. Air conditioning control chart for 1970 Pontiac.

frigeration system is turned off. The VENT position is useful on cool dry days when air entering the passenger compartment need not be cooled or dehumidified.

Whenever the air control lever is moved to a different position, the NORM-VENT lever will automatically return to the NORM position, which turns on the refrigeration system. In order to operate in the VENT position, the NORM-VENT lever must be reset after each movement of the air control lever.

Blower Control Lever: The blower control lever controls the speed of the blower which moves air into the passenger compartment. Whenever the system is operating, the blower will also operate at one of the four blower lever positions.

Temperature Control Lever: The temperature control lever regulates the temperature of the air entering the passenger compartment. Position of the temperature lever determines air temperature in any one of the five operating positions of the air control lever.

General Motors cars also have automatic temperature controls at extra cost. This type of system provides thermostatically controlled interior temperature and offers a wide range of personalized comfort. With this control, the driver can set the desired interior comfort level with a lever located on the air-conditioning control panel. The system will then maintain the set comfort level automatically, regardless of the weather. This type of control will be explained later on in this chapter.

The home mechanic can perform the tests required to determine if these controls are operating properly; begin the tests by following the procedures outlined below:

1. Turn the top (mode) lever to the far left—the OFF position. Move the blower lever to the far right which sets the blower switch on HIGH. Then move the bottom temperature lever as far as it will go to the left. At these settings, the compressor should not be running, and no air should be blowing through the system.

2. Move the mode lever to the DE ICE position; at this position the compressor should start running, the blower motor will be operating at high speed, and hot air should be coming from the heat outlet and the defrost nozzle.

3. Move the mode lever to HEAT. The compressor should continue to run if the control is operating properly, but the air flow should now change from the defrost nozzle to the heat outlet. However, a small amount of hot air will still be coming out of the defrost nozzle.

4. Move the mode lever to BI LEVEL and the temperature lever to the mid-position. The compressor should still be running and air will be coming out of all the outlets; the heat-outlet air should be slightly warmer than the air coming out of the air-conditioning outlets.

5. Move the mode lever to A/C and set the temperature lever to cool. The compressor is running and cooled outside air should be coming through the air-conditioning outlets.

6. Move the NORM-VENT switch to VENT. At this setting the compressor will stop running, but outside air will still be coming through the air-conditioning outlets. However, the air will be the same temperature as the outside air as there is no heating or cooling in this position.

7. Move the mode lever to INSIDE, if the unit is operating properly you will notice an increase in noise in the blower fan and the air flow rate will increase slightly. The compressor should be running.

8. Finally, move the blower switch to each position on the control panel. There should be a noticeable air-flow and noise change at each position.

If all the mode positions and tests described above operate as indicated, the controls are working properly.

The air-conditioning system found on cars manufactured by Chrysler is similar to the two previously described types, except that the Chrysler system uses a different method to select the mode of operation. The modes and various damper door positions are shown in the chart in Fig. 4-16. Notice in the chart that the selection is made possible by a series of pushbuttons labelled as shown on the top row of the chart opposite the heading "Button."

The vacuum selector valve, power connection, blower switch, electrical feed source, and the main compressor clutch switch are all included in the pushbutton switch assembly. A secondary compressor switch, which is mounted on the control assembly plates, is actuated by the temperature control lever. This switch runs the compressor in the HEAT and DEFROST modes when the temperature lever is approximately one-fourth or less the distance from COLD. The temperature-control slide lever operates a water valve through a self-adjusting cable. Cool temperatures are attained at the left position, and warm temperatures are obtained at the right position.

This system can be checked like the General Motors systems if you substitute the pushbutton operations for the slide movements given for the General Motors system.

The three systems (Ford, General Motors, and Chrysler) all operate in a similar fashion; any major differences were pointed out. For example, all of these types of systems use resistors to control the speed of the blower motor. The main difference is the location of the resistor; that is, the Ford and General Motors systems have the

CHRYSLER MANUAL A/C MODE CONTROL CHART

BUTTON	OFF	MAX.A/C	A/C	HEAT	DEFROST
INLET AIR DOOR (OPEN TO)	INSIDE	INSIDE	OUTSIDE	OUTSIDE	OUTSIDE
AIR-CONDITIONING DOOR	OPEN	OPEN	OPEN	CLOSED	CLOSED
HEATER DOOR	CLOSED	CLOSED	CLOSED	OPEN	CLOSED WITH AIR BLEED
DEFROSTER DOOR	CLOSED	CLOSED	CLOSED	CLOSED WITH AIR BLEED	OPEN
BLOWER SPEED	OFF	HI-MED LOW	HI-MED LOW	HI-MED. LOW	HI-MED. LOW
COMPRESSOR CLUTCH	ON	ON	ON	* OFF	*OFF

*COMPRESSOR CLUTCH MAY BE ON IN HEAT
AND DEFROST. TEMPERATURE CONTROL
LEVER SETTING OPTIONAL ON ALL MODES.

Fig. 4-16. Modes and various damper door positions for cars manufactured by Chrysler.

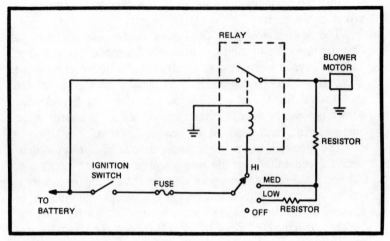

Fig. 4-17. A typical resistor consists of a set of terminals and resistor wire coil connected between them as shown here.

blower speed resistor located in the engine compartment while the resistor in the Chrysler system is located on the A/C instrument panel housing.

Regardless of where the resistor is located, it performs the same function for operating the heating and cooling system in the car in question. A typical resistor consists of a set of terminals with resistor wire coils connected between them as shown in Figs. 4-17 and 4-18. Each speed setting is connected to the resistor assembly by an individual wire from the blower switch. If any problems occur in the blower—such as the fan not operating on one or more speeds—the problem is usually in the wires, switch, or resistors. The switch is easily checked with an ohmmeter or simple continuity tester by placing one test lead on the voltage input terminal and the other test lead on the various position terminals as the switch is operated. Loose connections can be checked visually and the voltage can be checked at the resistor terminals to ensure that the wires are satisfactory. If all these tests check out, it stands to reason that one or both of the resistors are bad and must be replaced.

After placing new resistors in the system, if the remaining wiring, switch, etc., checks out, and the motor still does not function properly, chances are that the motor is bad and will have to be replaced. Most local dealers will have a replacement motor. However, the replacement can be time-consuming since the motor in most cars is hard to reach—requiring the removal and replacement of several other automotive parts. In some cases it may even mean removing the inner fender well and most of the duct under the well—very time-consuming. Always check with the service manual (available from the manufacturer of your car for about $15) before attempting such a replacement.

On manual control air-conditioning systems, temperature control is generally provided by the temperature control lever operating a blend-air door or a water valve, depending upon the make of the car and system. This door is usually cable-operated and mixes cooled air from the evaporator coil and heated air from the heater core in varying amounts. This control cable may be adjusted by first positioning the temperature lever on the coldest setting. Then adjust the turnbuckle until the cam roller is at the end of the cam slot. The cam should be on top of the air-conditioning unit under the instrument panel on General Motors products. It may be necessary to remove some of the car's parts under the dash or instrument panel in order to get to it. Finally move the temperature lever to full warm and then back to full cold. The cam should rest at the end of the slot when it is returned. If not, readjust the turnbuckle until it does so.

If the temperature cable should have to be replaced, it often means the removal of several other items under the instrument panel, such as the glove compartment or air ducts. For this reason, consult the car's service manual before attempting such an operation.

In some systems—Chrysler, for instance—the regulated vacuum powers a water valve rather than operating a blend-air damper door: the higher the vacuum, the greater amount of water flow through the valve and heater core. This results in a higher air temperature.

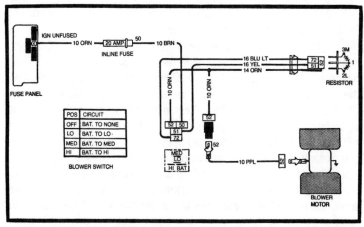

Fig. 4-18. Typical blower motor wiring diagram.

These systems described above use the reheat principle of temperature control which means that the air is first cooled and dehumidified by the evaporator and then reheated to a comfortable temperature by the heater. If the air discharged from the system is the same temperature as the inlet air, the system is operating as a dehumidifier. The air first passes through the cold evaporator, which cools and dehumidifies the air, and then through the heater core, which raises the temperature to the desired level.

Nearly all air-conditioning systems installed in modern automobiles utilize a safety-control device in order to protect the compressor from mechanical seizure and complete failure. This control disengages the compressor clutch when the refrigerant charge is lost. General Motors, for example, calls this device a "super-heat switch." It's mounted on the rear head of the compressor. It operates similarly to the thermal cutout installed on most electric heating units. When this switch senses both high-suction gas temperature and low-suction gas pressure resulting from a certain amount of refrigerant loss, the contacts in the switch close, energizing the heater, and the thermal fuse link in the clutch circuit melts permanently, turning off the compressor. Before the fuse link can be replaced, the location and cause of the refrigerant leak must be corrected and the system must be recharged as described elsewhere in this book.

Chrysler systems utilize a low-pressure cutoff switch connected in series in the clutch wire lead. Upon sensing a low refrigerant charge, the normally closed contacts open the compressor clutch circuit. This type of switch automatically resets after the leak has been detected, repaired, and the system has been recharged. This switch also shuts off the compressor when the ambient temperature is below 32°F—another helpful safety device.

Automatic temperature control systems are standard on the luxury cars and may be installed in the less expensive models as an option at additional cost. This type of system automatically maintains the selected temperature inside the car regardless of the weather on the outside. In warm weather, the control provides the right amount of cooling; on cold days it provides the right amount of heat; and on mild days, it performs a blending operation. Other features include automatic blower speed control; that is, it selects high fan speeds for a fast change of temperature when the car is first turned on and as the car approaches the preset temperature, the blower speed slows down. However, such systems (as of this writing) do not have an automatic defrost cycle—the driver must operate this mode manually. Rather than using the high or low temperature ratings as on the manually operated systems, the automatic temperature-control systems have a dial that is calibrated in actual degrees Fahrenheit of temperature.

The diagram shown in Fig. 4-19 is the basic circuit for all systems, although the controls will vary from car to car. In general, all systems have sensors made up of thermistors—a resistor that changes its value as the temperature changes. These are wired in series and will change in value as the ambient temperature, the inside temperature, and the control dial are changed.

An amplifier is also used in all systems. This boosts the weak current flowing through the sensor circuit and sends it to the transducer, which converts the electrical energy to mechanical energy. This mechanical energy takes the vacuum from the engine reservoir or supply tank through a source port of the rotary switch, and a certain amount of control vacuum is transmitted to the vacuum motor through port 2 of the master vacuum relay and then out of port 1. The vacuum which opens the 1 and 2 ports comes from a separate source, such as the control panel selector switch, to port 5.

The vacuum motor regulates the control vacuum and changes the mode from full cooling to full heat as the condition requires. As the vacuum motor's shaft moves, the resistance of the feedback pot changes. The amplifier resistance of the sensor string and feedback pot circuit must remain the same for all modes of operation. The feedback pot then compensates the amplifier for the other changes in the sensor string, which tells the amplifier whether or not the condition is satisfied.

The vacuum motor also operates the blend-air door and the water valve automatically. (These are the same devices that were operated with control levers in the manual systems described earlier in this chapter.) When the vacuum motor shaft moves to operate these devices, it also engages the blower speed contacts and operates the blower fan.

Another control device operated by the vacuum motor is the rotary vacuum valve. This valve distributes vacuum to other vacuum motors for mode changes and opens the heater water valve.

The in-car sensors are placed behind a small grille in the car's instrument panel so they will be able to sense an average in-car temperature and not the air discharging from the air outlets. However, they must have some air flowing over them in order for them to operate properly. The device used to supply this air is called an aspirator. In general, the aspirator is a nozzle which is attached to an opening in the ductwork or some similar place. As the air flows

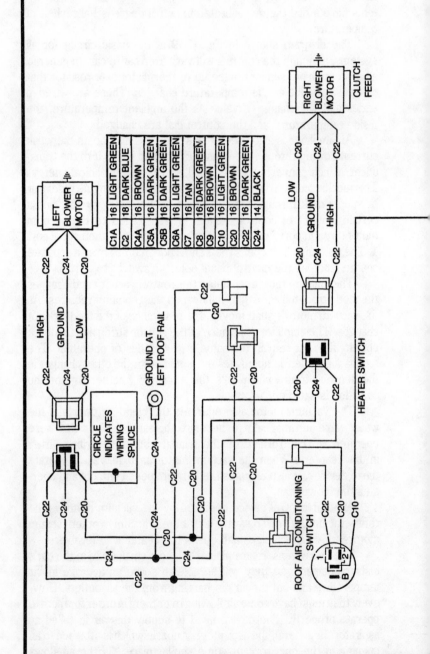

C1A	16	LIGHT GREEN
C2	18	DARK BLUE
C4A	16	BROWN
C5A	16	DARK GREEN
C5B	16	DARK GREEN
C6A	16	LIGHT GREEN
C7	16	TAN
C8	16	DARK GREEN
C9	16	BROWN
C10	16	LIGHT GREEN
C20	16	BROWN
C22	16	DARK GREEN
C24	14	BLACK

LEFT BLOWER MOTOR

RIGHT BLOWER MOTOR

CLUTCH FEED

HIGH   GROUND   LOW

LOW   GROUND   HIGH

CIRCLE INDICATES WIRING SPLICE

GROUND AT LEFT ROOF RAIL

ROOF AIR CONDITIONING SWITCH

HEATER SWITCH

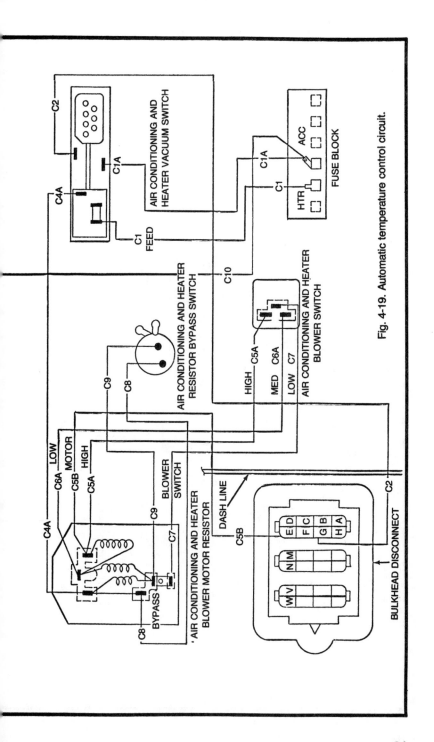

Fig. 4-19. Automatic temperature control circuit.

91

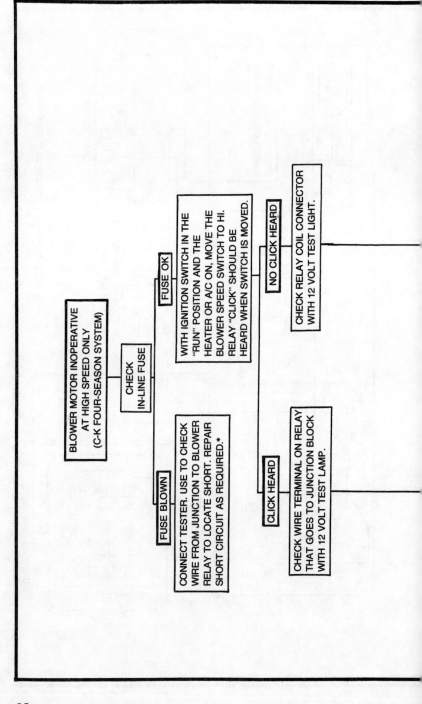

BLOWER MOTOR INOPERATIVE AT HIGH SPEED ONLY (C-K FOUR-SEASON SYSTEM)

CHECK IN-LINE FUSE

FUSE OK

FUSE BLOWN

WITH IGNITION SWITCH IN THE "RUN" POSITION AND THE HEATER OR A/C ON, MOVE THE BLOWER SPEED SWITCH TO HI. RELAY "CLICK" SHOULD BE HEARD WHEN SWITCH IS MOVED.

CONNECT TESTER. USE TO CHECK WIRE FROM JUNCTION TO BLOWER RELAY TO LOCATE SHORT. REPAIR SHORT CIRCUIT AS REQUIRED.*

NO CLICK HEARD

CLICK HEARD

CHECK RELAY COIL CONNECTOR WITH 12 VOLT TEST LIGHT.

CHECK WIRE TERMINAL ON RELAY THAT GOES TO JUNCTION BLOCK WITH 12 VOLT TEST LAMP.

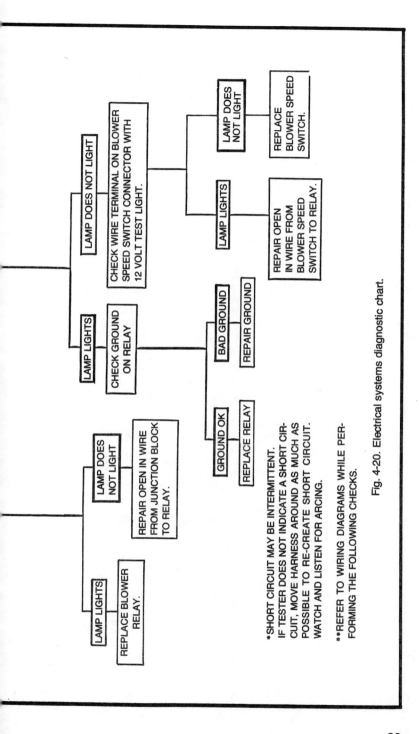

LAMP LIGHTS

REPLACE BLOWER RELAY.

LAMP DOES NOT LIGHT

REPAIR OPEN IN WIRE FROM JUNCTION BLOCK TO RELAY.

GROUND OK

REPLACE RELAY

BAD GROUND

REPAIR GROUND

LAMP LIGHTS

CHECK GROUND ON RELAY

LAMP DOES NOT LIGHT

CHECK WIRE TERMINAL ON BLOWER SPEED SWITCH CONNECTOR WITH 12 VOLT TEST LIGHT.

LAMP LIGHTS

REPAIR OPEN IN WIRE FROM BLOWER SPEED SWITCH TO RELAY.

LAMP DOES NOT LIGHT

REPLACE BLOWER SPEED SWITCH.

*SHORT CIRCUIT MAY BE INTERMITTENT. IF TESTER DOES NOT INDICATE A SHORT CIRCUIT, MOVE HARNESS AROUND AS MUCH AS POSSIBLE TO RE-CREATE SHORT CIRCUIT. WATCH AND LISTEN FOR ARCING.

**REFER TO WIRING DIAGRAMS WHILE PERFORMING THE FOLLOWING CHECKS.

Fig. 4-20. Electrical systems diagnostic chart.

```
┌─────────────────────────────────────────┐
│ COMPRESSOR CLUTCH INOPERATIVE** │
└─────────────────────────────────────────┘
        ┌──────────────┐
        │ CHECK FUSE │
        └──────────────┘
    ┌──────────────┐
    │ FUSE BLOWN │
    └──────────────┘
```

WITH IGNITION SWITCH IN "RUN" POSITION,
AND A/C "ON", CONNECT TESTER AND
LOCATE SHORT IN ONE OF THE
FOLLOWING WIRES OR COMPONENTS. RE-
PLACE A SHORTED WIRE OR DEFECTIVE
SWITCH.

C-K MODEL SYSTEMS

1. WIRE FROM FUSE PANEL TO MASTER
   SWITCH (ON CONTROL).
2. MASTER SWITCH.
3. WIRE FROM MASTER SWITCH TO
   THERMOSTATIC SWITCH.
4. THERMOSTATIC SWITCH.
5. WIRE FROM THERMOSTATIC SWITCH
   TO DISCHARGE PRESSURE SWITCH.
6. DISCHARGE PRESSURE SWITCH.
7. WIRE FROM DISCHARGE PRESSURE
   SWITCH TO COMPRESSOR CLUTCH
   SOLENOID.

G MODEL SYSTEMS

1. WIRE FROM FUSE PANEL TO
   AMPLIFIER.
2. AMPLIFIER.
3. WIRES FROM AMPLIFIER TO THERMIS-
   TER.
6. DISCHARGE PRESSURE SWITCH.
7. WIRE FROM DISCHARGE PRESSURE
   SWITCH TO COMPRESSOR CLUTCH
   SOLENOID.

MOTOR HOME UNIT

1. WIRE FROM FUSE PANEL TO BLOWER
   SWITCH.
2. BLOWER SWITCH.
3. WIRE FROM BLOWER SWITCH TO
   THERMOSTATIC SWITCH.
4. THERMOSTATIC SWITCH.
5. WIRE FROM THERMOSTATIC SWITCH
   TO COMPRESSOR CLUTCH SOLENOID.

ELECTRICAL SYSTEM DIAGNOSTIC CHART

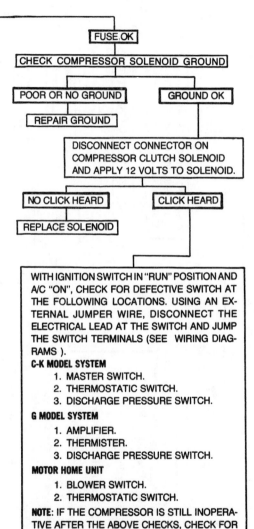

FUSE.OK

CHECK COMPRESSOR SOLENOID GROUND

POOR OR NO GROUND

REPAIR GROUND

GROUND OK

DISCONNECT CONNECTOR ON COMPRESSOR CLUTCH SOLENOID AND APPLY 12 VOLTS TO SOLENOID.

NO CLICK HEARD

REPLACE SOLENOID

CLICK HEARD

WITH IGNITION SWITCH IN "RUN" POSITION AND A/C "ON", CHECK FOR DEFECTIVE SWITCH AT THE FOLLOWING LOCATIONS. USING AN EXTERNAL JUMPER WIRE, DISCONNECT THE ELECTRICAL LEAD AT THE SWITCH AND JUMP THE SWITCH TERMINALS (SEE WIRING DIAGRAMS).

C-K MODEL SYSTEM
1. MASTER SWITCH.
2. THERMOSTATIC SWITCH.
3. DISCHARGE PRESSURE SWITCH.

G MODEL SYSTEM
1. AMPLIFIER.
2. THERMISTER.
3. DISCHARGE PRESSURE SWITCH.

MOTOR HOME UNIT
1. BLOWER SWITCH.
2. THERMOSTATIC SWITCH.

NOTE: IF THE COMPRESSOR IS STILL INOPERATIVE AFTER THE ABOVE CHECKS, CHECK FOR POWER FEED AT EACH COMPONENT SINCE TWO OR MORE COMPONENTS ARE DEFECTIVE OR THERE IS AN OPEN IN THE WIRES CONNECTING THE COMPONENTS.

Fig. 4-20. cont.

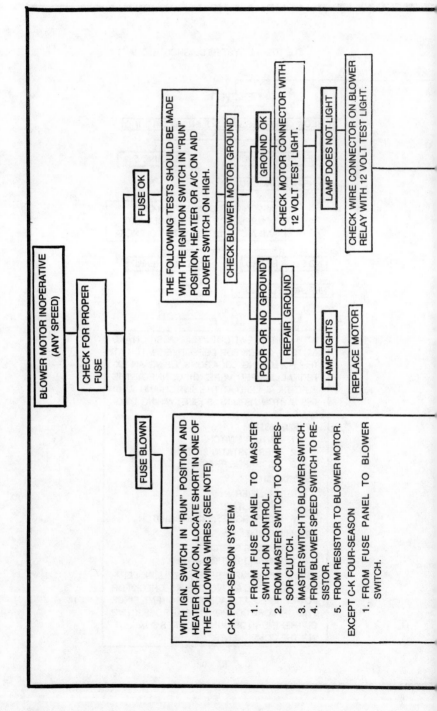

BLOWER MOTOR INOPERATIVE (ANY SPEED)

CHECK FOR PROPER FUSE

FUSE OK

THE FOLLOWING TESTS SHOULD BE MADE WITH THE IGNITION SWITCH IN "RUN" POSITION, HEATER OR A/C ON AND BLOWER SWITCH ON HIGH.

CHECK BLOWER MOTOR GROUND

GROUND OK

CHECK MOTOR CONNECTOR WITH 12 VOLT TEST LIGHT.

LAMP DOES NOT LIGHT

CHECK WIRE CONNECTOR ON BLOWER RELAY WITH 12 VOLT TEST LIGHT.

POOR OR NO GROUND

REPAIR GROUND

LAMP LIGHTS

REPLACE MOTOR

FUSE BLOWN

WITH IGN. SWITCH IN "RUN" POSITION AND HEATER OR A/C ON, LOCATE SHORT IN ONE OF THE FOLLOWING WIRES: (SEE NOTE)

C-K FOUR-SEASON SYSTEM

1. FROM FUSE PANEL TO MASTER SWITCH ON CONTROL.
2. FROM MASTER SWITCH TO COMPRESSOR CLUTCH.
3. MASTER SWITCH TO BLOWER SWITCH.
4. FROM BLOWER SPEED SWITCH TO RESISTOR.
5. FROM RESISTOR TO BLOWER MOTOR.

EXCEPT C-K FOUR-SEASON

1. FROM FUSE PANEL TO BLOWER SWITCH.

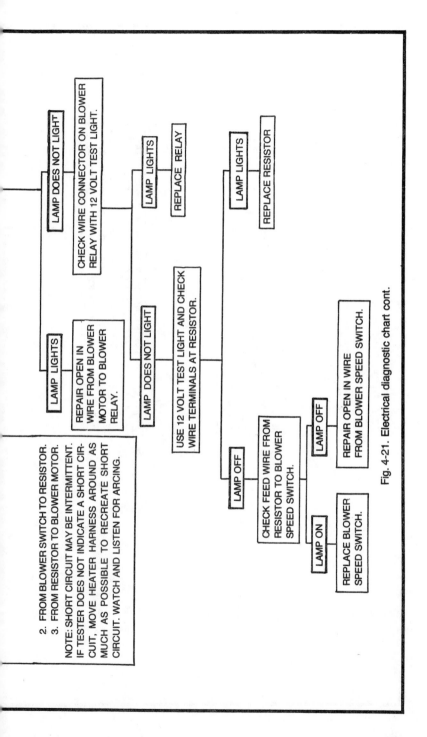

LAMP DOES NOT LIGHT

CHECK WIRE CONNECTOR ON BLOWER RELAY WITH 12 VOLT TEST LIGHT.

LAMP LIGHTS

REPLACE RELAY

LAMP DOES NOT LIGHT

USE 12 VOLT TEST LIGHT AND CHECK WIRE TERMINALS AT RESISTOR.

LAMP LIGHTS

REPLACE RESISTOR

LAMP LIGHTS

REPAIR OPEN IN WIRE FROM BLOWER MOTOR TO BLOWER RELAY.

LAMP OFF

CHECK FEED WIRE FROM RESISTOR TO BLOWER SPEED SWITCH.

LAMP ON

REPLACE BLOWER SPEED SWITCH.

LAMP OFF

REPAIR OPEN IN WIRE FROM BLOWER SPEED SWITCH.

2. FROM BLOWER SWITCH TO RESISTOR.
3. FROM RESISTOR TO BLOWER MOTOR.

NOTE: SHORT CIRCUIT MAY BE INTERMITTENT. IF TESTER DOES NOT INDICATE A SHORT CIRCUIT, MOVE HEATER HARNESS AROUND AS MUCH AS POSSIBLE TO RECREATE SHORT CIRCUIT. WATCH AND LISTEN FOR ARCING.

Fig. 4-21. Electrical diagnostic chart cont.

ELECTRICAL SYSTEM DIAGNOSTIC CHART

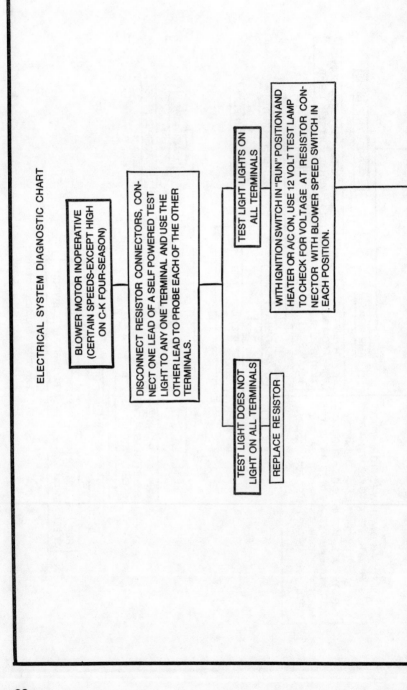

BLOWER MOTOR INOPERATIVE
(CERTAIN SPEEDS-EXCEPT HIGH
ON C-K FOUR-SEASON)

DISCONNECT RESISTOR CONNECTORS, CONNECT ONE LEAD OF A SELF POWERED TEST LIGHT TO ANY ONE TERMINAL AND USE THE OTHER LEAD TO PROBE EACH OF THE OTHER TERMINALS.

TEST LIGHT LIGHTS ON ALL TERMINALS

WITH IGNITION SWITCH IN "RUN" POSITION AND HEATER OR A/C ON, USE 12 VOLT TEST LAMP TO CHECK FOR VOLTAGE AT RESISTOR CONNECTOR WITH BLOWER SPEED SWITCH IN EACH POSITION.

TEST LIGHT DOES NOT LIGHT ON ALL TERMINALS

REPLACE RESISTOR

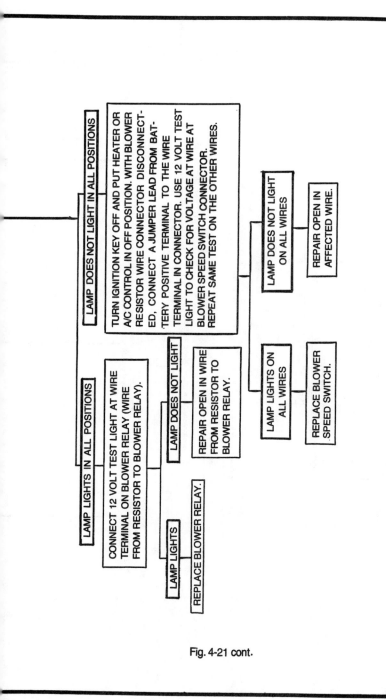

LAMP DOES NOT LIGHT IN ALL POSITIONS

TURN IGNITION KEY OFF AND PUT HEATER OR A/C CONTROL IN OFF POSITION. WITH BLOWER RESISTOR WIRE CONNECTOR DISCONNECTED, CONNECT A JUMPER LEAD FROM BATTERY POSITIVE TERMINAL TO THE WIRE TERMINAL IN CONNECTOR. USE 12 VOLT TEST LIGHT TO CHECK FOR VOLTAGE AT WIRE AT BLOWER SPEED SWITCH CONNECTOR. REPEAT SAME TEST ON THE OTHER WIRES.

LAMP DOES NOT LIGHT ON ALL WIRES

REPAIR OPEN IN AFFECTED WIRE.

LAMP LIGHTS ON ALL WIRES

REPLACE BLOWER SPEED SWITCH.

LAMP LIGHTS IN ALL POSITIONS

CONNECT 12 VOLT TEST LIGHT AT WIRE TERMINAL ON BLOWER RELAY (WIRE FROM RESISTOR TO BLOWER RELAY).

LAMP DOES NOT LIGHT

REPAIR OPEN IN WIRE FROM RESISTOR TO BLOWER RELAY.

LAMP LIGHTS

REPLACE BLOWER RELAY.

Fig. 4-21 cont.

99

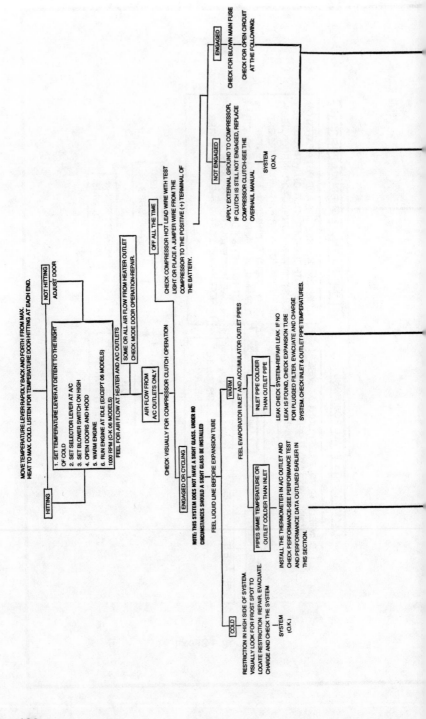

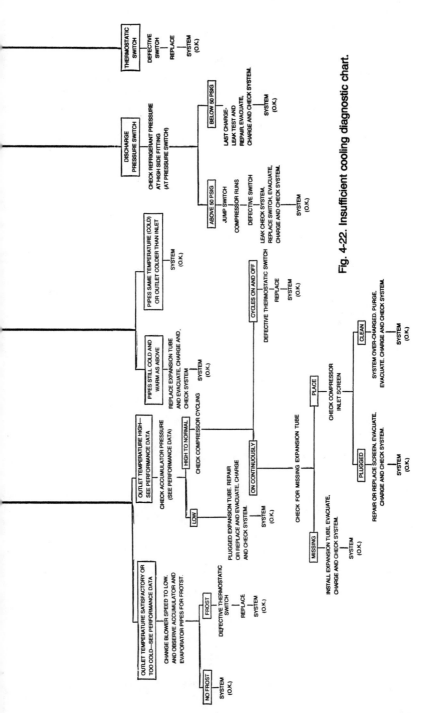

Fig. 4-22. Insufficient cooling diagnostic chart.

through the nozzle, a suction is created at the fitting on the opposite end of the nozzle and draws air through a hose and over the in-car sensor.

Servicing automatic temperature-control systems requires a basic knowledge of the particular system's operation. A description of the system's operation can be found in the manufacturer's service manual, or by consulting the section on servicing automatic temperature control systems in Chapter 5. Figures 4-20 through 4-22 will aid in diagnosing electrical and other air conditioner malfunctions.

Chapter 5

Troubleshooting The Automotive Air-Conditioning System

Although a stem-to-stern servicing job on an automotive air-conditioning system is usually beyond the capabilities of most home mechanics, there are a number of service and repair jobs within their reach. This chapter covers the most common problems found in the automotive air-conditioning system and the procedures for solving them. Even if you find that some of the jobs are beyond your capabilities (probably due to the lack of proper tools), you will still have an idea of what the trouble is. When you point out the problems to the mechanic who will repair the trouble, much time and money can be saved.

The problems and the solutions for correcting them are aimed at both the add-on and factory-installed units. Some of the problems—like an inadequate cooling system—are more typical of cars with the add-on unit while other problems could be typical of both types.

OVERHEATED ENGINE

The addition of an air-conditioning system in your car will always have some effect on its normal operation. This is especially true of the car's cooling system when an add-on type unit is utilized; factory-installed units normally have made provisions to absorb the additional load on the cooling system.

At the first sign of engine overheating, check for a loose fan belt (see Fig. 5-1). The most accurate way of doing this is to use a belt

Fig. 5-1. At the first sign of engine overheating, check for a loose fan belt. With the engine off, push down on the belt with your thumb or finger in the middle of the longest belt span. The belt should not depress more than 1/2 inch for normal operation.

tension gauge to see if the belt tension is somewhere between 60 and 80 pounds. If you do not have a belt tension gauge, a rule of thumb is to push down on the belt with your finger in the middle of the longest belt span. The belt should depress not more than 1/2 inch for normal operation on most cars. If either one of these tests shows that the belt is loose, retension the belt to the recommended tension.

Should the fan belt tension prove to be correct, check for a faulty pressure cap on the car's radiator (Fig. 5-2). A certain amount of pressure is required in the car's cooling system to allow the water to absorb higher temperatures without boiling. If this pressure is not maintained, the water will boil at a temperature lower than required for the engine's operation, and probably flow out the radiator's overflow pipe—causing the cooling system to become low on water. Replace the cap if this is found to be defective.

The next logical step would be to check the radiator thermostat. Replace it it necessary.

Perhaps your cooling fan is not large enough for the job it is to perform. If your engine still overheats after checking the previously mentioned items, take a look at the fan, and also at your condenser and radiator. Clean bugs, dirt, paper, leaves, and the like from the condenser and radiator with a garden hose. If this doesn't solve the engine heating problem, install a new five-bladed fan (Fig. 5-3).

104

COMPRESSOR FAILS TO ROTATE PROPERLY

The first logical step is to check the tension on the drive belt (Fig. 5-4). As was recommended for testing fan belts, a belt tension gauge is the most accurate method. If you do not have a belt tension gauge, push down on the belt with your finger in the middle of the longest belt span. If the belt depresses more than 1/2 inch (for most cars), the belt is too loose and needs to be tightened.

If the compressor drive belt tension seems to be set correctly and the compressor still fails to operate properly, it could be caused by very high head pressure. This is usually due to an overcharge of refirgerant. If so, see Chapter 10 for correcting the situation.

Also check pulley belts for wear caused by nicked pulleys or improper pulley alignment, and for fractured cord caused by applying

Fig. 5-2. Check for a faulty pressure cap on the car's radiator.

Fig. 5-3. If your engine still overheats, take a look at the fan; install a new 5-bladed fan if necessary.

too much side pressure during installation (Fig. 5-5). Smooth out any nicks found in the pulleys or replace; realign pulleys if they are out of alignment. In any case, the worn pulley belts should be replaced.

If you're still having trouble with the compressor rotating properly, look for a slipping clutch. The slip could be caused by low

Fig. 5-4. If compressor fails to rotate properly, first check the tension on the drive belt.

Fig. 5-5. Also check pulley belts for nicks, improper pulley alignment, or fractured cord.

voltage on the clutch circuit, in which case the faulty wiring (Fig. 5-6) should be corrected by following suggestions found in Chapter 4. Grease on the clutch face could be causing the trouble; if so, clean the face with carbon tetrachloride or a similar cleaning agent.

Assuming that the clutch voltage is OK, but the clutch is still inoperative, check for an open field coil in the clutch and replace it if found to be defective. Worn brushes or dirty slip rings could also be

Fig. 5-6. If you're still having trouble with the compressor rotating properly, look for a slipping clutch which could be caused by faulty wiring on the clutch circuit.

causing the trouble. Don't overlook a damaged clutch bearing—this is not common, but does happen. If found to be defective, replace.

UNUSUAL NOISE IN ENGINE COMPARTMENT

Every car owner is going to experience this problem sometime during the life of the car. The first suggestion is to check for something loose—brackets, bolts, braces, etc. Tighten all bolts with a torque wrench and then check pulley alignment.

Damaged bearings in the idler pulley or clutch could be another cause of excessive noise in the engine compartment. Check these by conventional methods and replace any that are worn. Also check the clutch retaining bolt and all pulleys as well as the crankshaft. Tighten any that are found to be loose.

If a dull knock or thump occurs in the compressor, chances are there is excessive oil in the crankcase. This is known as oil pumping and occurs infrequently; when it does, it usually corrects itself. However, if the pumping is persistent, check the oil in the crankcase; if it is excessive, remove sufficient oil to bring the level to normal. When opening the crankcase to the air, the pressure should be balanced and afterwards purged.

Should the noise from your compressor be a squeaking, hammering or clanking noise, it is probably caused by insufficient oil in the crankcase (Fig. 5-7). If this is the case, add sufficient oil to the

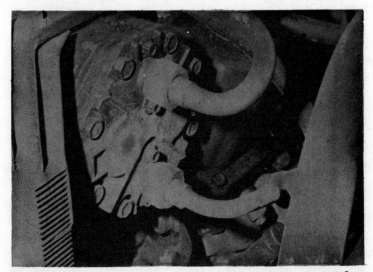

Fig. 5-7. Should the noise from your compressor be a squeaking, hammering or clanking noise, it is probably caused by insufficient oil in the crankcase.

crankcase to bring it to normal. However, before doing this, make certain that the refrigerant charge in the system is sufficient; an insufficient refrigerant charge can create a low oil level in the crankcase. Again, when opening the crankcase to the air, the pressure should be balanced and afterwards purged as described elsewhere in this book.

Continue your check for noise by examining the evaporator to see if it could be flooded, allowing liquid refrigerant to reach the compressor. You could also have a broken compressor valve. The ordinarily noisy discharge valve makes a clicking noise, while a stuck valve or a valve with insufficient lift makes a dull thud, in most cases. Also, with a stuck valve the walls of the cylinder will be warm. Noisy discharge valves are usually caused by insufficient or too much lift.

DEFECTIVE EVAPORATOR BLOWER MOTOR

As with any electrical device, when it doesn't operate, always check the fuse first. However, if you find that the fuse is blown, do not replace it until you first check for a short circuit within the electrical system—something caused the fuse to blow. If neither is found to be the problem, check for loose or broken wiring and correct any defects. Continue on to the switch controlling the circuit and replace with a new one if this is found to be defective.

The problem could be mechanical rather than electrical. For example, worn bearings or a tight shaft could render the evaporator blower motor inoperative. If this seems to be the case, lubricate and check for dirt in the bearings. If the blower wheels are bent, this may also cause the motor to function improperly. In most cases it is best to replace them rather than try to straighten them.

DISCHARGE PRESSURE OVER 250 POUNDS

The most likely cause of high discharge pressure is an overcharge of refrigerant. If this is the case, you will also probably have a frosted suction line, poor refrigeration, and oil pumping in the compressor. You can remedy the situation, however, by purging the unit until the proper level of refrigerant is obtained.

Air entering the system is another cause of high discharge pressure. When this is suspected, test all joints and other possible places for leaks, bleed the system, evacuate and recharge. Usually, if a leak is found, it can be corrected by tightening the joint.

An overheated condenser, due to a slipping fan belt or a clogged air passage, is another common cause of boosting the discharge pressure to over 250 pounds. Obviously, the fan-belt tension should be corrected, and if clogged air passage through the condenser is noticed, clean bugs and dirt from the condenser fins with a garden hose. Straighten any fin that may become bent in the process.

Kinks in hoses or a clogged filter will restrict the liquid flow in the liquid line from the condenser and cause excessive discharge pressure. Check these items and correct if necessary.

LOW DISCHARGE PRESSURE

The main cause of low discharge pressure is an undercharge of refrigerant, which is indicated by bubbles or foam present in the sight glass (provided on most systems). Further symptoms of an undercharge of refrigerant may include poor refrigeration, suction pressure less than normal, and oil level in the compressor lower than normal.

Before adding any new refrigerant, test all joints in the system for possible leaks. You might even want to test the entire system for leaks as small holes in the lines are possible. If no leak is discovered or if the leak can be corrected by tightening the joint, add the necessary amount of refrigerant to bring the system to normal. See Chapter 10.

If the leak cannot be corrected by tightening the joint, repair the leak in an appropriate manner and then recharge the system with the correct amount of refrigerant to bring the system back to normal. Again, see Chapter 10.

Damaged compressor valves or dirt under the valves will also cause low discharge pressure. To correct, first isolate the compressor and then remove the valve plate. Clean the valves or replace the valve plate. Replace the gaskets. In reassembling, be sure to clean all parts with carbon tetrachloride or some similar solution, and assemble the compressor, using new gaskets and other new parts where necessary. Never use a valve on which the slightest scratch appears and always assemble the parts properly mated.

In some cases, it may be necessary to replace only a blown gasket on the valve cover. In other instances, however, the compressor itself may be damaged, such as having a broken piston or piston rings. Place a screwdriver against the crankcase with your ear against the end of the handle. Listen for a knock inside the compressor. You probably won't be able to tell exactly which part is loose or broken until the compressor is disassembled, but you will at least know something is loose or broken beforehand.

Isolate the compressor from the rest of the system and disassemble the compressor. If you find that certain parts are broken or in need of repair, you will probably be better off either replacing the entire compressor or sending the damaged one back to the factory for repairs. The job is a little too complicated for the average home mechanic. When you do put the compressor back in operation, be certain that you have the correct amount of oil in the crankcase.

LOW SUCTION PRESSURE

The main cause of low suction pressure in your car's air-conditioning system is low air supply through the evaporator; in most cases this can be remedied by cleaning the air filter or air ducts—an easy job for almost anyone. In some cases, the low air supply may be due to the evaporator blower motor; the inoperative motor should be replaced or repaired. The evaporator fins and coils may be very dirty which will restrict the flow of air over them. This problem can also be remedied very easily—merely clean them and flush with water.

Looking further down the list, a suction control valve stuck open will most definitely cause low suction pressure, so test for this problem if the previously described remedies did not cure the ailment. Replace the valve if necessary. Don't overlook the possibility of a defective evaporator coil thermostat. If your tests indicate that the thermostat is on the blink, the fastest way to correct this is to replace the defective one with a new one. Chapter gave troubleshooting procedures for testing thermostats and other controls related to the car's air-conditioning system.

If an undercharge of refrigerant is indicated by bubbles or foam in the sight glass, this could be the cause of low suction pressure. Before adding refrigerant, check all joints and other possible areas for leaks; if no leaks are evident or the leak has been corrected, add the proper amount of refrigerant.

An expansion valve showing frost probably means that moisture is freezing within the valve, which is another cause of low suction pressure. In this case, install a new drier, and evacuate and recharge the system. The expansion valve inlet screen could be clogged causing the same trouble. Remove the screen, clean with carbon tetrachloride or some similar cleaning solution, and replace the screen.

Should the low suction pressure continue, look for an inoperative expansion valve; the valve will either be stuck closed or the feeler bulb will have lost its charge. To check, warm the feeler bulb by holding it in your hand a few minutes. If the suction pressure does not change, replace the expansion valve.

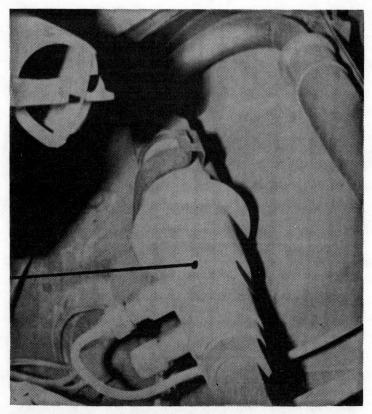

Fig. 5-8. Intermittent cooling could be caused by an erratic suction control valve or a partially stuck expansion valve.

A restriction anywhere in the liquid line is another possible cause of low suction pressure. Normally the line will show signs of frost at or near the point of restriction. If this seems to be the cause of your problem, merely locate the restriction and repair it.

INTERMITTENT COOLING

Although there are a number of reasons for this problem, the most probable cause is an erratic suction control valve. Therefore, this test should be made first and the valve should be replaced if necessary. An erratic or partially stuck expansion valve could also be causing the problem; test and replace this valve if necessary (see Fig. 5-8).

Intermittent cooling may be caused by the compressor rotating intermittently. This problem was discussed earlier in this chapter and can be caused by the compressor drive belt slipping, very high head pressure (caused by an overcharge of refrigerant), a slipping clutch, or other problems. Use the remedies given earlier in this chapter for correcting these faults; that is, check the wiring, clutch, drive belt, and thermostat.

HIGH SUCTION PRESSURE

If the suction line on your system shows signs of frost, you probably have high suction pressure in your system. First check to see if the feeler-bulb clamp on the suction line is loose. If so, clean all contact surfaces of the suction line and feeler bulb and then tighten the clamp.

Next look for a non-closing expansion valve. Symptoms will be a frosted suction line near the compressor and a flooded evaporator. If this is the case, replace the expansion valve. The compressor drive belt could also be slipping—adjust the belt according to the instructions given earlier in this chapter.

A check of the electrical circuit is in order next as the magnetic clutch could be slipping, which would cause high suction pressure. Check for correct voltage to the clutch coil (see Chapter 4). Also clean the clutch surfaces.

Another possible cause of high suction pressure is a leaking or broken compressor valve. Valve kits are available for replacing defective valves if this seems to be the problem.

In most cases, the average home mechanic will not want to attempt rebuilding or repairing a defective compressor unit. You will probably want to trade the defective one in on a factory-rebuilt model or purchase a new unit. However, for those of you who like a challenge, the job is within the capabilities of those who are relatively competent and who have a well-equipped tool kit or can borrow or rent the necessary tools. All that is needed is the proper service manual (obtainable from the factory) and a supply of parts to replace those that are defective or worn. If you should get into a jam, you can usually obtain assistance from one of the local shops; perhaps a call to the manufacturer will be all that is necessary.

Some servicing techniques for automatic temperature controls follow.

SYSTEM OPERATES AT MAXIMUM COOLING ONLY

This can be a mechanical or electrical problem, so the diagnosis should be separated into parts to determine which is causing the problem. Begin by disconnecting the programmer electrical connector while the system is running; observe the programmer movement

Fig. 5-9. Service valve on compressor line used for charging and testing the system.

through the slot at the bottom of the programmer cover. If the programmer remains in the maximum air-conditioning position, remove the multiple vacuum connector and check for supply vacuum at the black hose. If no vacuum exists or it is lower than 15 inches of mercury, check for leaks or loose connections in the vacuum hose assembly. If the vacuum supply is all right, the programmer itself is malfunctioning. In this case, remove the programmer cover and inspect for obvious disconnections; use a tester to analyze and correct the problems as recommended in the manufacturer's service manual.

During the initial test, if the programmer moved to the maximum heater position when the electrical connector was disconnected, the defect is external and not in the programmer itself. You may want to check the following items:

1. Shorted sensors.
2. Shorted or miscalibrated temperature dial.
3. A short in the sensor circuit wires.

SYSTEM OPERATES AT MAXIMUM HEATING ONLY

In most cases, the problem will be in the electrical wiring, not mechanical. To determine whether the problem is internal (inside the programmer) or external, set the temperature dial to 65° and the control lever to the VENT position with the system operating.

114

Observe the programmer through the slot located in the lower half of the programmer cover to see if the programmer now moves to the maximum air-conditioning position. If it does, the problem is one of the following:

1. Disconnected or defective sensors.
2. Open circuit in the wiring of the sensor circuit.
3. Disconnected terminal in the three-way connector located under the instrument panel on the right-hand side near the programmer.

During the initial test, if the programmer did not move when the control was set to the VENT position, the problem lies in one of the following areas:

1. Defective or disconnected temperature dial.
2. Open circuit between the control head and the programmer.
3. No electric power to the programmer. Check the yellow wire with a voltmeter.
4. No ground at amplifier.
5. Defect within the programmer assembly that should be tested with an analyzer as recommended by the manufacturer's service manual.

BLOWER SPEED AND MODE SHIFTS DURING ACCELERATION

This problem is either in the vacuum-checking relay inside the programmer or a leaking programmer vacuum motor. To determine which, remove the programmer electrical connector to force the programmer to maximum heating, that is, full vacuum. Then remove the vacuum hose assembly connector. The programmer should remain in the maximum heat position; if it doesn't, pinch the programmer vacuum motor supply hose with a pair of small pliers while removing the electrical connector. If the programmer still moves, the vacuum motor is leaking. If the programmer does not move, the checking relay is defective. If only the mode shifts during acceleration without any blower change, the check-valve portion of the checking relay is probably defective.

DIAL SETTING DOES NOT PROVIDE CORRECT TEMPERATURE

This is an indication of incorrect calibration and can be best corrected with a tester designed especially for this. Check and reset the temperature dial, the feedback potentiometer in the programmer, the temperature door link adjustment, and the sensor string.

Refer to the instruction sheet included with the tester for further details.

INSUFFICIENT HEATING AND COOLING

This problem can be caused by several different systems and you should first determine which area to pursue. Begin by checking the compressor clutch. If it is not operating, check your service manual for troubleshooting the low refrigerant detection system. Check for a clean sight glass and cold suction line which indicates no cooling. Check the engine coolant level if no heating is present. Check the temperature of the heater hoses by touch—with the engine hot—to see if hot water is entering the heater core (in the case of no heating). Check the air flow at the AUTO and HI lever settings.

BLOWER SPEEDS AND MODE SHIFT OCCURS WITHOUT TEMPERATURE CHANGE

Check the connection of the air mix damper-door link to the programmer shaft and to the air-door crankarm.

SYSTEM OPERATES ONLY AT LOW BLOWER SPEED

This problem probably indicates an open or disconnected blower relay or a poor connection at the six-way connector, the programmer, or control head. You can trace out the blower circuit by using the electrical wiring diagram in the service manual.

NO BLOWER OPERATION AT ANY SETTING

First check the 15 amp fuse and then look for open or disconnected wiring at the blower motor or at the radio capacitor in series with the blower-motor feed wire. The motor could be stalled due to misaligned blades or some obstacle in the fan. Also check the six-way connector near the programmer.

Any other problem with the blower motor is usually due to open wiring or a defective relay, blown fuse, etc. Use the wiring diagram to check out the entire system, beginning at the fuse and power supply.

NO HEATER TURN-ON IN COLD WEATHER EXCEPT IN VENT AND DEF

This problem indicates an electrical disconnection at the heater turn-on switch or a defective switch. If the trouble is not found at either of these locations, check the wiring diagrams to trace the wiring for other possible disconnections.

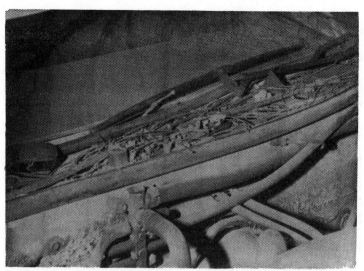

Fig. 5-10. Check vacumm hoses for leaks or a leaky connection if controls are not functioning properly. Also clean leaves and other debris from the outside air vents.

IMMEDIATE HEATER TURN-ON IN COLD WEATHER

A defective heater turn-on or in-car switch is the most probable cause of this problem.

AIR CONDITIONING DELAYED IN WARM
WEATHER UNTIL ENGINE WARMS UP

This will occur with a defective in-car switch or open wiring elsewhere in the system.

DAMPER DOOR ACTUATION PROBLEMS

Since vacuum is required to operate the damper doors, always check the vacuum hose connections for leaks. Work from the defective item back towards the vacuum source.

HEATER WATER VALVE CONTROL PROBLEMS

The water valves are also actuated by vacuum, so again check for leaks starting from the inoperative valve back to the vacuum source.

COMPRESSOR ELECTRICAL PROBLEMS

If insufficient or no cooling is the problem, chances are that the problem lies in the compressor electrical circuit. Check for a blown

117

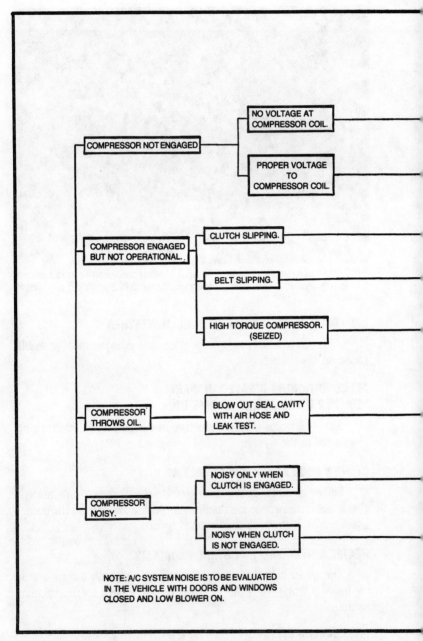

COMPRESSOR NOT ENGAGED
- NO VOLTAGE AT COMPRESSOR COIL.
- PROPER VOLTAGE TO COMPRESSOR COIL.

COMPRESSOR ENGAGED BUT NOT OPERATIONAL.
- CLUTCH SLIPPING.
- BELT SLIPPING.
- HIGH TORQUE COMPRESSOR. (SEIZED)

COMPRESSOR THROWS OIL.
- BLOW OUT SEAL CAVITY WITH AIR HOSE AND LEAK TEST.

COMPRESSOR NOISY.
- NOISY ONLY WHEN CLUTCH IS ENGAGED.
- NOISY WHEN CLUTCH IS NOT ENGAGED.

NOTE: A/C SYSTEM NOISE IS TO BE EVALUATED IN THE VEHICLE WITH DOORS AND WINDOWS CLOSED AND LOW BLOWER ON.

thermal fuse or a disconnected wire at the thermal fuse. Continue checking for a blown 15 ampere fuse in the fuse block, electrical disconnection at the compressor clutch coil, grounded clutch coil,

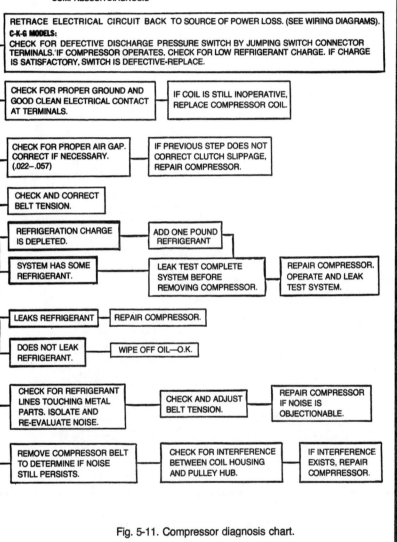

COMPRESSOR DIAGNOSIS

RETRACE ELECTRICAL CIRCUIT BACK TO SOURCE OF POWER LOSS. (SEE WIRING DIAGRAMS).
C-K-G MODELS:
CHECK FOR DEFECTIVE DISCHARGE PRESSURE SWITCH BY JUMPING SWITCH CONNECTOR TERMINALS. IF COMPRESSOR OPERATES, CHECK FOR LOW REFRIGERANT CHARGE. IF CHARGE IS SATISFACTORY, SWITCH IS DEFECTIVE-REPLACE.

CHECK FOR PROPER GROUND AND GOOD CLEAN ELECTRICAL CONTACT AT TERMINALS.

IF COIL IS STILL INOPERATIVE, REPLACE COMPRESSOR COIL.

CHECK FOR PROPER AIR GAP. CORRECT IF NECESSARY. (.022–.057)

IF PREVIOUS STEP DOES NOT CORRECT CLUTCH SLIPPAGE, REPAIR COMPRESSOR.

CHECK AND CORRECT BELT TENSION.

REFRIGERATION CHARGE IS DEPLETED.

ADD ONE POUND REFRIGERANT

SYSTEM HAS SOME REFRIGERANT.

LEAK TEST COMPLETE SYSTEM BEFORE REMOVING COMPRESSOR.

REPAIR COMPRESSOR. OPERATE AND LEAK TEST SYSTEM.

LEAKS REFRIGERANT

REPAIR COMPRESSOR.

DOES NOT LEAK REFRIGERANT.

WIPE OFF OIL—O.K.

CHECK FOR REFRIGERANT LINES TOUCHING METAL PARTS. ISOLATE AND RE-EVALUATE NOISE.

CHECK AND ADJUST BELT TENSION.

REPAIR COMPRESSOR IF NOISE IS OBJECTIONABLE.

REMOVE COMPRESSOR BELT TO DETERMINE IF NOISE STILL PERSISTS.

CHECK FOR INTERFERENCE BETWEEN COIL HOUSING AND PULLEY HUB.

IF INTERFERENCE EXISTS, REPAIR COMPRRESSOR.

Fig. 5-11. Compressor diagnosis chart.

electrical disconnection at the compressor ambient switch, or an electrical disconnection at the three-way electrical connector inside the car. There could also be a defective compressor ambient switch,

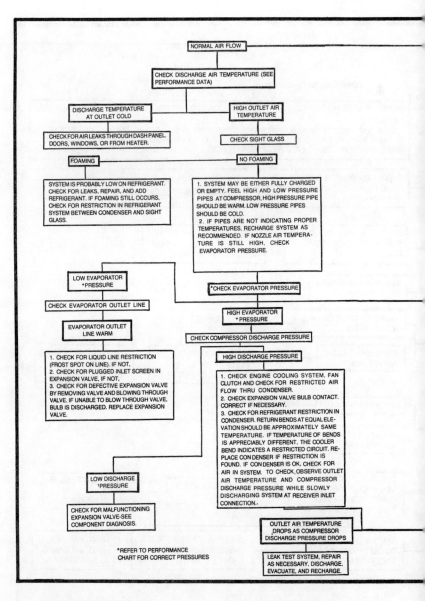

NORMAL AIR FLOW

CHECK DISCHARGE AIR TEMPERATURE (SEE PERFORMANCE DATA)

DISCHARGE TEMPERATURE AT OUTLET COLD

HIGH OUTLET AIR TEMPERATURE

CHECK FOR AIR LEAKS THROUGH DASH PANEL, DOORS, WINDOWS, OR FROM HEATER.

CHECK SIGHT GLASS

FOAMING

NO FOAMING

SYSTEM IS PROBABLY LOW ON REFRIGERANT. CHECK FOR LEAKS, REPAIR, AND ADD REFRIGERANT. IF FOAMING STILL OCCURS, CHECK FOR RESTRICTION IN REFRIGERANT SYSTEM BETWEEN CONDENSER AND SIGHT GLASS.

1. SYSTEM MAY BE EITHER FULLY CHARGED OR EMPTY. FEEL HIGH AND LOW PRESSURE PIPES AT COMPRESSOR, HIGH PRESSURE PIPE SHOULD BE WARM. LOW PRESSURE PIPES SHOULD BE COLD.
2. IF PIPES ARE NOT INDICATING PROPER TEMPERATURES, RECHARGE SYSTEM AS RECOMMENDED. IF NOZZLE AIR TEMPERATURE IS STILL HIGH, CHECK EVAPORATOR PRESSURE.

LOW EVAPORATOR *PRESSURE

*CHECK EVAPORATOR PRESSURE

CHECK EVAPORATOR OUTLET LINE

HIGH EVAPORATOR *PRESSURE

EVAPORATOR OUTLET LINE WARM

CHECK COMPRESSOR DISCHARGE PRESSURE

HIGH DISCHARGE PRESSURE

1. CHECK FOR LIQUID LINE RESTRICTION (FROST SPOT ON LINE). IF NOT,
2. CHECK FOR PLUGGED INLET SCREEN IN EXPANSION VALVE, IF NOT,
3. CHECK FOR DEFECTIVE EXPANSION VALVE BY REMOVING VALVE AND BLOWING THROUGH VALVE. IF UNABLE TO BLOW THROUGH VALVE, BULB IS DISCHARGED. REPLACE EXPANSION VALVE.

1. CHECK ENGINE COOLING SYSTEM, FAN CLUTCH AND CHECK FOR RESTRICTED AIR FLOW THRU CONDENSER.
2. CHECK EXPANSION VALVE BULB CONTACT. CORRECT IF NECESSARY.
3. CHECK FOR REFRIGERANT RESTRICTION IN CONDENSER. RETURN BENDS AT EQUAL ELEVATION SHOULD BE APPROXIMATELY SAME TEMPERATURE. IF TEMPERATURE OF BENDS IS APPRECIABLY DIFFERENT, THE COOLER BEND INDICATES A RESTRICTED CIRCUIT. REPLACE CONDENSER IF RESTRICTION IS FOUND. IF CONDENSER IS OK, CHECK FOR AIR IN SYSTEM. TO CHECK, OBSERVE OUTLET AIR TEMPERATURE AND COMPRESSOR DISCHARGE PRESSURE WHILE SLOWLY DISCHARGING SYSTEM AT RECEIVER INLET CONNECTION.

LOW DISCHARGE PRESSURE

CHECK FOR MALFUNCTIONING EXPANSION VALVE-SEE COMPONENT DIAGNOSIS.

OUTLET AIR TEMPERATURE DROPS AS COMPRESSOR DISCHARGE PRESSURE DROPS

*REFER TO PERFORMANCE CHART FOR CORRECT PRESSURES

LEAK TEST SYSTEM, REPAIR AS NECESSARY, DISCHARGE, EVACUATE, AND RECHARGE.

a misconnected heat control, or open wiring elsewhere in the system.

The procedures given in this chapter have purposely been kept brief. For further details about the procedures described, check the index of this book—most are covered in step-by-step detail in other chapters—or refer to Figs. 5-11 and 5-12.

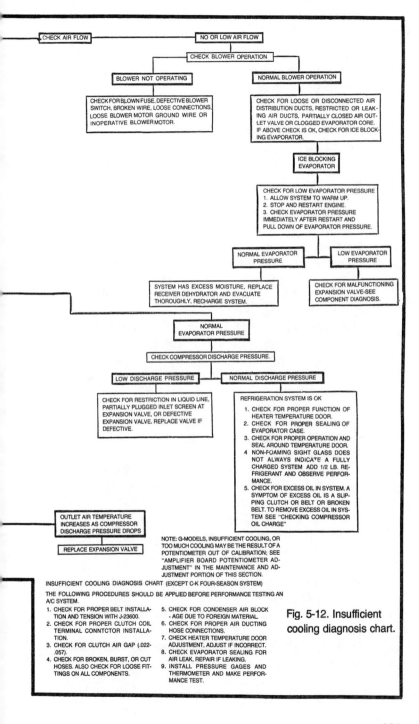

CHECK AIR FLOW ── NO OR LOW AIR FLOW

CHECK BLOWER OPERATION

BLOWER NOT OPERATING

CHECK FOR BLOWN FUSE, DEFECTIVE BLOWER SWITCH, BROKEN WIRE, LOOSE CONNECTIONS, LOOSE BLOWER MOTOR GROUND WIRE OR INOPERATIVE BLOWER MOTOR.

NORMAL BLOWER OPERATION

CHECK FOR LOOSE OR DISCONNECTED AIR DISTRIBUTION DUCTS, RESTRICTED OR LEAKING AIR DUCTS, PARTIALLY CLOSED AIR OUTLET VALVE OR CLOGGED EVAPORATOR CORE. IF ABOVE CHECK IS OK, CHECK FOR ICE BLOCKING EVAPORATOR.

ICE BLOCKING EVAPORATOR

CHECK FOR LOW EVAPORATOR PRESSURE
1. ALLOW SYSTEM TO WARM UP.
2. STOP AND RESTART ENGINE.
3. CHECK EVAPORATOR PRESSURE IMMEDIATELY AFTER RESTART AND PULL DOWN OF EVAPORATOR PRESSURE.

NORMAL EVAPORATOR PRESSURE

SYSTEM HAS EXCESS MOISTURE, REPLACE RECEIVER DEHYDRATOR AND EVACUATE THOROUGHLY, RECHARGE SYSTEM.

LOW EVAPORATOR PRESSURE

CHECK FOR MALFUNCTIONING EXPANSION VALVE-SEE COMPONENT DIAGNOSIS.

NORMAL EVAPORATOR PRESSURE

CHECK COMPRESSOR DISCHARGE PRESSURE.

LOW DISCHARGE PRESSURE

CHECK FOR RESTRICTION IN LIQUID LINE, PARTIALLY PLUGGED INLET SCREEN AT EXPANSION VALVE, OR DEFECTIVE EXPANSION VALVE. REPLACE VALVE IF DEFECTIVE.

NORMAL DISCHARGE PRESSURE

REFRIGERATION SYSTEM IS OK
1. CHECK FOR PROPER FUNCTION OF HEATER TEMPERATURE DOOR.
2. CHECK FOR PROPER SEALING OF EVAPORATOR CASE.
3. CHECK FOR PROPER OPERATION AND SEAL AROUND TEMPERATURE DOOR.
4. NON-FOAMING SIGHT GLASS DOES NOT ALWAYS INDICATE A FULLY CHARGED SYSTEM ADD 1/2 LB. REFRIGERANT AND OBSERVE PERFORMANCE.
5. CHECK FOR EXCESS OIL IN SYSTEM. A SYMPTOM OF EXCESS OIL IS A SLIPPING CLUTCH OR BELT OR BROKEN BELT. TO REMOVE EXCESS OIL IN SYSTEM SEE "CHECKING COMPRESSOR OIL CHARGE"

OUTLET AIR TEMPERATURE INCREASES AS COMPRESSOR DISCHARGE PRESSURE DROPS

REPLACE EXPANSION VALVE

NOTE: G-MODELS, INSUFFICIENT COOLING, OR TOO MUCH COOLING MAY BE THE RESULT OF A POTENTIOMETER OUT OF CALIBRATION; SEE "AMPLIFIER BOARD POTENTIOMETER ADJUSTMENT" IN THE MAINTENANCE AND ADJUSTMENT PORTION OF THIS SECTION.

INSUFFICIENT COOLING DIAGNOSIS CHART (EXCEPT C-K FOUR-SEASON SYSTEM)

THE FOLLOWING PROCEDURES SHOULD BE APPLIED BEFORE PERFORMANCE TESTING AN A/C SYSTEM.

1. CHECK FOR PROPER BELT INSTALLATION AND TENSION WITH J-23600.
2. CHECK FOR PROPER CLUTCH COIL TERMINAL CONNTCTOR INSTALLATION.
3. CHECK FOR CLUTCH AIR GAP (.022-.057).
4. CHECK FOR BROKEN, BURST, OR CUT HOSES. ALSO CHECK FOR LOOSE FITTINGS ON ALL COMPONENTS.

5. CHECK FOR CONDENSER AIR BLOCK - AGE DUE TO FOREIGN MATERIAL.
6. CHECK FOR PROPER AIR DUCTING HOSE CONNECTIONS.
7. CHECK HEATER TEMPERATURE DOOR ADJUSTMENT, ADJUST IF INCORRECT.
8. CHECK EVAPORATOR SEALING FOR AIR LEAK, REPAIR IF LEAKING.
9. INSTALL PRESSURE GAGES AND THERMOMETER AND MAKE PERFORMANCE TEST.

Fig. 5-12. Insufficient cooling diagnosis chart.

POINTS TO REMEMBER

1. The inside of the refrigeration system is completely sealed from the atmosphere. If that seal is broken at any point, the system will soon be damaged.

2. Complete and positive sealing of the entire system is vitally important. This sealed condition is absolutely necessary to retain the chemicals and keep them in a pure condition.

3. All parts of the refrigeration system are under pressure at all times, whether operating or idle, and any leakage points are continuously losing refrigerant and oil.

4. The leakage of refrigerant can be so silent that the complete charge may be lost without warning.

5. Refrigerant gas is heavier than air and will rapidly drop to the floor as it flows from a point of leakage.

6. The pressure in the refrigeration system may momentarily become as high as 480 pounds per square inch.

7. The total refrigeration charge circulates through the entire system at least once each minute.

8. The compressor is continually giving up some lubricating oil to the circulating refrigerant and depends upon oil in the returning refrigerant for continuous replenishment. Any stoppage or major loss of refrigerant will therefore damage the compressor.

9. The extreme internal dryness of a properly processed refrigeration system is maintained by drying material in the receiver-drier or accumulator holding tightly onto the tiny droplets of residual moisture.

10. The attraction of the drying material for moisture is so powerful that if the receiver or accumulator is left open, moisture will be drawn in from the outside air.

11. Water added to the refrigeration charge will start chemical changes that can result in corrosion and eventual breakdown of the chemicals in the system. Hydrochloric acid is one result of mixing R-12 with water.

12. Air in the refrigerant system may start reactions that can cause malfunctions.

13. The drying agent in the receiver-drier is activated silica alumina.

14. The inert gas in the expansion valve-capillary line is carbon dioxide.

Chapter 6
Checking The
Refrigerant Charge

Previous chapters have covered just about every type of repair or servicing job within the capabilities of the average handyman with conventional hand tools. This chapter, on the other hand, begins with a description of air-conditioning servicing normally handled by the trained automotive air-conditioning mechanic whose shop is equipped with special tools to handle all types of servicing and repairs. If you have the proper tools (or can borrow them) there is really no reason why you can't perform these repairs just like a pro—provided the instructions given are followed step-by-step.

Due to the potential hazards involved in the use of certain refrigerants and high-pressure equipment, you should not attempt any of the service work described herein unless you understand the contents fully, have access to the proper tools, and know exactly how to use them. Even diagnostic checks can prove harmful if you don't know what you're doing.

For the reasons outlined in the preceding paragraph, a few preliminary precautions are in order before proceeding further.

1. When servicing any part of an air-conditioning system, always wear safety goggles. When refrigerant escapes into air, it evaporates so rapidly that it tends to freeze anything it touches. If it gets into the eyes it can cause blindness!

2. Keep a bottle of sterile mineral oil and a container of weak boric acid solution near your work. If any refrigerant gets into your eyes, wash it out instantly with a few drops of mineral oil, followed by the weak boric acid solution. Then get to a doctor immediately.

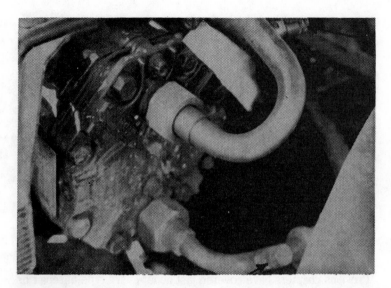

Fig. 6-1. Service valves mounted on either the compressor or the refrigerant tubing near the compressor, as shown here, enable you to check the refrigerant charge.

3. Never use an excessive amount of heat on or near any part of the air-conditioning system while the system contains a charge of refrigerant. To do so could cause an explosion. Furthermore, when refrigerant vapor comes in contact with an open flame (like that used in a leak detector torch), it is converted into a dangerously toxic gas. Avoid inhaling the fumes from the leak detector and keep all other flames well away from any parts on an air-conditioning system.

4. When discharging the refrigerant from an air-conditioning system, discharge it in the open air—with plenty of ventilation—and away from any foliage or pets. Since discharged refrigerant displaces all air in the immediate vicinity, it could possibly cause suffocation if the area is not ventilated properly. Always maintain good ventilation around the area in which you are working.

5. When charging a system with refrigerant, always keep the tank or can in an upright position to ensure that refrigerant gas (and not refrigerant liquid) will enter the air-conditioning system. Serious damage could occur if the liquid did enter the system.

You have become familar with some of these precautions from previous chapters and you will see some of them again in chapters to follow. When you do come across them, read them over again; observing them is the *only* way to make working on air conditioners safe.

Service valves mounted on either the compressor or the refrigerant tubing near the compressor (as shown in Fig. 6-1) enable you to check the refrigerant charge with a manifold gauge such as the one shown in Fig. 6-2. The hose from the low-pressure gauge of the manifold is connected to the low-pressure refrigerant tubing or service valve, and the hose from the high-pressure gauge is attached to the high-pressure service valve on the compressor or the refrigerant tubing. Both gauges indicate pressure in pounds per square inch; the low pressure gauge will also indicate a vacuum which will be useful for vacuuming the system as described in Chapter 8.

Each of the two valves on the manifold operate in three positions: when backed off (turned counterclockwise) all the way, the system operates normally; when opened to the midway position, the operation of the system can be checked with the gauges; when the valves are turned fully clockwise, the system is shut off from the compressor—isolating it completely. Figure 6-3 shows a cross section of the valve.

To check the refrigerant charge with the manifold gauges, close both valves on the manifold (turn them fully clockwise). Connect the high-pressure gauge hose to the high-pressure or discharge side of the compressor and the low-pressure gauge hose to the suction or low-pressure side of the compressor. When you are certain that these connections are secure, crack both service valves on the

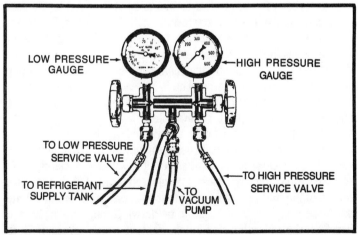

Fig. 6-2. Typical manifold gauge used to test the refrigerant charge. Courtesy of Ford Motor Co.

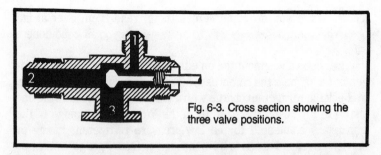

Fig. 6-3. Cross section showing the three valve positions.

compressor. A special wrench is normally required to perform this operation. Both gauges should read between 60 and 80 psi at 70°F ambient temperature when the engine is not running. If little or no pressure is indicated, the refrigerant charge has been lost from the system.

If you suspect the charge is low—due to other indications explained later in this chapter—connect a container of R-12 to the hose that is connected to the center port on the manifold gauge. Open the refrigerant cylinder and purge the hose of air. Open the two manifold gauges to allow the refrigerant to enter the system until the gauges stabilize; close the valve on the manifold as well as on the container of refrigerant.

Then, with a leak detector (Fig. 6-4), check all connections, the compressor, and other parts of the system. Since R-12 is practically odorless and does not react with other gases or vapors at room temperatures, it is impossible to test for leaks by volatile chemical means such as the reaction of ammonia with sulphur dioxide. Therefore, leaks in an automotive air-conditioning system are best tested with a gas torch with a special attachment. This special leak detector is constructed so that the air intake to the flame is through a rubber tube known as the search hose. As the tube is brought near the place to be tested for leaks, the burning flame produces a suction, drawing air and refrigerant to the flame. The R-12 reacts with the copper ring around the flame causing the flame to change from blue to green (for a big leak) or to orange (for a small leak).

The initial leak test should be made with a pressure of approximately 30 psi on the system. In using the tester, hold the inlet of the search hose as close to the joint as possible without blocking off the air to the torch. Slowly proceed completely around each joint with the end of the tube, remembering that an appreciable length of time may be required for the sample to be drawn through the hose, and therefore the indication will not be instantaneous. Since R-12 is much heavier than air, the drift of the refrigerant is downward from a leak. The presence of leaking refrigerant may therefore often be detected below a leak when it cannot be detected from above.

Test all tubing joints, assemblies such as expansion valves, the compressor, and the condenser. If no leaks are found, admit more refrigerant and allow the pressure to increase in 20-pound steps until saturation pressure for the existing ambient temperature is reached, testing for leaks after each step. Never exceed 90 psi during the tests, however.

If a leak is found, mark the spot, but do not stop there—other leaks could be in the system. While you have the testing torch working, you might as well go ahead and check the entire system. Once the leak(s) are found, repair them by acceptable methods as described elsewhere in this book.

Other methods of checking the refrigerant charge include the use of a sight glass in the receiver-drier, by means of high and low petcocks on the receiver-drier, or by feeling the outside of the receiver-drier to determine the level of the liquid within. A brief description of these methods follows.

Fig. 6-4. Leak detector for checking all connections and other parts of the system for refrigerant leaks.

127

USING THE SIGHT GLASS

To be most effective in checking the refrigerant charge, the sight glass should be located in the liquid line as close as possible to the receiver-drier outlet service valve.

Before noting the appearance of the liquid flow past the glass, the compressor should be started to increase the head pressure to normal operation. Once operating, if clear liquid is flowing past the glass, sufficient refrigerant should be in the system. However, false indications have been noted for both sufficient and insufficient charges when using this method.

A false indication of sufficient refrigerant can be illustrated as follows. Assume that you check your system during cool weather when both the discharge and the suction pressure is low. The sight glass would probably be clear because there is sufficient liquid in the receiver-drier to cover the outlet opening. However, at higher pressures, during warmer weather, a greater amount of refrigerant will be carried in the vapor state in both the evaporator and the receiver-drier with a consequent reduction in the liquid level in the receiver-drier. The charge is then insufficient since there is not enough liquid in the receiver-drier to cover the receiver outlet opening.

A false indication of insufficient refrigerant can occur with the condenser operating at a low discharge pressure. Since the temperature of the car engine and the ambient air (on a very hot day) may be above the saturation temperature of the liquid refrigerant, it is possible for the liquid refrigerant to absorb enough heat from the engine to result in some vaporization in the line and the appearance of bubbles in the sight glass. This is especially true if the sight glass is located beyond the strainer at some distance from the condenser because the normal pressure drop in the line and strainer will increase the amount of vaporization in the line.

The possibility of a false indication can be overcome by temporarily increasing the discharge or head pressure to higher than that at which the system normally operates. This can be done by placing a piece of cardboard over the condenser to stop the air circulation.

Where the receiver-drier is equipped with high and low level petcocks, the refrigerant level should be above the level of the lower petcock and below the level of the higher petcock. When it's momentarily opened, liquid should boil out of the lower petcock while only vapor should be discharged from the upper petcock.

Another method used for determining the liquid level inside the receiver-drier is feeling the outside of the receiver while the com-

Fig. 6-5. One method of determining the liquid level inside the receiver-drier is to feel the outside of the receiver while the compressor is running and the discharge pressure is being rapidly increased.

pressor is running and the discharge pressure is rapidly increased by placing a piece of cardboard over the condenser (Fig. 6-5). During a rise in head pressure, the temperature of the vapor above the liquid rises with the discharge pressure while the temperature of the liquid rises more slowly.

Directly after a rise in discharge pressure, a very distinct temperature difference can easily be felt between the area below the liquid level and the area above the liquid level. At this time the liquid level can be determined within reasonable limits.

TESTING THE CONDENSER FOR LEAKS

The condenser itself should be carefully tested for leaks at a discharge pressure higher than that at which it normally operates. Close off the air and allow the discharge pressure to build up until the condenser is cut off by the high-pressure control. Then proceed to test every gasketed or soldered joint on the unit. Also test the seal and the various plugs. If the unit is equipped with a safety valve, test the outlet of the valve to make sure that the valve is holding.

If a leak is found in the high-pressure side of the condenser, it will be necessary to remove the refrigerant before attempting to repair the leak. The refrigerant charge can be removed from the condenser by utilizing the refrigerant compressor itself.

Connect an empty refrigerant cylinder that is large enough to hold the entire refrigerant charge to the receiver outlet service valve (Fig. 6-6). If a cylinder of sufficient size is not available, several small

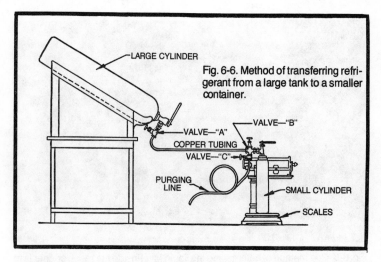

Fig. 6-6. Method of transferring refrigerant from a large tank to a smaller container.

cylinders can be used in succession, care being taken not to fill the cylinders full, as an area must be left in the cylinders for expansion of the liquid as the temperature rises.

Stand the refrigerant cylinder in a bucket of cold water to cool the refrigerant as it flows into the cylinder, thereby reducing the pressure in the cylinder.

Close the outlet service valve and open the refrigerant cylinder valve. Run the compressor and pump the evaporator and refrigerant lines down to cut-out pressure. This will also raise the discharge pressure and cause the liquid refrigerant in the receiver to flow into the refrigerant cylinder.

Now very carefully operate the low-pressure control manually and run the compressor intermittently so that the suction pressure is reduced to slightly below atmospheric pressure, being careful to run the compressor only a few revolutions at a time to prevent oil slugging.

Open the receiver outlet service valve and allow the refrigerant gas which remains in the receiver to flow into the evaporator and refrigerant lines until the pressures equalize. Since the evaporator had previously been pumped down to less than atmospheric pressure, the resultant pressure will be low. Close the receiver outlet service valve. The remainder of the refrigerant charge may now be purged to the atmosphere provided it is R-2.

Another sign of low refrigerant charge in an automotive air-conditioning system is low suction pressure accompanied by an icing evaporator; low suction pressure being that the suction gauge may read a vacuum indicating evaporator lacks refrigerant.

Chapter 7

Testing For

Internal Malfunctions

If your air-conditioning system doesn't come up to par after you have checked all external conditions as outlined in Chapter 5, then it's time to look further—for internal malfunctions. Troubleshooting this part of the system is going to require a manifold gauge set (Fig. 7-1) to test for suction, refrigerant pressure, and to uncover other possible internal causes of trouble.

A manifold gauge set consists of two gauges. One is a pressure gauge which reads from 0 to approximately 500 pounds. The other is a compound gauge which reads from a vacuum of 30 inches of mercury up to 0 inches and then reads pressures from 0 pounds to 225 pounds or so. The pressure gauge is used to measure the pressure in the high side of the refrigeration system, while the compound gauge is used to measure low pressure or vacuum in the low side of the system.

These two gauges are conveniently mounted in a manifold which has three fittings to which hoses may be connected. A cross section of a typical manifold with the gauges attached is shown in Fig. 7-2. This drawing shows the center port isolated from both gauge openings. However, the low side of a refrigeration system may be connected to the center port of the manifold by opening the hand valve on the low-pressure side, or the high side of the system may be connected to the center port by opening the hand valve on the high-pressure side. If both valves are opened simultaneously with the manifold connected to a refrigeration system, there is a path from the high side to the low side through the block assembly.

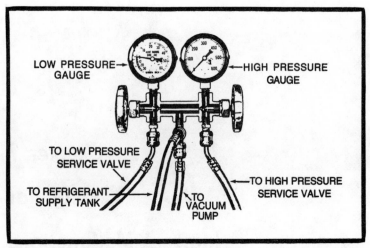

Fig. 7-1. Manifold gauge set used to test for suction, refrigerant pressure, and to uncover other possible internal causes of trouble.

The manifold gauge has several uses for troubleshooting and servicing automotive air-conditioning systems. Hoses are run from the manifold fittings to the high and low sides of the refrigeration system for performing various tests on the system as will be explained later. The center port is used to connect a container of refrigerant for recharging; to bleed air or remove refrigerant from a system; or as a connection for a vacuum pump in applying a vacuum to a system.

The vacuum gauge may also be used to check parts of the car's operation other than the refrigerant system. Vacuum lines and vacuum motors—both single- and double-action—which provide power for air dampers for the car's heating and ventilation system can be checked using the vacuum gauge.

OPERATIONAL TEST OF SYSTEM

With the car engine idling, turn the air-conditioning controls to maximum cooling and run for approximately 15 minutes to allow sufficient time for all parts to become completely stabilized. You can determine if the system is fully charged by use of the test gauges and the sight glass. Discharge pressure should read from 180 psi to 220 psi or higher—depending upon ambient temperature and the type of unit being used. The sight glass—as discussed previously—should be free of bubbles. The low-side pressure should read approximately 15 psi to 30 psi, again depending on the ambient temperature and the unit being tested.

A system operating normally will indicate a high-side gauge reading between 150–170 psi with an 80°F ambient. The same system will register 210–230 psi with an ambient of 100°F. No two systems will register exactly the same, which requires that allowances for variations in head pressures must be considered. Following are the most important normal readings the serviceman will encounter during the season. These pressures and their ambient relationship should be committed to memory for quick reference.

Ambient	High-Side Pressure
80°F.	150–170 psi
90°F.	175–195 psi
95°F.	185–205 psi
100°F.	210–230 psi
105°F.	230–250 psi
110°F.	250–270 psi

The high side of the system should be uniformly hot to the touch throughout. A difference in temperature will indicate a partial blockage of liquid or gas at this point. The low side of the system should be uniformly cool to the touch with no excessive sweating of the suction line or low-side service valve. Excessive sweating or frosting of the low-side service valve usually indicates that the expansion valve is allowing an excessive amount of refrigerant into the evaporator. This condition will not necessarily be applicable to those units installed on General Motors products which use a suction throttling valve. On these systems, the line from the valve to the compressor will normally drop to a much lower pressure than the evaporator pressure as the suction throttling valve closes, resulting in the occurrence of moisture or frosting on this line. This is a normal reaction in this type of system and is the result of the STV, and the compressor having approximately 35% more capacity than previous models.

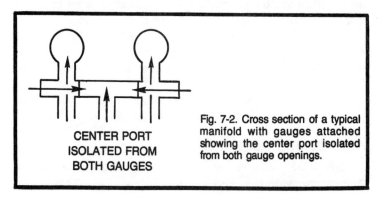

CENTER PORT
ISOLATED FROM
BOTH GAUGES

Fig. 7-2. Cross section of a typical manifold with gauges attached showing the center port isolated from both gauge openings.

These factors often cause the line from the valve to the compressor to drop into a partial vacuum under normal operation.

The following is designed to acquaint the reader with gauges as diagnostic instruments. The most common malfunctions are included with their effects both on high- and low-side pressures. A careful study of these and preceding pages will eliminate much of the mystery of the air-conditioning system.

THE COMPRESSOR TEST

Attach the manifold gauge to the high and low sides of the compressor service valves as discussed previously; make certain that the valves are completely closed. After attaching properly, back-seat the high-pressure service valve fully counterclockwise while the low-pressure service valve is turned fully clockwise.

Crank the engine and let it idle; then turn the air-conditioning control to maximum cooling for 30 seconds, and turn it completely off. The low-pressure gauge on the manifold should reach 20 inches of mercury within this period of time and should remain below zero for at least a minute after the compressor is shut off. Performance other than stated here means either a blown gasket or leaking valves—requiring servicing or replacement.

LOW REFRIGERANT CHARGE

Little or no cooling from the evaporator and excessively low readings on the low- and high-side gauges indicate a low refrigerant charge. No bubbles appearing in the sight glass and warm discharge air from the evaporator is a further indication of a low refrigerant charge.

To repair, first leak-test the system (because the system has lost refrigerant). It may be necessary to add a partial charge of refrigerant to perform the test. Then purge the system of refrigerant to assure that the system will not be contaminated with air and moisture. Repair any leaks following applicable repair procedure.

You should also check the compressor oil level as the compressor may have lost some oil. The system should then be evacuated—using a vacuum pump—to remove all air and moisture from the system.

Recharge the system with new refrigerant and continue the performance test as described earlier in this chapter.

INSUFFICIENT REFRIGERANT CHARGE

When the air conditioner is not providing adequate cooling, and both the low- and high-side gauges read too low, this is an indication of an insufficient refrigerant charge. Other signs of this malfunction will be bubbles streaming in the sight glass and the discharge air from the evaporator being only slightly cool.

To repair, first leak-test the system as the system has lost refrigerant. It is generally accepted that air conditioners lose some refrigerant between seasons. Purge the system of refrigerant to assure that the system will not be contaminated with air and moisture. Repair any leaks following applicable repair procedure.

You should also check the compressor oil level as the compressor may have lost some oil. The system should then be evacuated—sing a vacuum pump—to remove all air and moisture from the system.

Now charge the system with new refrigerant and continue performance test as described earlier in this chapter.

AIR IN SYSTEM

When there is insufficient cooling from the evaporator, and the low-side pressure constant will not drop, and the high-side pressure gauge is slightly high, there is air and moisture present instead of a full refrigerant charge. This condition is further recognized by the sight glass being free of bubbles or showing only an occasional bubble, the suction line being warm to the touch, and the evaporator discharge air being only slightly cool.

To repair, first leak-test the system because a leak has allowed the entry of air. Make sure you check the compressor seal closely. Purge the system of refrigerant because it has been contaminated with air and moisture. Then replace the receiver-drier.

You should also check the compressor oil level as the compressor may have lost some oil. The system should then be evacuated—using a vacuum pump—to remove all air and moisture from the system.

Now fill the system with new refrigerant and continue the performance test as described previously in this chapter.

CONDENSER MALFUNCTION

Should the interior of your car not cool properly, and your engine is overheating at the same time, chances are your condenser is malfunctioning. This is especially true if the low-side gauge reading is too high (it should read between 15–20 psi) and the high-side gauge is reading too high (above 215 psi). Bubbles may also appear in the sight glass and the liquid line will be very warm. Warm discharge air from the evaporator—rather than the normal sharp cold air—will just about insure that the problem is caused by a condenser malfunction.

Begin repairs by inspecting for loose or worn drive belts which will cause the engine to overheat as well as excessive head pressure. Continue by inspecting the condenser itself for clogged air passages or bug screens. Both will restrict ram air flow causing improper condenser action and engine overheating.

Incorrect clearance or mounting of the condenser will also restrict the air flow over the radiator fins and coils, creating high head pressure and engine overheating. Therefore, inspect the condenser to be sure that you have enough clearance between the condenser and the radiator. Follow necessary procedures to correct any trouble found, then inspect the clutch-type fan for proper operation—if you have this type of fan on your car. End the initial check with an inspection of your radiator pressure cap to see if it is operating properly.

After examining all these items, and correcting any defects, the pressure gauges on the manifold should read normal. However, if they do not, continue the diagnosis by following this order of tests:

1. Inspect the air-conditioning system for an overcharge of refrigerant; excess refrigerant will cause excessive system pressures and engine overheating during low speeds in hot weather.
   a. Purge refrigerant until bubbles stream in the sight glass and both low- and high-side gauges drop below normal pressures.
   b. Add new refrigerant until bubbles disappear and pressures are normal. You may even want to add 1/4 pound of extra refrigerant for reserve.
   c. If the system is normal, continue performance test. If not, proceed to step No. 2.
2. Remove and inspect condenser for oil clogging.
   a. Purge the refrigerant, then remove the condenser and use compressed air to force oil from the condenser.
   b. Follow procedures to replace the condenser and the receiver-drier; evacuate and charge the system.

Follow procedures given earlier in this chapter for giving a performance test to the complete system. Upon completion, the system should function properly.

EXPANSION VALVE MALFUNCTION

One of the reasons that the automotive air conditioner fails to cool the car is a malfunction of the expansion valve. The manifold gauges should both read too high (above 30 psi for the low-side gauge and above 205 psi for the high-side gauge). Further symptoms of this condition will include warm discharge air from the evaporator and heavy sweat on the suction hose and the evaporator.

When the expansion valve malfunctions, it either allows too much refrigerant through the evaporator or restricts the flow of refrigerant. In the first instance, inspect the expansion valve to see if the valve is stuck in the open position or the thermal bulb contact is loose or corroded. To test this bulb, loosen it from the tailpipe. With the motor running, and the air-conditioning controls adjusted for maximum cooling, spray liquid R-12 over the thermal bulb while watching for the low-side gauge to drop into vacuum. Once the vacuum reading is obtained, warm the bulb with your hand and repeat the procedure. Clean the surface between the bulb and the tailpipe, then clamp the bulb to the tailpipe and tighten the clamp securely.

If little or no reduction in pressure is observed on the low-side gauge, the valve is defective and must be replaced. To replace the expansion valve, purge refrigerant from the system as outlined in Chapter 8 and then follow the manufacturer's instructions for replacing the valve.

Once the installation is completed, evacuate the system using a suitable vacuum pump; follow applicable procedure for the type of equipment used. Then charge the system (see Chapter 10) with new refrigerant and performance-test the system as outlined earlier in this chapter.

If the expansion valve is restricting refrigerant flow, both the low-side and high-side gauges will read too low, and the discharge air from the evaporator will be only slightly cool—not a sharp cold feel as when it is operating normally. Heavy sweat or frost on the expansion-valve inlet is another clue that the valve is restricting the flow of refrigerant.

When the inlet of the expansion valve reveals sweat or frost, the inlet screen is probably clogged. Purge refrigerant from the system, remove and clean the screen, and then replace. Evacuate the system and charge with new R-12 refrigerant following procedures as outlined in Chapter 10.

If the inlet end of the expansion valve is found to be warm to the touch, the valve is partially closed and should be operated by force to see if this will solve the problem. If not, the valve will have to be replaced. Evacuate and charge the system using new R-12. Then continue performance test as outlined earlier in this chapter.

HIGH SIDE RESTRICTION

Little cooling from the evaporator could mean that a restriction is in the high side of the cooling system. When this condition exists, both the low-side and the high-side gauges will read too low. The compressor will evacuate refrigerant from the evaporator faster than it can enter—causing too-low pressures. The condenser and receiver-drier become a storage container and hold the refrigerant charge. Ram air will subcool the refrigerant because it is not moving at a high rate of flow, and therefore the high-side gauge pressure will drop. A normal capacity condenser will give the above indications. However, too small a condenser and/or receiver-drier (or an overcharged system, for that matter) will cause the high-side gauge pressure to be normal or excessively high.

Further indications of this condition will be only slightly cool air discharging from the evaporator and heavy sweat or frost appearing on the receiver-drier or liquid line.

The restriction in the receiver-drier or liquid line could be due to loose rubber in the liquid line which clogs the receiver-drier. Purge the system of refrigerant and remove the part restricting the flow of refrigerant. Repair or replace the defective part and reinstall the part according to the manufacturer's recommendations. Evacuate the system with a suitable vacuum pump, and then charge the system with new refrigerant. A performance test should also be performed on the system before placing it back in service.

The condition just described is known as a starved coil. A flooded evaporator is just the opposite; that is, too much refrigerant is passed through the evaporator coils, resulting in unexpanded liquid passing into the suction line and into the compressor. Liquid refrigerant in the compressor can result in damage to the reed valves and pistons. A flooded evaporator will contain too much refrigerant for efficient heat absorption in the evaporator coil and will result in inefficient evaporation and poor evaporator cooling.

Gauge pressure readings on the low side of the system readily indicate either condition. Too low a reading on the low-side gauge accompanied by quick frost formation on the fins with too little cool air emitted from the evaporator indicates a starved coil. A flooded coil is indicated by too high a pressure and excessive sweating of the evaporator coils and suction hose.

ABNORMAL PRESSURE GAUGE READINGS

Low Suction Pressure, Head Pressure Normal

1. Thermostat defective.
2. Screen in expansion valve clogged.

3. Restriction between receiver and expansion valve.
4. Moisture in system.
5. Expansion valve closed if low pressure gauge reads a vacuum.

High Suction Pressure, Head Pressure Normal

1. Improper operation of expansion valve.
2. Sensing element of expansion valve defective or making improper contact.

High Suction Pressure, Low Head Pressure

1. Compressor defective.
2. Compressor reed valve defective.

Excessive Head Pressure

1. Air in system or excessive charge of refrigerant in system.
2. Condenser air passages clogged.
3. Restriction in condenser, dehydrator, filter, or any high-pressure line.
4. Excessive oil in compressor.
5. Engine overheating.

Chapter 8
Vacuuming The Auto
Air-Conditioning System

Once an air-conditioning system has been drained of refrigerant in order to make repairs, it is vitally important that the system be vacuumed before recharging. This is normally accomplished with a set of manifold gauges and a vacuum pump. The latter must be capable of pulling a strong enough vacuum that the boiling point of water is below the surrounding temperature. With such a pump (although it's relatively expensive), all moisture and air may be pumped from a refrigeration system that has been opened to the atmosphere either for repair or because of a leak.

The manifold gauges are connected to the system so that the high and low sides of the gauges correspond to the high and low sides of the refrigeration system as shown in Fig. 8-1. The center port is connected to a vacuum pump and then all valves of the manifold are opened and the pump is started. Continue pumping until the low-side gauge indicator drops down below zero, indicating the presence of a good vacuum within the refrigeration system. This will probably take from 15 to 20 minutes to accomplish.

If the system contains refrigerant, it will, of course, have to be bled before vacuuming the system. To do this, connect the manifold gauge set to the service fittings on the compressor. Connect the inlet-suction line (low-pressure compound gauge) to the side of the compressor where the refrigerant enters as it comes from the evaporator. Then connect the high-pressure gauge line to the side of the compressor through which refrigerant passes on its way to the condenser; this is known as the discharge line. Make sure all the valves on the manifold gauges are closed at this point.

Connect a third hose or line to the center or exhaust port and run the opposite end of the exhaust line to a safe place where the refrigerant can be discharged without causing damage. Choosing a proper area for the discharging is extremely important because:

1. Refrigerant discharged into the open air evaporates so rapidly that it tends to freeze anything that comes in contact with it. This includes your skin and eyeballs! This rapid evaporation also causes all air within the immediate vicinity to be displaced. If proper ventilation is not provided, it could cause suffocation.

2. Certain refrigerants will kill all vegetation as well as birds and pets with which they come into contact in any quantity. So if you're releasing them in the air, be careful to keep them away from these.

With the discharge hose located in a safe place, you are now ready to discharge the system. With your safety goggles on, crack the service valves on the compressor, and carefully open both valves on the manifold. Open them only slightly to allow the refrigerant to discharge slowly—if the refrigerant is allowed to rush out too rapid-

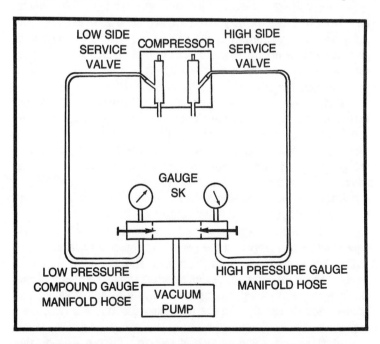

Fig. 8-1. Manifold gauge set connected to high and low sides of the refrigeration system and a vacuum pump connected to the center port.

ly, it will carry the oil in the compressor out with it. When the needle indicator of the pressure gauge reads zero, the system is clear.

Remove the refrigerant discharge line from the middle or discharge port on the manifold and connect a vacuum pump line to this port. Open both valves of the manifold all the way and start the vacuum pump, letting it run for at least 15 or 20 minutes. At higher elevations, it may be necessary to run the pump longer. Also remember, for every 1000 feet of altitude above sea level, the vacuum-gauge reading will drop 1 inch. When the indicating needle on the pressure gauge drops below zero (to approximately 28 inches of mercury), you have a good vacuum.

When the evacuation is completed, close both valves on the manifold and turn off the vacuum pump. Disconnect the vacuum pump from the center hose. The system is ready for recharging as explained in Chapter 10. When both gauges stabilize at the recommended psi, close both manifold valves, turn off the valve at the refrigerant container, and disconnect it from the center hose.

As an added precaution, the entire system should be checked again with a leak detector to make certain that no leaks are present—especially when repairs have been made or components have been replaced. After you're certain that no leaks exist, let the refrigerant charge remain in the system for about 30 minutes to allow this charge of refrigerant to pick up any moisture that may have remained in the system during the initial evacuation. After this time period, discharge and evacuate the entire system again.

It may seem unnecessary to many to perform the discharge and recharge operation twice, but the importance of eliminating moisture in the system cannot be overemphasized. To illustrate, moisture in the presence of refrigerant and oil forms hydrochloric acid and sludge that will damage internal working parts and lead to eventual failure of the entire system. A small drop of moisture, for example, can freeze in the expansion valve, restricting refrigerant to the evaporator and resulting in poor cooling.

Air-conditioning systems require a number of other special procedures when preparing the system for repair service and when putting the system back into operation. The following will cover many of these procedures, beginning with purging refrigerant from the system, evacuation, charging the system, and isolating the compressor for service. All are necessary for satisfactory system repair.

Start the engine and let it idle at 1500 to 1750 rpm. Connect the manifold gauges to the high and low sides of the system and move the air-conditioning controls to maximum cooling. Operate the system in this manner for about 15 minutes before shutting off both the engine and the air-conditioning system.

Bleed off the old refrigerant by opening the low-side manifold valve slightly with the discharge hose placed in a container, drained with running water, or a similar suitable place for discharging. Remember, do not ever discharge the R-12 near an open flame as a toxic gas can result.

Now open the high-side manifold valve slightly—only enough to drain the refrigerant from the system. If the refrigerant is drained too rapidly, oil may be drawn from the compressor.

When refrigerant ceases to come from the hose, close both manifold shut-off valves; both gauges should read 0 psi.

Your next step is to evacuate the system by using a suitable vacuum pump. Connect the vacuum pump to the manifold gauges (assuming they are still connected to the high and low sides of the air-conditioning system). This operation is performed by removing the cap from the vacuum-pump hose connector and installing the center hose from the manifold gauges to the vacuum-pump connector. Then open the high- and low-side gauge manifold valves and turn on the vacuum pump. This should be operated a minimum of 30 minutes to insure proper air and moisture removal. Watch the compound gauge to see that the system pumps down into a vacuum.

The system should reach 28–29 1/2 inches of mercury in not over five minutes, but if it doesn't, check all connections and leak-test if necessary. When a vacuum is reached, close the hand valves and shut off the vacuum pump. Then watch the compound gauge to see that the gauge does not rise faster than 1 inch of mercury every 5 minutes. This checks the system's ability to hold vacuum. If the compound gauge rises faster than this, install a partial charge of R-12 and leak-test as described earlier. Then purge the system and repeat the steps just given.

If the system holds vacuum within the specifications, fully charge the system with refrigerant as described in Chapter 10.

A charge station may also be used to evacuate the air-conditioning system, but this is strictly a professional tool not normally found around the home mechanic's shop. Still, for those of you who have access to a charging station, here's how the job is done.

Connect the high and low manifold gauges to the high and low sides of the air-conditioning system to purge the system as described previously. Then connect the center hose to the vacuum pump (built into the charging station). Open both high- and low-side gauge valves on the charging station and engage the on/off switch to the vacuum pump according to the directions of the specific charging station being used. The system should pump down to 28–29 1/2 inches of mercury in not more than 5 minutes. If not, the system is in need of repair.

The pump should be operated at least 30 minutes to insure that all air and moisture is removed from the system. When this is accomplished, close the high- and low-side gauge valves on the charging station and turn off the vacuum pump. However, the compound gauge should be watched to see that the gauge rises no faster than 1 inch of mercury every 4 or 5 minutes. If a faster rate is observed, repairs on the system will probably be necessary. If the rise rate is within the specifications, fully charge the system with refrigerant as described in Chapter 10.

If a vacuum pump is not available, and it becomes necessary to evacuate your air-conditioning system, you can use the air-conditioning compressor as a pump. However, this is not recommended if any other means are available. In fact, prolonged use of the compressor as a vacuum pump will prove detrimental to its function; no manufacturer recommends this procedure for their compressor.

Connect the manifold gauges to the high and low sides of the system as described previously and open *only* the high-side hand valve. Start the engine and idle at a slow speed (500 rpm). When the compound gauge registers 20–25 inches of mercury, close the hand valves immediately. You will note that this is somewhat lower than the previous reading (28–29 1/2 inches of mercury), but the car engine will seldom pump down to greater than 25 inches of mercury. If the compressor is allowed to run after it has reached this rating, it will increase wear and possibly cause damage to the compressor as it is operating without sufficient lubrication.

Once the manifold valves have been closed, shut off the engine and watch the compound gauge to see that the gauge does not rise faster than 1 inch of mercury every 5 minutes. If the pressure does rise faster than this, install a partial charge of refrigerant and test the system for possible leaks. Repair any that are found, purge the system, and repeat the evacuating procedures as outlined. If the gauge reading is satisfactory, charge the system with refrigerant as outlined in Chapter 10.

ISOLATING THE COMPRESSOR FROM THE SYSTEM

On air-conditioning systems having both a high-side and a low-side service valve, the compressor may be isolated—retaining the refrigerant in the system—while service work is being performed on the compressor or the car motor. To perform this, attach the

144

manifold gauges to the system, crank the car engine, and turn the air-conditioning control to maximum cooling. Operate the system in this manner for approximately 15 minutes.

Slowly close the low-side service valve until the low-side gauge reads 0 psi, then turn the engine off. Now completely close the low side service valve and then close the high-side valve. Purge refrigerant from the compressor by cracking the low side hand manifold until both gauges read 0 psi. This purging action should be done slowly to prevent pulling oil from the compressor.

You may now remove the service gauges from the service valves and also the service valves from the compressor in order to perform any work that may be required. After the work is completed, reinstall the service valves to the compressor, purge air from the compressor by cracking the high-side service valve for not more than 3 seconds with high-side hose capped and the low-side hose connector open.

Connect gauges to the service valve connectors and purge air from the hoses before continuing the performance test as described in Chapter 7. Mid-position the service valves and continue testing the system; adjust controls for maximum performance.

CRANKSHAFT SEAL REMOVAL

One of the repairs that can be performed in a relatively short period of time when the compressor is isolated is the replacement of the crankshaft seal. To perform this repair, isolate the compressor, then loosen the oil filler plug to relieve the pressure in the compressor. Remove the magnetic clutch before removing the seal-plate retaining screws and the seal plate. Next remove the carbon seal ring and the seal housing assembly from the crankshaft. Finally, replace the seal with a new one and reverse the procedure to reassemble the apparatus.

DISCHARGING THE SYSTEM

It was just explained how to isolate the compressor in order to perform a variety of repairs without evacuating the entire system. However, you cannot remove any other refrigerant-carrying part within the system without first discharging the refrigerant. Note that we didn't say evacuating the system, merely discharging the system. Discharging the refrigerant doesn't completely empty the system, but does relieve the pressure so that the system may be opened.

In order to discharge an air-conditioning system, connect the manifold gauges to the high and low sides of the compressor with both manifold gauge valves closed and both service valves on the compressor back-seated. Connect the hose from the center valve of the manifold to some safe discharge area. Then slowly open the outlet gauge valve to connect the high-pressure side of the compressor to the discharge hose. This valve should only be cracked, to let the refrigerant escape slowly as a vapor.

If the refrigerant is allowed to discharge too rapidly, compressor oil may come out with the refrigerant. Watch the open end of the hose and reduce the flow if you see compressor oil coming out with the refrigerant.

As soon as the refrigerant is discharged, back-seat the service valves on the compressor once more and close the manifold gauge valves. This will help prevent air and moisture from entering the system.

Remember to exhaust the refrigerant in a safe area; never discharge the refrigerant into any work area, and never get near refrigerant without wearing safety goggles.

After discharging and recharging an air-conditioning system, you may want to check the oil level in the compressor in case oil has been pulled out during the discharging process. After the system has been charged, and operated at maximum output for at least 15 minutes—at an engine speed of approximately 1500 rpm—stop the engine. Isolate the compressor as discussed earlier in this chapter and remove the oil filler plug very slowly to release any trapped pressure.

Insert a clean dipstick—designed for the compressor being tested—in the oil filler hole until it bottoms in the crankcase. If necessary, turn the compressor crankshaft slightly by hand to allow the stick to reach the bottom. Remove the stick and read the oil level—comparing the reading with that recommended in the service manual accompanying the car or air-conditioning system.

If more oil is required in the compressor, use only the type recommended by the manufacturer of the compressor; never use engine or transmission oil. Replace the filler plug, evacuate the compressor, and connect it into the system. You should also check around the filler plug opening for possible refrigerant leaks. Do this with either a flame leak detector or a dye solution.

Systems not having service valves installed on or near the compressor must be purged of refrigerant before the oil level may be checked. This may be done after the system has been discharged.

Adding oil to General Motors compressors requires a little different procedure. Connect the manifold gauges as described previously with the high-side compressor service valve mid-positioned;

front-seat the low service valve. You will then need an oil charging line consisting of 10 inches of 1/4-inch copper tubing with flare fittings (see Chapter 13) to connect to the center manifold connector. Tighten this fitting with the proper size wrench and then purge air from the oil charging line by opening the high-side hand manifold valve slightly for not more than 3 seconds. Place the open end of the charging line in the oil and close the high-side hand manifold valve, placing the oil and the manifold gauge in a secure position before continuing.

Start the engine and operate at idle speed while the air-conditioning controls are set in maximum cooling position. The engine should pump the system to 10 inches of mercury. However, if the system does not hold a vacuum, check and tighten all connections before continuing.

Open the low-side manifold valve and put 2 ounces of oil into the system. Close the valve, remove the oil charging line, and cap the center connection, tightening it securely.

The process is continued by purging oil from the manifold gauge. Open the high-side gauge manifold valve followed by the low-side manifold gauge valve. Then close both valves. You will have to stabilize the system by mid-positioning the compressor service valves and operating the engine at 1600 rpm for about 5 minutes while the air-conditioning controls are set in the maximum cooling position.

Open the oil test valve and add 2 ounces of oil at a time until the correct oil level is obtained.

Chapter 9

The Receiver-Drier Unit

The function of the receiver-drier is basically to store the condensed refrigerant until it is fed to the evaporator; the level of the stored refrigerant varies depending upon the cooling load requirements. The receiver-drier also contains a filter element designed to remove small amounts of moisutre and dirt that might get into the system.

Several types of receiver-driers are used in automotive air-conditioning systems, but most consist of a cylindrical steel shell as shown in Fig. 9-1. The operation of all types is identical; that is, the "used" refrigerant enters the inlet valve, flows downward through filter pads and a drying agent, and is then sucked up through the pickup tube and routed to the expansion valve of the evaporator.

A safety device is usually located in the receiver-drier to protect the system from abnormally high pressures that could cause failure or ruptures of the system components. This safety device is normally in the form of a metal plug with a very low melting point. If the plug's melting point is reached, the plug softens and is blown out—relieving the pressure. Some systems, however, utilize a compressor pressure-release valve in place of the receiver fusible plug.

Problems occurring in the air-conditioning system that are directly related to a faulty receiver-drier almost always require that the receiver-drier be replaced. Here are a few common complaints.

EXCESSIVE MOISTURE IN SYSTEM

If you find that your air-conditioning system cools satisfactorily during the early morning hours or late evening, but does not cool

Fig. 9-1. Several types of receiver-driers are used in automotive air-conditioning systems, but most consist of a cylindrical steel shell as shown here.

during the hot part of the day, excessive moisture in the air-conditioning system could be the trouble.

To diagnose this complaint, attach the high- and low-pressure gauges to the high and low side of the air-conditioning system. If moisture is present in the system, the low-side gauge will read between 15 and 30 psi or may drop into vacuum while performing the test. The high-side gauge reading will be around 205 psi, but if the low side drops into vacuum, the high-side pressure will drop also.

Continue your diagnosis by feeling the discharge air while performing the test. If the discharge air feels sharp initially, but warms while the low side is in vacuum, your system almost certainly has excessive moisture in the system; that is, the drier is saturated with moisture and releases this moisture (during high ambient temperature) which collects in the expansion valve orifice and freezes to stop refrigerant.

To repair, first purge the system of refrigerant because this will be contaminated with moisture. Remove the existing receiver-driver from the system and install a new one. Then evacuate the entire system to remove the moisture. During the evacuating process, the pump-down time will probably have to be increased as much as four or five times due to the moisture in the system. If you cannot pump down the system for at least one hour, you will have to sweep the system. Attach and operate the vacuum pump for about 15 minutes and then shut the pump off. Add half of the refrigerant charge and operate the system in maximum cooling position for about 10 minutes to allow the refrigerant to pick up any moisture in the system. Purge the system and pump down 15 more minutes with the vacuum pump. You are now ready to charge the system.

Charge the system with new refrigerant by following procedures outlined in Chapter 10. Then perform a performance test as explained in Chapter 7.

SYSTEM CONTAMINATED WITH AIR

Another problem which usually requires replacement of the receiver-drier is air and moisture in the system. The first sign of this problem will be that the system does not cool properly. When the manifold gauges are attached, the low-side reading will be too high and the high-side gauge reading will be higher than normal.

When this problem occurs, purge the system of refrigerant because this will be contaminated with air and/or moisture. You will also have to remove and replace the receiver-drier; the drying agent will have reached saturation point and must be removed from the system as evacuation cannot remove moisture from the drier.

Evacuate the system for air and/or moisture removal with a vacuum pump that is capable of creating a deep vacuum. Pump down the system for a minimum of 30 minutes. If heavy moisture is suspected, it is advisable to sweep the system as explained in "Excessive Moisture In System."

Charge the system with new R-12 refrigerant by following procedures outlined in Chapter 10. Then follow the performance test as described in Chapter 7.

REPLACING REED VALVE PLATE ON COMPRESSORS

Occasionally the reed valve must be replaced on automotive air-conditioning compressors. While individual reeds are available, it is recommended that the complete reed plate—as an assembly—be replaced because often the old plate will be warped during service, and reinstalling this plate will result in failure of the new reeds and compressor.

Begin the installation by isolating the compressor as described previously in this book, or purge the entire system of refrigerant if your compressor does not have both high- and low-side service valves. Whichever method you use, the next step will be to remove the bolts holding the compressor head to the compressor body. If your compressor has service valves, these should be unbolted and lifted off with the hoses attached before removing the compressor head. Then tap the extruding flange on each side of the head to loosen it from the compressor body. The valve plate may then be easily lifted from the compressor body, and then separated from the compressor head. Clean the old gasket from the compressor head and body; you will want to replace it.

Use clean refrigeration oil on the new gaskets as the use of other sealers on gaskets will result in excess sealer being picked up by refrigerant and deposited in screens throughout the system. Complete clogging of the expansion valve screen has been known to result from using sealers—causing the air-conditioning system to fail completely.

Coat the new gasket between the reed plate and the compressor liberally with refrigeration oil and install the gasket on the aligning pins on the compressor body. Then install the new reed plate on the aligning pins of the compressor body and press it into place.

Next coat the head gasket liberally with refrigeration oil and install this gasket on the alignment pins of the compressor body. Press the compressor head into place and screw in the head bolts, which should be tightened finger tight.

Use a torque wrench to tighten the bolts to the specification listed in the service handbook or manual. Coat the new mounting gaskets with refrigeration oil and install on the compressor head. Again install the bolts with your fingers and then tighten with a torque wrench according to the specification; torque inner bolts first, then outer bolts.

You are now ready to return the air-conditioning system to service. If you isolated the compressor to make the replacement, follow the procedure for reconnecting it. On the other hand, if the system was discharged, evacuate the system (Chapter 8) and charge the system as described in Chapter 10. Continue performance-testing the system until controls are adjusted for maximum performance.

REPLACING CLUTCH BEARING

The clutch bearing will more than likely be the part on your air-conditioning system that will need replacing more often than any of the others. Though these assemblies differ from car to car and from manufacturer to manufacturer, the following procedure is quite applicable to most of them—with a few variations.

Begin the operation by removing the clutch retaining bolt from the compressor shaft by striking the side of your wrench with a quick hammer blow with the clutch engaged momentarily. Then loosen the belt tension adjustment and remove the belt from pulley. Install a 5/8 × 2 1/2-inch bolt into the threaded center of the hub. A shorter bolt may be required on some installations because of the tight working area between the clutch hub and the shroud.

Tighten this bolt against the end of the compressor shaft until the clutch assembly is loosened sufficiently to be lifted from the compressor. On clutch assemblies not threaded in center of hub, the bolt obviously cannot be used. Instead, unscrew the clutch retaining bolt approximately half its length and then use a brass or steel hammer to strike the bolt with a light, sharp blow while holding the clutch assembly with one hand. Remove the bolt and lift off the clutch assembly when the clutch is loosened on the shaft.

Never use any type of wheel puller on pressed steel pulleys as unequal pressure caused by the wheel puller can result in damage to the pulley and the armature.

Your next step will be to remove the hub and armature from the bearing inner race. Begin this procedure by removing the hub retaining snap-ring from inside the clutch assembly; the spacer should also be lifted off if present. Thread the $5/8 \times 2 1/2$-inch bolt into the hub from inside the clutch assembly and drive the hub out of the inner race using a brass or steel hammer. Remove the bolt from the hub and separate the armature and hub from the bearing. Finally, clean and inspect all pieces for excessive wear or damage and lay to one side.

Scoring between the armature and rotor plates is to be expected and is permissible. However, if they are worn to such an extent that solid contact is not possible, the clutch assembly must be replaced with a new one.

Remove the bearing from the pulley by pressing the hub and armature from the bearing inner race. Clean and inspect and lay to one side. Remove the bearing retainer lock-ring from each side of the bearing. Clutch assemblies that do not use lock-rings to retain the hub in the bearing inner race are constructed with a sliding fit in the bearing. When disassembling this type, omit all previous steps regarding its removal.

Either spiral-locks or snap-rings will be used. Instead of the outer retainer ring, some assemblies use a shield installed in the outer side of the pulley which requires that the bearing be removed from the inner side of the pulley if the shield is retained by the bearing.

Continue this phase of the operation by driving the old bearing from the pulley—being careful not to damage the shield if it is present. Clean and inspect the pulley for excess wear in the bearing seat as excessive wear and damage to the pulley will require that the clutch assembly be replaced.

Install the retainer ring or shield into the outer side of the pulley. Press the replacement bearing into the pulley by exerting pressure on the outer race of the bearing until the lock-ring groove is exposed. Then install the bearing retainer ring in the groove of the pulley.

Again use the 5/8 × 2 1/2-inch bolt and install it into the front of the hub to protect the springs and armature. Press the hub into the inner bearing race with a suitable size sleeve such as a pipe or socket wrench. Install the spacer and lock-ring on the hub if it is used.

Adjust the air gap between the armature and rotor by loosening the lock-nuts on the outer face of the clutch assembly. Alternately adjust the set screws until a .05 to .06 air gap is obtained between the armature and rotor. Then tighten the lock-nuts, which will hold the set screw stationary. Recheck the air gap and readjust if tightening the lock-nuts altered the air gap.

Clean the inner bore of the hub and the crankshaft to insure even contact between surfaces before installing the clutch assembly to the compressor crankshaft. Then align the key-way in the hub with the key in the crankshaft and press the clutch assembly into place. Install the clutch retaining bolt in the crankshaft and tighten to approximately 20 ft-lbs with a torque wrench. Adjust the belt to the correct tension and the job is complete.

CLEANING BURNOUTS WITH A HAND PUMP SPRAYER

The Freon Products Lab has devised a procedure for cleaning up a small system after a burnout occurs which is based on the Calclean Sprayer No. 300 manufactured by Calgon Company, Pittsburgh, Pa.

Before beginning the flushing procedure, the pump will have to be prepared for use. Do not use the hose supplied with the sprayer as Freon 11 refrigerant will dissolve it. Therefore, with either threaded or soldered fittings, tee an inexpensive 0–60 psi pressure gauge into the sprayer discharge pipe at the top end of the pipe. Then solder or fit a common, inexpensive water valve into the discharge pipe above the pressure gauge tee. Next fit or solder a line to the outlet of the valve so that a hose can be connected from the sprayer discharge pipe to the refrigeration system to be cleaned. The hose tubing should be at least 3/8-inch diameter and made of an approved material like synthetic gasoline hose, Tygon tubing, etc. If you're in doubt about the material of your hose, soak a sample of the hose in Freon 11 for 4 to 8 hours; then check for discoloration of the Freon 11 and damage to the hose. If none occurs, the hose should be safe to use with the pump.

Begin the cleaning operation by removing the pump from the sprayer—keeping the pump handle crosswise to the slot in the pump top. Pulling up slightly, turn the handle counterclockwise until the entire pump is removed from the tank.

Add Freon 11 to the tank by pouring the refrigerant into the funnel opening on the tank. Use about 15 pounds of Freon 11 per horsepower, but do not fill the tank more than three-quarters full. Now reinstall the pump into the tank by lowering the pump through the funnel opening, turning the pump handle clockwise until the top of the pump locks under the inner lip of the funnel.

Remove the burned-out compressor from the system and connect the sprayer to the compressor discharge line on the system with a suitable hose. Also add a suitable hose to the compressor suction line on the system and run the other end of the hose to an open container about the same size as the sprayer tank. Hose clamps, flares, or threaded connections can be used.

Close the valve on the sprayer discharge pipe and pump the sprayer to 25 or 35 psi pressure. Then open the sprayer valve to allow the Freon 11 to be pushed through the system into the open container. When the pressure drops to zero, remove the pump from the sprayer. Repeat the previous steps (adding more refrigerant to the tank, etc.) and flush out the system until the new Freon 11 appears very clean. The Freon 11 from the final flush should be clear and should not be acidic when tested with DuPont Acidity Test Paper.

Disconnect the sprayer and hoses from the system and purge the system with Freon 12 or Freon 22 (see Chapter 12) to blow any Freon 11 from the system. Then reassemble the system as recommended by the manufacturer, being sure to evacuate the system properly.

Most of the components of an automotive air-conditioning system can be repaired, but receiver-driers are replacement items rather than repair items. The receiver-drier must be replaced when any of the following occurs: (1) the compressor fails because the receiver-drier will become clogged with burned oil, metal chips, etc.; (2) a clogged filter, which can be recognized by feeling the inlet and outlet of the receiver-drier; the outlet will be appreciably cooler than the inlet; (3) a system leak that has caused the system to be without charge for a long period of time, because moisture and air will be allowed to enter the system through the leak; (4) any opening in the system that has allowed moisture to enter the system; (5) a blown or ruptured fusible plug, unless the fusible material is incorporated in a removable plug.

Before replacing the receiver-drier, the system must be discharged and swept with a test charge. The purpose of the sweep-test charge is to pressurize the system so that a leak test can be made. The sweep-test charge also serves the purpose of drying the system or sweeping out trapped moisture. Repairs and component replacement must be completed before charging with the sweep-test charge.

Begin the test by closing both gauge-set manifold valves and opening the gauge-set manifold needle valve. Then attach the free end of the long hose used for discharging to the refrigerant-dispensing manifold. Attach a single can of R-12 to the dispensing manifold. Place the refrigerant in a pan of water at approximately 125°F.

With the vehicle windows open and hood up, operate the engine at about 1200 rpm for about five minutes. Then turn the air-conditioning system on and the fan switch to the high position. Return to the manifold gauge and slowly open the left-hand manifold valve to meter the refrigerant into the system. When the full can of refrigerant has been metered into the system, close the gauge-set manifold valves and the refrigerant manifold valve.

If the system has been opened for repair or has accidentally lost its charge, a complete leak test must be made to make sure the system is sealed. Stop the engine and disconnect the test hoses and adapters from the compressor service ports.

If the system is free of leaks, or after correcting a leak, remove the sweep-test charge. Close the refrigerant manifold valve so that any refrigerant remaining in the container is sealed. Remove the long test hose from the refrigerant manifold. Insert the free end of this test hose into an exhaust system outlet and then open the right-hand gauge-set manifold valve a fraction of a turn to let the sweep-test charge escape slowly. Allow the system to discharge until the discharge-pressure gauge registers zero. Open the left-hand gauge valve to allow any refrigerant trapped in the suction side of the system to escape.

Now the receiver-drier can be removed by simply unscrewing the refrigerant lines. When installing the new receiver-drier, use a new gasket and tighten the connections to approximately 12 ft-lbs. However, do not overtighten since this might damage the gasket.

Since the system has been opened to the atmosphere, it is absolutely essential that the system be swept with refrigerant and evacuated or "vacuumed" (see Chapter 8) to remove all the air and the moisture. If any appreciable amount of air remains in the system when it is charged, the trapped air will concentrate near the top of the condenser and cause abnormally high discharge pressures. Air in the system will also reduce the condenser's ability to condense the refrigerant gas and supply adequate liquid refrigerant to the evaporator. After the system has been evacuated, you may want to leak-test. Then your system will be ready for recharging, described in the next chapter.

Evacuation of the system is started by connecting the gauge-set manifold to the compressor and the long test hose from the gauge-set manifold center connection to the vacuum pump. Open both gauge-set manifold valves and also the needle valve. Then start the vacuum pump and operate until the evaporator suction gauge registers at least 26 inches of vacuum. If the system is tight and the pump in good condition, the vacuum will go as low as 28 inches, which is even better. Continue running the vacuum pump for at least five minutes after reaching the proper vacuum.

Close both gauge-set manifold valves, turn off the vacuum pump and remove the test hose from the vacuum pump. Leave the gauge-set manifold connected to the compressor for charging the system.

A special refrigerant dispensing manifold that permits charging three full cans of refrigerant at one time is the type recommended for recharging the air-conditioning system. Attach the center hose from the gauge-set manifold to the refrigerant dispensing manifold. Turn the refrigerant manifold valves completely counter clockwise so that they are fully open. Remove the protective caps from the refrigerant manifold.

Screw the refrigerant cans into the manifold and be sure that the manifold-to-can gasket is in place and in good condition. Tighten the can and the manifold nuts to 6 to 8 ft-lbs with a torque wrench. Continue by turning the three refrigerant manifold valves completely clockwise to puncture the cans and close the manifold valves. Now turn the refrigerant manifold valves counterclockwise to open them.

Momentarily loosen the charging hose at the gauge-set manifold to allow the refrigerant gas to purge air out of the charging hose.

Place the three cans of refrigerant into a pan containing hot water at a temperature of about 125°F. Then start the engine and adjust the speed to about 1200 rpm.

The system is charged through the suction side of the compressor by slowly opening the left-hand guage-set manifold valve. Adjust the valve as necessary so the charging pressure does not exceed 50 psi. Maintain the temperature of the water in the pan by adding warm water as necessary.

When all three cans of refrigerant are completely empty, close the gauge-set manifold valves and the refrigerant manifold valves. If more than three cans of refrigerant are necessary to fully charge the system, repeat the previous steps.

Always keep the refrigerant manifold valves capped when they are not in use. Also keep a supply of extra refrigerant-can-to-refrigerant-manifold gaskets on hand so that gaskets can be replaced periodically. This will insure a good seal without excessive tightening of the can or the manifold nuts.

CAUTION: Replacement receiver-drier units must be sealed while in storage as the drying agent used in these units is so hungry for moisture that it can saturate quickly upon exposure to the atmosphere. When installing a drier, have all the tools and supplies ready for quick reassembly to avoid keeping the system open any longer than necessary.

Chapter 10
Recharging The System

When refrigerant has been drained for tests or repairs, or needs replenishing, the air-conditioning system must be recharged. There are several methods that can be used to charge an automotive air-conditioning system, but always follow the manufacturer's instructions, recommendations, and specifications when doing so. The amount of the refrigerant charge will also vary depending on the manufacturer and model of the system. However, a nameplate—normally on the compressor—will tell just how much and which type of refrigerant to use in your system. The correct amount of refrigerant is very important because a smaller charge than recommended affects the system's cooling efficiency, while an overcharge may endanger the compressor.

The most convenient way to recharge an air-conditioning system—especially when done by the home mechanic—is to purchase the refrigerant in 15-ounce cans. The cans are sealed at the factory and you will need a special can-tapping valve to open them. Figure 10-1 shows a single-can tapping valve.

The most convenient way for the home mechanic to charge his own air-conditioning system is to purchase one of the inexpensive kits at an auto supply house. Most sell for around $5.00. The kit will contain a 14-oz. can of R-12 refrigerant, a safety dispensing valve a charging hose—all you'll need to do the job. Remember that the can of refrigerant is under pressure and may explode if misused.

CAUTION

1. Do not attempt to add refrigerant until you fully understand the procedure. To do so could be harmful or fatal.
2. Do not attempt to charge a system having over 170 psi pressure.
3. Do not attempt to charge through the discharge side of the compressor.
4. Do not connect to the high-pressure side of the compressor. Charge the system only through the low-pressure side, otherwise the refrigerant can may explode when the compressor is running.
5. Do not expose the refrigerant to heat or store in temperatures above 120°F.
6. Do not puncture or incinerate the containers.
7. Keep them out of the reach of children.

Methods were given in Chapter 6 on how to check for low refrigerant. But let's briefly review a simple procedure to determine if your car's air-conditioning system needs charging. Crank up the engine and turn on the air-conditioning controls to maximum cooling. Look at the front of the compressor to see if it is turning. If the pulley on the front of the compressor is not turning, check the V-belt to see if it is worn or loose; replace or adjust as necessary. Next cycle the air conditioner off and on to see if the electric clutch is operating. If it is not engaging and disengaging you must determine the cause. This could be caused by a blown fuse, loose wire, bad clutch, etc. If you cannot determine the causes, seek professional help. Also check the blower; if no air is being blown out of the air conditioner inside the car, determine the cause (blown fuse, loose wire, bad switch, etc.).

DETERMINING CONDITION OF COOLANT CHARGE

Check the sight glass—located on top of the receiver-drier, on the storage tank connected to the condenser core in front of the car

Fig. 10-1. A single can-tapping valve used for adding refrigerant to air-conditioning systems.

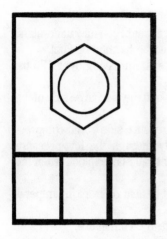

Fig. 10-2. Appearance of sight glass if system is fully charged.

radiator, attached to the fender well of the car, or on the side of the V.I.R. valve (General Motors late models).

To read the status of the charge, operate your air conditioner for 5 to 10 minutes at maximum cooling. Absence of bubbles may indicate either a fully charged or a completely empty system. Cycle the system off and on rapidly; if bubbles do not appear during cycling, the system is fully charged (Fig. 10-2).

If there are no bubbles, carefully add only part of a can (1/2 or less) of refrigerant. Check the sight glass again to see the condition of the charge. If no bubbles are seen after adding R-12, do not attempt to fill the system. Seek professional help.

If a steady stream of heavy or large bubbles is visible, the system is very low on charge and may take one or more 14-oz. cans of R-12 (Fig. 10-3).

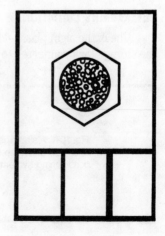

Fig. 10-3. Appearance of sight glass when system needs charged.

If streaks of oil appear on the sight glass, this indicates a complete absence of R-12 and the entire system needs recharging. See Fig. 10-4.

To determine if the system is completely without R-12, run the engine at a very fast idle and cycle the magnetic clutch on and off. Bubbles should be seen during the off cycle. If none are seen, the system needs to be completely recharged. Before attempting to completely recharge your system, correct all leaks. This can be done by using a red dye/R-12 mixture. For best results, we suggest you have the system completely evacuated before charging.

PREPARING KIT FOR USE

Remove the valve body from the valve adapter and make sure that the puncturing device is up, as shown in Fig. 10-5. Snap the valve adapter into the top of the R-12 can by using sufficient pressure (with your hands) to force the lips of the valve under the lip of the can as shown in Fig. 10-6.

Make sure the puncturing device is all the way in the up position and then screw the valve body into the valve. Check to be sure it is down tight against the top of the can. Now puncture can top and open the valve to release a small amount of R-12, then immediately close the valve again. See Figs. 10-7 and 10-8.

Attach the charging hose (Fig. 10-9) to the dispensing valve and you're ready to proceed to charging the system.

CONNECTING THE HOSE

Locate the low-pressure side of the compressor. Charge the system only through the low-pressure side of the compressor, also

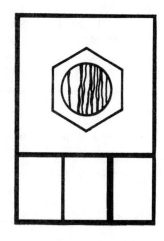

Fig. 10-4. Appearance of sight glass (streaks of oil) which indicates the entire system needs recharging.

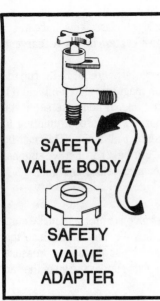

Fig. 10-5. Remove valve body from the valve adapter and make certain that the puncturing device is not down as shown here.

SAFETY VALVE BODY

SAFETY VALVE ADAPTER

known as the suction side. Do not attach the charging hose to the high-pressure side of the compressor. Serious injury may result. Because of the large number of manufacturers of compressors and the many different models, you must be particularly careful to locate the valve.

On some compressors the word "suction" will be stamped on the compressor head. After removing the protective cap, attach your charging hose to the low-side (suction) compressor fitting. Even in partially charged systems, the low-pressure side of the compressor should be cold to the touch. If you cannot determine which connection is the low-pressure (suction) fitting, do not attempt to charge the system without professional help.

After attaching the charging hose to the low-pressure side of the compressor, you are now ready to charge the system. Open the dispensing valve on the can. Start the car and set it at fast idle. Turn

Fig. 10-6. Snap valve adapter onto top of R-12 can using sufficient pressure to force lips of the valve under the lip of the can.

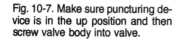
Fig. 10-7. Make sure puncturing device is in the up position and then screw valve body into valve.

the air conditioner to maximum cooling position (blower and thermostat).

Charge the system by opening the dispensing valve all the way until the can is empty or the sight glass on the receiver-drier is clean, which may require more than one can. Automotive air-conditioning units normally have a capacity of three cans. Do not overfill—damage to the compressor can result. Turn the valve to the OFF position. Remove the hose and replace the protective cap.

There are several other methods that can be used to charge an automotive air conditioner. In an automotive air conditioner, the charge is critical to ±1/2 pound. This leeway of one pound is above the amount of excess refrigerant that can be held in a receiver.

Automotive air conditioners require different amounts of charge depending on the manufacturer and model. The charge varies from two pounds of refrigerant for small compacts to over five pounds of refrigerant for a large limousine. It is important that the charge be correct as the cooling efficiency will drop if the system does not have a full charge; if there is too much refrigerant in the system, the compressor may be damaged.

Most pro shops use a charging station which provides an accurate measure of the refrigerant charge and is recommended by most manufacturers. The charging station includes a vacuum pump, man-

PUNCTURE NEEDLE

Fig. 10-8. Location of puncturing needle.

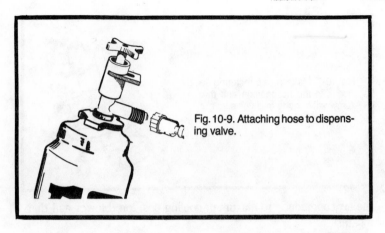

Fig. 10-9. Attaching hose to dispensing valve.

ifold gauge set, charging cylinder, and a supply of refrigerant, mounted on a portable platform. The charging cylinder usually consists of a glass cylinder used to measure refrigerant. There are scales calibrated for weight and temperature for several refrigerants. Pressure gauges are used to measure the temperature of liquid refrigerant in the cylinder. Both the vacuum pump and the charging cylinder are connected to the center port of the manifold gauge set.

To use this apparatus, first evacuate the system. Then close the manifold valves and the vacuum pump valve and turn off the vacuum pump. Determine the proper charge for the system—either from the data plate on the compressor or the service manual. Find the charge weight on the R-12 scale attached to the station to determine the approximate level of the liquid refrigerant in the charging cylinder. Open the valves on the refrigerant cylinder and the bottom of the charging cylinder so the liquid refrigerant flows into the charging cylinder. It may be necessary to crack the bleed valve at the top of the charging cylinder to allow the refrigerant to flow. While filling the cylinder, it will be necessary to close the bleed valve periodically to allow boiling to subside so the refrigerant level in the charging cylinder can be accurately read.

When the level of liquid refrigerant approaches the desired point, close the bleed valve and the lower cylinder valve. Read the temperature on the cylinder pressure gauge and find the exact level desired. Open the lower valve and fill the charging cylinder to the correct level. When the level is correct, close all valves.

Continue by opening the charging-cylinder valve and let liquid refrigerant fill the line. Open the high manifold valve and allow all of the liquid refrigerant to enter the system. If the full charge will not enter the system, close the high manifold valve. Start the engine and run at a slow idle with the air conditioner turned to maximum cooling. When the low-pressure gauge drops to 30 psi, crack the low manifold valve to let the rest of the charge enter the system. Watch the low-pressure gauge and keep the gauge below 50 psi by regulating the low manifold valve. Closing the valve will lower the pressure and prevent liquid refrigerant from reaching the compressor while it is operating.

Finally, when all of the charge has entered the system, close all valves. The system is now charged and should be performance-tested before the gauge lines are disconnected.

When using refrigerant from bulk—as from a drum—you will need a scale that can weigh the filled drum with accuracy to one ounce. Then, connect the drum to the center hose of the manifold gauge set after evacuating the system, leaving the gauges attached. Open the valve on the refrigerant drum and loosen the center hose connection at the manifold for two or three seconds to purge the air from the line.

Next, weigh the drum very carefully. Determine the full charge and subtract this amount from the present weight of the drum. The new weight is what the scale will read when the full charge has entered the system. Start the car and set the air conditioner for maximum cooling. Open the low manifold valve and watch the scale very carefully. When the scale indicates that a full charge of refrigerant has been withdrawn from the drum, close the low manifold valve. Allow about five minutes for the air-conditioning system to stabilize, and then run a performance test as described in Chapter 7.

PRECAUTIONS IN HANDLING REFRIGERANTS

1. When moisture comes in contact with the refrigerant, the moisture freezes in the low side. Therefore, it is of the greatest importance that every precaution be used to prevent moisture, which is present in the air, from coming in contact with the refrigerant.
2. Use only dehydrated and filtered refrigerants supplied in moisture-proof cans. They should never be allowed to lie around exposed to the air.
3. Refrigerant R-12 may be released into the open air.
4. Refrigerant cylinders should be plugged or capped when not in use. Empty cylinders should not be used for refrigerant unless they are dry, clean and meet the following test: remove the pipe plug, fill the opening with R-12 and open the valve very slightly. If the refrigerant blows out of the

opening or sucks into the cylinder, the cylinder is suitable to use. Never heat a cylinder of refrigerant unless it is attached to a unit and all the valves are open.

5. Never fill service cylinders full as there is a possibility of bursting them when the temperature rises.

6. If it is not suitable to release the refrigerant into the open air, it may be released in running water. When doing so, put the end of the hose or tubing well inside the drain pipe of a sink, laundry tub, or something similar, and allow the water to flow rapidly.

Chapter 11
Transmission Cooling

If you're one to haul a trailer behind your car, you already know that transmission overheating is a problem. A transmission oil cooler can easily be installed and is designed to cool transmission oil during sustained high-speed driving, pulling heavy loads, mountain driving, and related conditions of transmission stress. The oil cooler will guard against overheating, but will never overcool the transmission oil, even in winter months.

The recommended method of mounting is the "in-series" (Fig. 11-1) installation which utilizes the existing cooling system and complies with all new car warranties.

The "replacement" installation (Fig. 11-2) method should only be made if the existing cooling system is damaged and repair costs are too high. The replacement installation may void new car warranties and will provide less cooling than the in-series installation.

The three mounting positions are:

1. In front of the radiator and air-conditioning condenser. 100% of GVW Rating (Fig. 11-3).
2. Between the radiator and condenser. 75% of GVW Rating (Fig. 11-4).
3. Behind the radiator 60% of GVW Rating (Fig. 11-5).

Tools required for installation of oil coolers on cars with 5/16-inch steel transmission lines adaptable for use with quick-connect coupler are:

Container	to catch oil during line connection
Funnel	to aid in adding transmission oil
Screwdriver	to attach hose clamps

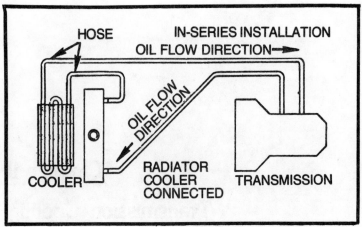

Fig. 11-1. Diagram of in-series installation of transmission oil cooler.

Side cutters	to cut off excess mounting rods
Transmission oil	to replenish transmission oil
1/2-inch wrench	to brace radiator fitting
5/8-inch wrench	to remove transmission line from radiator
Hacksaw	to cut fan shroud (position #3 only)

Additional tools necessary for applications not using quick-connect coupler are:

Flaring tool or drift punch	to flare ends of transmission oil line
Small round file or emery cloth	to remove sharp edges
Steel tube cutter or hacksaw	to cut selected transmission oil line

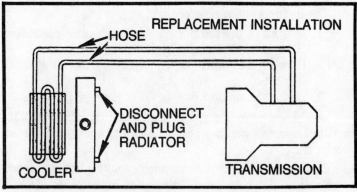

Fig. 11-2. Diagram of replacement installation of transmission cooler.

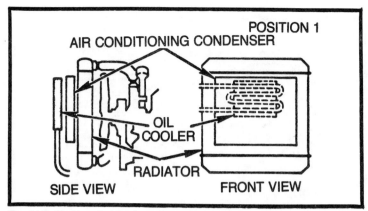

Fig. 11-3. Front and side view of mounting in front of the radiator and air-conditioning condenser. This mounting gives 100% of GVW rating.

Before beginning the installation, set the hand brake and block the wheels.

TRANSMISSION OIL LINE IDENTIFICATION

The oil return line is usually the oil line (1) located toward the rear of the transmission (see Fig. 11-6) and the oil line (3) farthest from the lower radiator hose (5) (see Fig. 11-7). If the oil return line cannot be identified in the above manner, use either of the following methods to identify the oil return line.

a. Start the engine *while the engine is cold*.
b. Place the transmission shift lever at DRIVE.

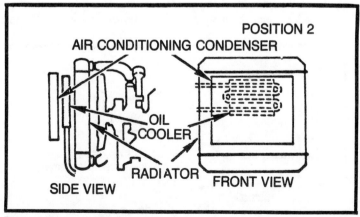

Fig. 11-4. Front and side views of mounting between the radiator and condenser for 75% of GVW rating.

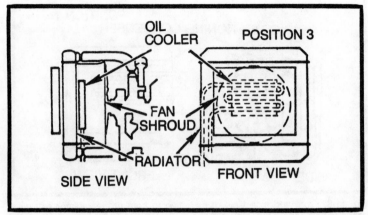

Fig. 11-5. Front and side views of mounting behind the radiator for 60% of GVW rating.

c. Identify the oil return line by feeling both oil lines (3 and 4). The coolest line is the oil return line.

d. Stop the engine.

When disconnecting the oil line, hold the adapter fitting (2) with another wrench to avoid damage to the radiator.

a. Place a container under the oil line and disconnect it.

b. Start the engine, place the shift selector in DRIVE position.

c. Identify the direction of oil flow. Oil must be pumped from the radiator side for proper in-series connection.

d. Stop the engine immediately.

e. If oil flowed from the radiator fitting during test, insert a quick-connect adapter for later hose connection. If the

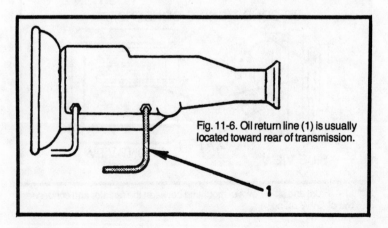

Fig. 11-6. Oil return line (1) is usually located toward rear of transmission.

quick-connect adapter does not fit the radiator fitting, re-connect the oil line to the radiator.

CAUTION: The oil cooler (6) must be installed at least 1 inch from the fan and 1/8 inch from the radiator (9) and air-conditioning condenser (8). Rubber hoses must be kept away from the fan, sharp edges, points of wear, and exhaust pipes. Look at Figs. 11-8 and 11-9 and proceed as follows:

1. Place clamps (3) on the ends of the hose (4) and push the hose onto the oil-cooler fittings (5) as shown in the detail diagram. Leave hose (4) in the loop—DO NOT CUT THE HOSE (4).
2. Position the clamps (3) 1/16 inch from the end of the hose (4). Tighten the clamps (3) until rubber pushes through the clamp slots and is flush with the surface of the clamp.
3. If mounting the oil cooler behind the radiator, loosen the fan shroud. Cut or drill a hole in the fan shroud for hose clearance. Install the shroud.
4. Attach adhesive cushion pads (7) to the oil cooler.
5. Break the locking nuts (2) off the mounting rods (10).
6. Place and hold the oil cooler (6) at installed position with the pads (7) facing the radiator or air-conditioner condenser (8). Insert the mounting rods through the radiator and/or condenser and then through the cooler.

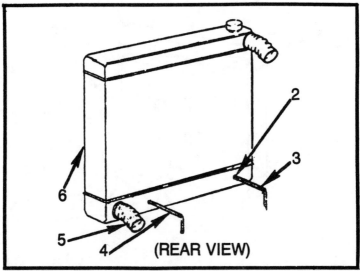

Fig. 11-7. Oil line is farthest from lower radiator hose (5) as shown in this example.

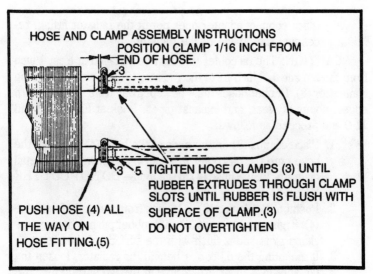

HOSE AND CLAMP ASSEMBLY INSTRUCTIONS

POSITION CLAMP 1/16 INCH FROM END OF HOSE.

3

5 TIGHTEN HOSE CLAMPS (3) UNTIL RUBBER EXTRUDES THROUGH CLAMP SLOTS UNTIL RUBBER IS FLUSH WITH SURFACE OF CLAMP.(3) DO NOT OVERTIGHTEN

3

PUSH HOSE (4) ALL THE WAY ON HOSE FITTING.(5)

Fig. 11-8. Hose and clamp assembly instruction.

7. Install the locking nut (2). Remove excessive mounting-rod length by cutting it off.
8. Repeat steps 5 thru 7 for the remaining ties.

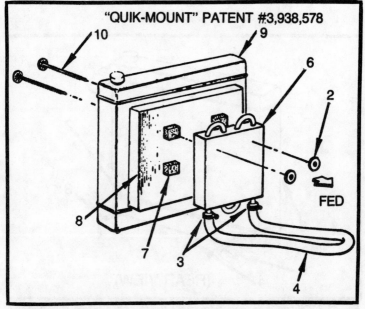

"QUIK-MOUNT" PATENT #3,938,578

FED

Fig. 11-9. Pictorial view of method of mounting cooler on radiator.

The directions below are for hose installation with the quick-connect coupler to be used on vehicles with 5/16-inch steel lines. (See Fig. 11-10.)

9. Install the quick-connect coupler to the radiator using appropriate male or female end if not done at time of oil line identification. Caution—use a wrench to support the radiator fitting—do not overtighten.

10. Position hose loop (4) next to quick-connect fitting and cut hose to length. Remove quick-connect fitting and push the hose onto the fitting at least one inch.

11. Position clamp (3) 1/4 inch behind the flared end of the quick-connect fitting and tighten it until rubber pushes thru the clamp slots.

12. Position the remaining hose next to the disconnected transmission line and cut it to length. The hose should be cut to fit 2 inches past the flared end.

13. Push the hose onto the transmission line at least one inch.

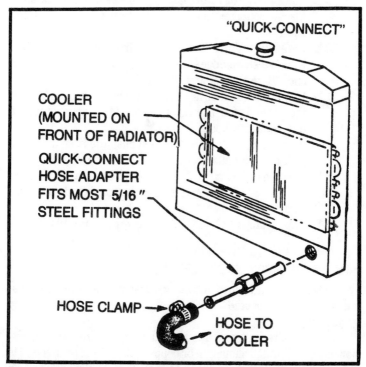

Fig. 11-10. Quick-connect hose adapter for use on vehicles with 5/16-inch steel lines.

14. Position hose clamp 1/4 inch behind the flared end of the transmission line, and tighten the clamp until rubber pushes thru slots.
15. Start the engine. Place the shift lever at the position indicated in the vehicle owner's manual for checking the transmission oil level.
16. Operate the engine at fast idle for 2 minutes. Check hose connections for leakage. If leakage is found, stop the engine and tighten the clamps.
17. Check the transmission oil level. Stop the engine and add oil if required. Caution: do not overfill the transmission.
18. Test-drive the vehicle.

If it is necessary to use the alternate method, here are the steps to take after Step 8. In carrying out these procedures, however, do not bend hose 4 to a radius of less than 2 inches. Hose 4 should be cut 2 inches longer than measured. Hose 4 must be kept away from the fan, sharp edges, points of wear, and exhaust pipes.

9A. Measure the oil return line (1) 4 inches from the radiator. Place a container under the oil return line (1) and cut the line (1).
10A. Carefully position the cut oil lines from radiator oil cooler. Remove sharp edges and burrs from the ends of the cut line. Flare the ends of the line.
11A. Place hose (4) at oil line (2) and measure 2 inches beyond the cut end of oil line (2). Cut hose (4). Repeat steps for the remaining hose.
12A. Place clamp (3) on hose (4) and push the hose at least 1 inch onto the oil line.
13A. Position the clamp (3) 1/4 inch beyond the flared end of oil line 2. Tighten clamp 3 until rubber pushes through the clamp slots.
14A. Repeat steps 12A and 13A for the remaining oil line hose.

HOW TRANSMISSION OIL COOLERS WORK

Most coolers are oil-to-air coolers; that is, heat from the transmission fluid is conducted to metal surfaces where it is carried away by passing air.

Most coolers feature a tube-and-fin design where the transmission oil flows through aluminum or copper tubes; heat from the oil is transferred to the tubing and then to long, thin aluminum fins which are bonded to the tubes.

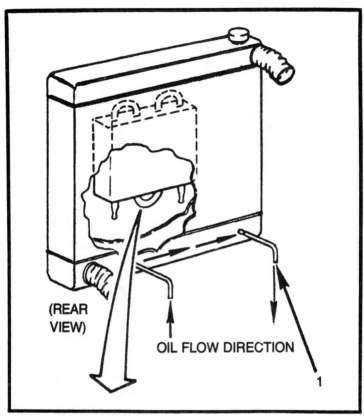

Fig. 11-11. Pictorial view of transmission oil lines; place container under oil return line (1) and cut oil return line (1).

A variation of this design has very short aluminum fins attached to a winding, multi-channel, oval tube—this is known as the "serpentine" tube-and-fin design. This design has more tube area and less fin area than usual tube-and-fin designs, though the cooling principle is the same.

Another type operates by circulating oil through wide shallow channels in stacked plates and is known as the stacked-plate design. Air passing above and below the plates—as oil circulates through them—carries the heat away from the oil.

The efficiency of transmission coolers is affected by several factors, but the quality of the fin-to-tube bond and the amount of turbulence created in the oil as it passes through the cooler's tubing seem to be the most important.

Some tube-and-fin transmission coolers are more efficient than others—the most efficient being those with a good mechanical bond.

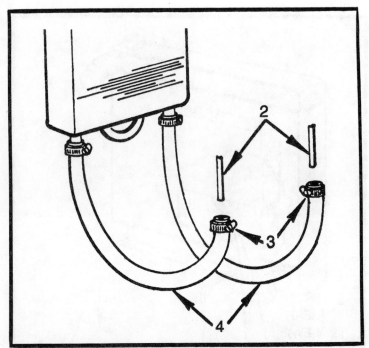

Fig. 11-12. Alternate method of installing the hoses for the cooling unit.

In a good mechanical bond, the tube is expanded hydrostatically or by means of a rod after the fins have been mounted. When the bond is carefully done, good heat-transfer efficiency results. On the other hand, when the bond is not performed with precision, only a fraction of the tube's surface lies in contact with the fin—the unit's heat-transfer efficiency is diminished.

The crimped-tube type of mechanical bond is inherently less efficient than the expanded-tube approach, as such a design provides fin contact with only a small portion of the tube's surface.

In a metallurgical bond, the tube and fin surfaces are connected by soldering, welding or brazing. As in a mechanical bond, ultimate efficiency depends on getting optimum surface contact between tube and fin.

It is claimed that some type of device is necessary to create turbulence in the oil as it flows through the tubing for optimum efficiency. When oil flows smoothly through the tube, only a small portion of it comes into contact with the tube surface, causing only the outside oil to become cool. The cool oil flows at a slower rate of speed than the hotter oil in the middle of the tube. The hotter oil passes through the tubing at a faster rate, preventing it from losing most of its heat. To prevent this problem, turbulence devices are installed in the system to keep the oil constantly tumbling and mixing so that it cools uniformly. The turbulence device also reduces the speed at which the oil passes through the cooler.

USE OF TRANSMISSION COOLERS IN WINTER

It is possible for a very efficient cooler (one that is oversized) in an unloaded car during the winter months to keep transmission oil temperatures so cool as to inhibit oil flow. Another problem is keeping oil temperatures so cool that moisture in the sump is not burned off. Sump temperatures should hit 140°F at least once or twice in a two-week period. If not, oil in the transmission sump of an unloaded car (one that is not towing a trailer) could collect harmful moisture.

There are ways to get around this problem, even if your transmission cooler is a little oversize for your car and load. The most obvious method is to disconnect the cooler during winter months, or remove it altogether. Models with quick-disconnect fittings that eliminate cutting the steel transmission line for an in-series installation are particularly well-suited for the removal of the system during winter months.

Another possibility is the use of some type of covering for the cooler. A painted cardboard sleeve that fits over the cooler and protects it from corrosive salts and other elements will work fine. This covering stops the flow of air over the condenser and neutralizes the cooling capacity. This covering will block some of the air passing through the radiator as well, but in cold winter weather that shouldn't be any problem.

Chapter 12

Refrigerants

Any fluid used as a cooling medium may be termed a "refrigerant." The term as used in this book may be defined as a chemical used in all types of automotive air-conditioning systems to produce a cooling effect or refrigeration by using the latent heat of vaporization of that particular chemical. This is known as a primary refrigerant. Brine or cold water may be circulated through some refrigeration systems and are often referred to as refrigerants. However, brine and cold water used in this way are not true refrigerants, but actually act as an agent to transfer heat from the substance to be cooled to the chemical refrigerant in the compression system. Any type of fluid used like the water just mentioned is known as the secondary refrigerant and must be cooled by the latent heat of the primary refrigerant.

HOW REFRIGERANTS WORK

The principles involved in the physical changes which produce refrigeration are the same for all chemical refrigerants used in compression-type cooling systems; discussion will be directed to these principles and their application in a typical automotive air-conditioning system. Following will be a description of the individual characteristics of the more popular types of refrigerants.

The refrigerating system described in Chapter 1 (see Fig. 12-1) embodies a perfect (but not reversible) cycle of operation. The refrigerant in the system is continually changing its physical state from liquid to vapor in the evaporator and from vapor to liquid in the condenser. During each period a certain amount of heat, partly from the refrigeration produced and partly during compression (from work converted into heat), is added to the refrigerant, and an equivalent amount of heat is abstracted from the refrigerant by some secondary refrigerant like water or—in the case of automotive air-conditioning systems—air. The typical cycle illustrated in Fig. 12-1 uses R-12 refrigerant, the most popular type of refrigerant used in automotive air-conditioning systems. However, the principles involved apply regardless of the particular refrigerant used, type of compressor, the type of power used, liquid control or evaporator. A review of this system's operation follows.

Since the evaporator is the place where the desired refrigeration effect takes place, this should be the starting point for the description of the system. The heat transfer is always from the higher temperature level to the lower temperature level; the heat travels, in most cases, by forced air to the evaporator surface, then by conduction through the evaporator shell to the refrigerant.

If any heat transfer is to take place between the substance passing over the surface of the evaporator and the refrigerant in the tubes of the evaporator, a temperature difference between the substance and the refrigerant must exist. The evaporator tubes contain R-12 in a liquid and a gaseous state. The temperature and therefore the pressure of the liquid refrigerant in the evaporator is

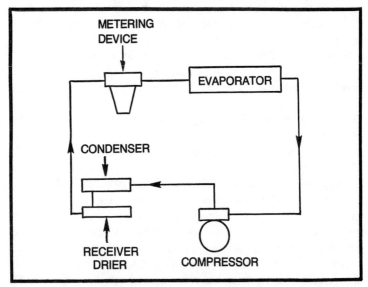

Fig. 12-1. The refrigeration system shown here embodies a perfect (but not reversible) cycle of operation.

179

determined by the temperature of the substance surrounding the evaporator. Therefore, a compressor—driven by the car's engine—is connected to the evaporator by a piping arrangement to pump some of the R-12 from the evaporator, which lowers the pressure in the evaporator. This simultaneously lowers the temperature, creating a temperature difference between the refrigerant and the substance surrounding the evaporator. A transfer of heat begins from the warmer substance to the cooler liquid refrigerant in the evaporator.

The action of the compressor removing gas from the evaporator keeps the pressure, the temperature, and therefore the boiling point of the liquid refrigerant lower than that of the substance around it; of course, the heat transferred cannot warm the cool liquid above its boiling point. The liquid refrigerant would then boil or vaporize from a liquid state to a gaseous state.

From the preceding paragraphs, we can readily see that most of the cooling of the substance surrounding the evaporator is accomplished by using the hidden heat of evaporation of the liquid refrigerant.

Each particular refrigerant requires a definite number of heat units to be added to a pound of its liquid to change it to a gas; the number of heat units for any individual refrigerant depends upon the temperature and pressure range under which the system is operating.

In a given system, to evaporate or boil the greatest amount of liquid refrigerant in the evaporator, it is necessary to keep all of the interior surface of the evaporator wet with liquid. When this condition is met, the gas that is evaporated from the liquid will leave the evaporator outlet at saturation temperature or the same temperature of the liquid in the evaporator. Under this condition undoubtedly there would be some drops of liquid entrained in the gas leaving the evaporator. These drops of liquid would boil or evaporate in the suction line where there would be no useful cooling effect obtained. This would also lower the capacity of the compressor in pounds of gas handled. However, by adjusting the flow of the refrigerant into the evaporator, the gas can be made to leave the evaporator in a slightly heated condition; that is, the gas temperature is slightly warmer than that of the gas just leaving the boiling liquid. The additional heat of the suction gas leaving the evaporator should not be much higher than 10°F if all the evaporator surface is to be used. If the gas leaving the evaporator is slightly heated, it will be 100% vapor and will not materially change the capacity of the evaporator outlet unless the heat difference is higher than 10°F.

Let's take an acutal condition. If the pressure in the evaporator is such that the boiling point of the liquid is 30°F and the gas leaving the evaporator outlet is 40°F, the gas would be heated 10°F above its saturation temperature of 30°F. This heated gas leaving the evaporator enters the heat exchanger, where it comes in contact with the warm liquid from the condenser passing through the liquid coil located in the path of travel of the gas. Since the liquid in the liquid coil is much higher in temperature than the 40°F suction gas, there is a transfer of heat from the warm liquid to the cooler suction gas. This transfer of heat gives two results: it cools the warm liquid in the coil and further heats the suction gas.

The cooling of the liquid is very advantageous while the heating of the gas increases its volume and is somewhat of a disadvantage. However, the suction gas will be heated in the suction line anyway by the hot cylinder walls and by the valve plate. Thus by the use of the heat exchanger, this waste is put to useful net refrigeration effect by sub-cooling the warm liquid before it enters the evaporator. A system has sufficient heat exchange when the suction gas leaving the heat exchanger is approximately the same temperature as the cooling air entering the condenser.

The heated suction gas leaves the heat exchanger and flows through the suction line by the pressure difference created by the compressor. The gas enters the compressor cylinder on the downward stroke through the compressor suction or inlet valve. If the suction gas is already heated to the condenser inlet-air temperature by the heat exchanger, it picks up very little additional heat on entering the compressor cylinder because this temperature is near the mean average temperature of most water- or air-cooled compressors. When the piston of the compressor reaches the bottom of the stroke and starts on the compression or upward stroke, the suction or inlet valve closes and the piston then begins to compress the gas. The piston continues on the upward stroke until the pressure in the cylinder above the piston is slightly greater than the pressure in the discharge tube. The gas then starts to flow out of the cylinder above the piston, through the compressor discharge valve, and continues to flow into the discharge tube until the piston reaches the top of its travel. After the piston has reached the top of its travel and gas no longer flows through the discharge or exhaust valve, the discharge valve closes against its seat, thus sealing off the discharge tube from the cylinder.

The volume of gas that can enter a given compressor cylinder on the suction stroke will depend upon the pressure in the cylinder at the end of the compression stroke, the ratio of clearance volume to total volume, the gas pressure at the inlet valve, and the inertia and the friction to gas flow of the compressor valves. The weight of gas that enters the compressor on a suction stroke depends directly on the volume and the density or weight per cubic foot of the particular refrigerant used.

Capacity for a given weight per stroke is affected by the speed of the compressor or number of strokes per minute. Higher pressure in the discharge tube will reduce capacity because the clearance-volume gas will require a larger portion of travel of the suction stroke to reduce the cylinder pressure to a point where the suction or inlet can open and permit gas to enter the cylinder. Therefore, less volume and weight is handled per stroke. Conversely, reduced pressure in the discharge tube increases the capacity. Lower suction pressure will reduce the capacity for two reasons: the piston must travel a larger portion of the suction stroke to obtain a lower pressure in the cylinder for the gas to enter the cylinder; the lower pressure also lowers the density of the gas, or each cubic foot of gas that enters the compressor weighs less than at a higher pressure. Therefore, by holding a constant discharge pressure and lowering the suction pressure, the capacity will decrease faster than by holding a constant suction pressure and raising the discharge pressure a similar amount. When the piston compresses the gas, the gas passes out through the discharge valve, through the discharge tube and into the oil separator. This discharge gas is super-heated and its density raised by compression. The heat content per pound of the discharge gas is considerably more than the heat content of the suction gas entering the compressor. The reason for this higher heat content of the discharge gas is the added heat of work by compression as well as some heat from the friction of the compressor parts. Therefore, by compression of the gas, its pressure and temperature are raised.

The high-pressure, high-temperature gas continues through the oil separator and passes into the condenser through the discharge tube. The purpose of the condenser is to remove sufficient heat to condense the high-pressure, high-temperature gas into a liquid state so it can be conducted to the evaporator and be used over again. In order to remove heat from this gas, its temperature must be raised higher than the cooling medium, which in this illustration is air. This action is accomplished by the compressor. The compressor continues to pump the refrigerant gas into the condenser under high pressure and density. This gas contains a definite quantity of heat units per pound. When more pounds and therefore more heat units are added to a given volume of gas, the temperature of that gas is raised.

This action continues until there is sufficient temperature difference between the gas and the cooling medium (air) to establish a heat flow between the gas and cooling medium so that the heat absorbed by the cooling medium is equal to the heat content of the gas delivered to the condenser. At this point, the discharge pressure becomes stable and the gas changes to a liquid. For a given condenser and compressor, the discharge pressure and condensing temperature are fixed by the temperature and quantity of cooling medium passed over the surface exposed to the gas, as well as the suction pressure of the system. The suction pressure helps determine the amount of heat delivered to the condenser. The total amount of heat to be absorbed by the cooling medium is always considerably more than the net cooling effect of the evaporator. This is caused by the superheat of the gas and the heat of work of compression added by the compressor. This additional heat to be removed by the condenser will vary for a given net refrigeration effect.

For example, in a system developing 12,000 Btus per hour at 35°F suction temperature, the heat to be absorbed by the condenser would be approximately 14,000 Btus per hour. In a system developing 12,000 Btus per hour at −21°F, the condenser would have to absorb approximately 24,000 Btus. The condenser surface and quantity of cooling medium must be modified in a manner to obtain a high-efficiency condensing temperature over a wide operating range of suction temperatures.

The liquid leaving the condenser passes out through the liquid line to the liquid coil in the heat exchanger and then to the liquid control valve. The liquid first passes through a sight glass which is usually used to determine whether there is sufficient liquid refrigerant in the system to insure a solid flow of liquid to the evaporator. The liquid passes through the refrigerant strainer to remove any free particles of scale dirt, etc., that may damage the liquid control valve seat.

The liquid then enters the liquid coil of the heat exchanger where it is sub-cooled by heat transfer from the warm liquid to the cool suction gas. The sub-cooling of the liquid reduces the heat content of the liquid and therefore its temperature. By lowering the temperature of the liquid before it enters the evaporator, the amount of liquid vaporized to cool the entering liquid to evaporator temperature is considerably reduced. This reduction in the quantity of liquid vaporized allows full-capacity heat transfer from the fluid passing over the evaporator. For a given heat transfer to the evaporator, the quantity of gas flowing through the evaporator tubes is also reduced, which in turn reduces the pressure drop between evaporator inlet and outlet. This reduction in pressure permits lower heat at the evaporator outlet without entrained liquid and also makes the adjustment of the liquid control valve easier.

The liquid enters the liquid control valve, where it is admitted to the evaporator at a lower pressure level and therefore lower temperature level. As stated above, part of the incoming liquid is vaporized at this point to cool the higher liquid temperature to the lower evaporator temperature. The liquid thus vaporized is sometimes called flash gas.

A standard numbering system is now used to identify all refrigerants commonly in commercial use. This system eliminates the trade names used by manufacturers such as Freon, Genetron, Isotron, etc. The numbering system consists of the captial letter R which represents refrigerant, followed by a number. In addition to the numbering system, a standard color code for each type of refrigerant has also been developed.

The most common refrigerant found in modern automotive air-conditioning systems—as well as other small air-conditioning and refrigeration systems—is R-12. This type of refrigerant may be used in reciprocating, rotary, and centrifugal compressors and is noncorrosive, nonflammable, nontoxic, and nonirritating. However, it is very important to keep moisture from contaminating this refrigerant since water is soluble in R-12; when it contains moisture, a corrosive effect on most metals will take place.

The second most widely used refrigerant is R-22. Its characteristics are similar to R-12 except that it is used only with reciprocating compressors. Again, moisture is a problem when allowed to contaminate this refrigerant.

When moisture comes in contact with either of these refrigerants, an acid is formed which will cause corrosion. Therefore, it is of the greatest importance that every precaution be used to prevent moisture, which is present in air, from coming into contact with the refrigerant.

The products of corrosion include metal salts and oxides that gum valves and coat the inner surface of the condenser and the evaporator. Such coatings reduce the effectiveness of heat transfer, thus reducing the capacity of the system. Gummed and leaky valves may cause complete failure of the system. Corrosion will cause clogged strainers and orifices, frozen pistons and rings, loose bearings, pitted needle valves, and leaky seals.

In addition to corrosion, freeze-ups are common in R-12 and R-22 systems that contain excessive moisture. The solubility of water with these two refrigerants is relatively low, and the solubility, in percent of water by weight, is rapidly reduced as the temperature of the refrigerant is lowered. The small quantity of water in excess of that which will dissolve in the refrigerant at a given temperature will freeze. Ice usually forms at the point of pressure change and, therefore, temperature reduction, or in extremely wet systems in the evaporator or coils carrying low-pressure refrigerant. Ice may not necessarily form or lodge where it will completely block the refrigerant flow. Such a condition depends upon the method of introducing the refrigerant into the evaporator.

Oil sludge may result from the acids formed by moisture. Certain types of refrigerants dissolve copper from brass or copper parts. These copper particles are carried in solution in the oil. Moisture or its acid does not affect the amount of this copper solution in the oil; however, the moisture or acid together with heat is a factor in throwing the copper out of solution, causing deposits of copper in the compressor. This copper plating will first be noticeable at the discharge valve where the highest temperature exists.

SOURCES OF MOISTURE

Excessive moisture in a refrigeration system may occur due to one or more of the following: (1) failure to remove sufficient air when starting up a new system; (2) faulty methods of charging new or old systems; (3) defective workmanship of piping system; (4) mechanical failure of some part of the system such as leaky condenser, leaky seal, cracked cylinder head, or leaky evaporator; (5) moisture on replacement service parts; and (6) wet oil or refrigerant and faulty service methods.

While the moisture in the air is a potential source of trouble, it is not so serious because the moisture will be removed with the air if not deposited upon the surface as free moisture. However, dry or moisture-laden air left in a system is serious, not only due to the moisture itself but due to the oxygen in the air. Air may slowly oxidize the refrigerant oil, combining with the hydrogen in the oil to form water. A cubic foot of air at zero pressure contains enough oxygen to form approximately 0.3 ounces of water. It is reasonable to assume that over a long period of time at elevated temperatures encountered in cylinder heads, some water will be formed from air and oil under conditions of operation.

The slight addition of moisture from any source may raise the moisture content of the refrigerant, which may cause trouble from corrosion or freeze-ups.

Do everything possible to keep moisture out of the refrigerant. If moisture does happen to be present, Chapters 8 and 9 give methods of removing moisture from automotive air-conditioning systems by both vacuum and chemical means.

Safety precautions cannot be overemphasized when working with refrigerants. Keep the following in mind at all times:

Always wear safety goggles when working with refrigerants or any part of the air-conditioning system.

When a leak is suspected in a system, always provide adequate ventilation before starting to work on the system.

Never allow a leak-detector flame to come close to your eyes or face. Certain refrigerants that come in contact with an open flame emit a toxic gas.

Always check the refrigerant specifications of your system against the type you're using to charge the system. One type of refrigerant should not be replaced with another type unless recommended by the manufacturer's specifications.

Never overfill a refrigerant cylinder as there is a possibility of the cylinder bursting when the temperature rises.

FIRST AID FOR REFRIGERANT ACCIDENTS

The following first aid for accidents should be followed:

Liquid

A. On the surface of the skin:
  1. Apply water liberally to the affected part.
  2. Dry the skin with a dry towel or cloth.
  3. Apply olive or mineral oil.
B. On clothing in front of wearer:
  1. Remove the person affected to fresh air.
  2. Lay the person on his back so that the gas will not rise to the face and be breathed.
  3. Remove the clothing.
C. Clothing saturated so that refrigerant penetrates to the skin:
  1. Apply liberal quantities of water by means of a hose, pail, or other suitable means to absorb the refrigerant, retard rapid evaporation, and prevent freezing of the flesh.
  2. Remove the clothing.
  3. Dry the skin with a dry towel or cloth.
  4. Apply olive or mineral oil.

D. Splashed in the eyes:
1. Lay the head back and pour water in the eyes, holding the eyelids open.
2. Place two drops of mineral oil or prime castor oil in each eye.
3. Wash the eyes with a 4% solution of boric acid or a 2% salt water solution.
E. Swallowing:
1. Dissolve one teaspoonful of bicarbonate of soda (baking soda) in a half-glass of water and swallow immediately.
2. Follow with a teaspoonful of mineral oil or olive oil.

Gas Inhalation

1. Remove the person affected to fresh air.
2. Bathe the face and head freely with cold water.

When applying water to the skin surface for refrigerant spills, use only lukewarm water. Never use hot water when trying to re-establish circulation, because hot water may cause sudden dilation of the blood vessels and cause them to rupture. If lukewarm water is not available, insulate the affected area with a bandage or towel so that the body heat will accomplish a thawing process. Furthermore, do not rub the area as doing so may also result in tissue damage.

IN ALL CASES SEE A PHYSICIAN WITHOUT DELAY!

Chapter 13

Miscellaneous Information

The information contained in this chapter gives several hints which will prove useful to both pro and hobbyist working with automotive air-conditioning systems.

REFRIGERANT TUBING

It is extremely important to run the refrigerant lines as direct and smooth as possible. This applies to replacement tubing for factory-installed units as well as installing tubing for add-on air-conditioning systems or transmission cooling systems.

Besides being careful not to puncture or kink refrigerant tubing when handling, care should be taken to keep it free from dirt, scale, and moisture; both ends of the tubing should be kept sealed until just before it is ready for use. Whenever a piece of tubing is left over from a roll, the ends should be pinched closed or otherwise sealed to keep it clean and dry. This is especially important during humid and cold weather. Any tubing that has been allowed to lie around for any length of time should not be used for refrigerant lines—you're certain to experience difficulty later on.

Precautions should be taken when bending refrigerant tubing. One-fourth- and 3/8-inch tubing may be bent by hand as shown in Fig. 13-1 while the larger sizes (1/2 inch and larger) should be bent only with a spring bender. To make bends in the larger sizes of refrigerant tubing, slip the spring bender over the pipe at the desired location as shown in Fig. 13-2. Then group the ends of the spring and make the bend across your knee as shown in Fig. 13-3.

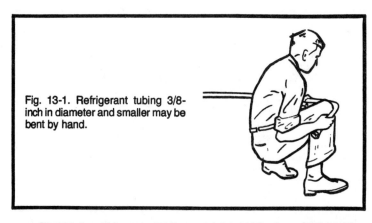

Fig. 13-1. Refrigerant tubing 3/8-inch in diameter and smaller may be bent by hand.

Should the tubing need to be cut, it is usually done with a tubing cutter as shown in Fig. 13-4. To operate, place the tubing (A) in the V-notch (B) of the tubing cutter tool and adjust the handle (C) until the cutting wheel (D) rests rather heavily on the tubing. Then turn the entire tool completely around the tubing and at the end of the revolution (and each succeeding revolution) tighten the handle a little more. Repeat this until the tubing is cut completely through—usually after only three or four complete turns.

When a flared connection is necessary, cut off the tubing square, loosen the two nuts of the tubing flaring tool (Fig. 13-5) so that the tubing can be slipped in the hole flush with the face of the clamp, and then retighten the nuts. Place a drop of refrigerant oil on the face of the male tool and place it over the tubing. Then turn the male tool down until the flare is made.

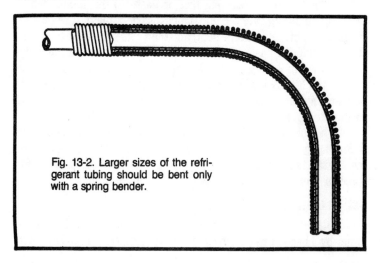

Fig. 13-2. Larger sizes of the refrigerant tubing should be bent only with a spring bender.

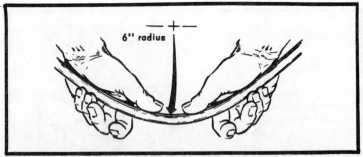

Fig. 13-3. With the spring bender slipped over the refrigerant tubing, make the bend across your knee.

In making the actual connection, use a few drops of refrigerant oil on the seat to help make a better seal. Care should be used at this point to guard against leaks. Be careful not to cross or strip the threads or put too much pressure on the tubing nut. Two wrenches must be used—one on the fitting and one on the nut.

If the fitting does not have a smooth seat, reseat it with a seating tool. To operate this tool, use the proper bushing (see instructions with the tool kit) and screw the tool onto the fitting. Turn down the knurled screw until the facing tool touches the fitting, and then turn the facing tool two or three times. This should be sufficient to reface the seat unless it is badly cut; in this case, repeat the operation.

A soldered tubing connection is made by first cutting the tubing squarely as with any other tubing connection. Thoroughly sand the inside of the fitting and about 1–1 1/2 inches of the tubing end. Then apply a light coat of soldering flux or paste to the tubing before inserting the fitting over the end. Once inserted, make sure that the tubing fits tightly against the seat, and then rotate it a little to ensure that the soldering paste is well distributed. Apply a blowtorch to the fitting to warm it up gradually and then apply tubing solder to the edge of the fitting. If the fitting is heated sufficiently, the solder will be drawn up inside the fitting between the walls of the fitting and the tubing. Remove the heat and apply more solder until the cavity is full.

If the solder does not show in a continuous ring at the end of the fitting, apply heat where it does not show until the solder creeps outward and seals the tubing. Allow the connection to cool slowly for three or four minutes before putting any strain on it.

USE OF LEAK DETECTOR

An R-12 leak can be located by the use of a leak detector—either by a halide torch or by an electronic leak detector. The torch

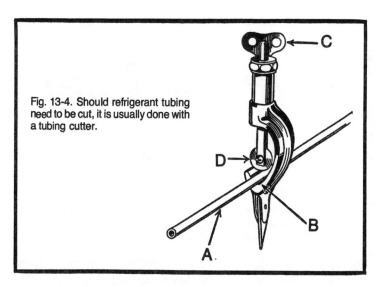

Fig. 13-4. Should refrigerant tubing need to be cut, it is usually done with a tubing cutter.

consists of a special propane burner, the air for which is taken in through a flexible search hose. When air only is taken into the tube, the flame of the torch burns blue. When a mixture of air and refrigerant is taken into the tube, the flame turns a bright green, while a high concentration of refrigerant turns the flame darker, to purple.

In using the leak detector torch, hold the inlet end of the search hose as close to the joint or connection as possible without blocking off the air supply to the torch. Slowly proceed completely around each joint with the end of the search hose, remembering that an

Fig.13-5. When a flared connection is necessary, a tubing flaring tool should be used.

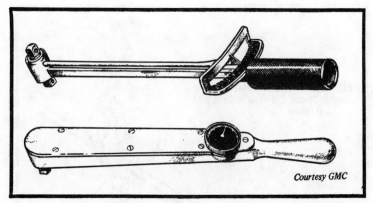

Fig. 13-6. Torque wrenches are necessary for working on some parts of automotive air conditioning systems as well as other sections of the car.

appreciable length of time is required for the sample to be drawn through the tube into the torch. Therefore, the result of the test is not instantaneous.

Since R-12 refrigerant is much heavier than air, the drift of R-12 is downward from a leak, requiring that the end of the hose be positioned a little below the point to be checked.

When the flame of a leak detector comes in contact with certain refrigerants, the gases which develop may be harmful. For this reason, never allow the fumes to come in contact with your nose or eyes.

An electronic leak detector operates by means of a special cell whose electrical characteristics change in the presence of certain refrigerants. It is used similarly to the torch detector except the electronic detector uses a battery-operated pump to suck air through a search hose or probe and passes it over the detection cell. If a refrigerant leak is present, the current through the cell will change, triggering a relay which activates a bell or buzzer to signal the presence of the leak.

USE OF TORQUE WRENCHES

Torque wrenches like the one illustrated in Fig. 13-6 are necessary for working on some parts of the automotive air-conditioning system as well as other sections of the car. The bolts and nuts securing the cylinder head and the air-conditioning compressor head are two examples of fasteners which must be tightened to certain specifications. Insufficient tightening will allow the bolt to loosen—with possible damage to the part—while too much tightening may cause distortion of the part and the possibility of stripped threads or

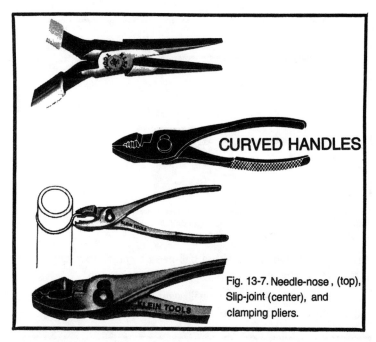

CURVED HANDLES

Fig. 13-7. Needle-nose , (top), Slip-joint (center), and clamping pliers.

broken fasteners. With a torque wrench, you can read on the dial the amount of torque being applied and thus tighten the fastener within specified limits.

MISCELLANEOUS TOOLS

It is unnecessary for the home mechanic to purchase tools and equipment of the type normally used only by the professional automotive air-conditioning mechanic, as the home mechanic will not be using them often enough to justify paying for them. Always keep the assortment of tools matched to the level of competence and to the kinds of automotive air-conditioning maintenance that will most often be performed.

Many of the necessary tools can already be found in your assortment of tools at home. If not, items such as pliers, hammers, screwdrivers, and an electric drill will also find other uses for repair around the home; they can double for duty in the home and on your car.

Besides the basic tools previously mentioned, you should acquire pairs of needle-nose, slip-joint, and clamping pliers as shown in Fig. 13-7. Try to vary the lengths and weights of screwdrivers and stock both common (top) and Phillips types (Fig. 13-8). You probably already have a standard claw hammer (top of Fig. 13-9), but this

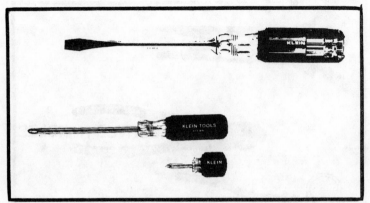

Fig. 13-8. Make sure you have the proper size and type of screwdriver. Distorted screwheads are a sure sign of sloppy workmanship.

should be supplemented with a ball-peen hammer (center), and a rubber or plastic mallet.

Other tools the beginner will want to acquire for repairs and maintenance on automotive air-conditioning systems will include

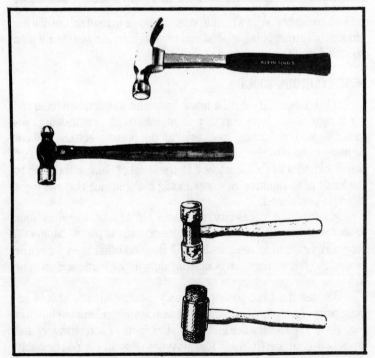

Fig. 13-9. Claw and ball-peen hammers, and both a plastic and rubber mallet.

Fig. 13-10. Set of Allen wrenches.

Allen wrenches (Fig. 13-10), box wrenches (Fig. 13-11), chisels (Fig. 13-12), a hacksaw (Fig. 13-13), combination wrenches (Fig. 13-14), punches (Fig. 13-15), and socket wrenches (Fig. 13-16). Metal files, an extension cord, and a work light will also prove useful.

One item that's not usually considered to be a tool can be the most useful aid any home mechanic ever owned for servicing the automotive air-conditioning system as well as other car systems; it's the manufacturer's service manual for your particular make and model of car. Such a manual will give the number and location of all parts in your car's system, the specifications for adjusting them, and all particulars necessary for their removal and installation. Although the manual may presume more knowledge than you have, such a manual will prove invaluable when used in combination with this book.

Special tools for servicing the automotive air-conditioning system as described in previous chapters usually will not be used

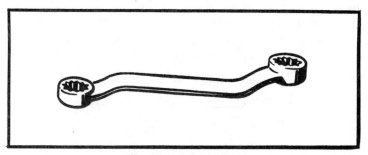

Fig. 13-11. Box wrench.

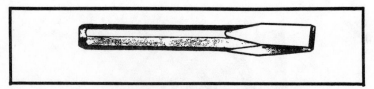

Fig. 13-12. Metal cutting chisel.

enough to justify their expense. However, most of these can be rented for a few dollars at most rental stores. These stores not only provide high-quality equipment, but their employees usually have enough mechanical knowledge to offer advice along with their tools.

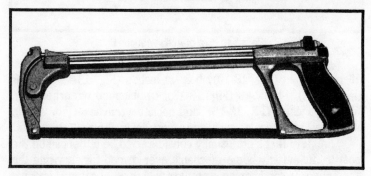

Fig. 13-13. Typical hacksaw.

If there are others in your neighborhood who want to service their own automotive air conditioners, perhaps all of you could go together and share the costs of these special tools; the initial cost per person would then make the investment worthwhile. You may even be able to find an automotive club near your home which you could join. You would then be able to have both tools and advice at your disposal. On the same order, U-Fix-It shops are becoming quite common in the metropolitan areas. These are garages where space, tools, and in many cases, trained supervisory personnel can be rented by the hour.

Many home mechanics may not want to purchase special tools to troubleshoot the car's air-conditioning system because they think

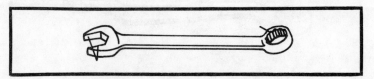

Fig. 13-14. Combination wrench.

196

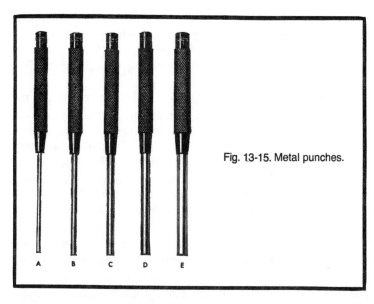

Fig. 13-15. Metal punches.

that the tool would only be used a few times each year and therefore would be a bad investment. However, many of the so-called special tools may also be used for testing car systems other than the air-conditioning system. You may even find a use for many of the tools for general repairs around the home.

For example, a vacuum gauge can be purchased at any of the automotive supply houses for about $5 and can be used to check the vacuum system operating your damper doors and other items which pertain to the car's air-conditioning system. The gauge can also be used for general tune-up tests on your car as well as many other

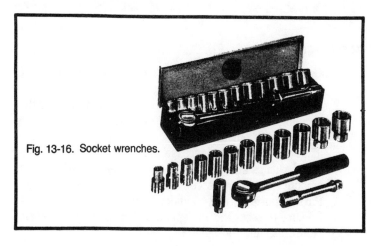

Fig. 13-16. Socket wrenches.

applications. The following will give several uses of the vacuum gauge to show how this inexpensive instrument can more than pay for itself. It is not the only "special" tool which the home mechanic will find useful for jobs other than checking the air-conditioning system.

For tune-up tests, the vacuum gauge is connected directly to the engine's intake manifold. The vacuum here is controlled by the engine's valves, piston rings, head gasket, timing, speed, and the throttle position. The reading on the gauge and the movement of the needle will detect many problems in the engine and may be used to select the proper idle mixture. Begin by selecting a vacuum hose on the car that is connected directly to the intake manifold. Remove this hose and install the vacuum-gauge test hose to this point.

Some vacuum circuits have a built-in bleed to limit the maximum vacuum in that circuit. To check if the point you have connected the hose to has such a bleed, temporarily connect the gauge to the manifold and start the engine. You are looking for a circuit where the vacuum at idle is between 15 and 22 inches as the engine is accelerated and decelerated.

When using the vacuum gauge, remember that readings have been calibrated for use at sea level. For all altitudes higher than sea level, readings will drop by 1 division on the dial for every 1000 ft. over sea level. Thus, a reading of 20 inches of mercury at sea level would be only 19 inches at 1000 ft., 18 inches at 2000 ft., etc.

TUNE-UP TESTS

This test is a quick way to determine if the engine has any mechanical problems—burnt valves, a blown head gasket, broken rings, or a cracked block or head—which will affect the engine's compression.

Cranking Vacuum

1. Ground out the coil's high tension lead so the engine will not start.
2. Crank the engine and watch the vacuum gauge. If the vacuum indicated is very low (less than 1 inch), you may have to back out the idle-speed screw or disconnect the idle stop solenoid to increase the reading. Cranking vacuum readings are normally between 2 and 10 inches. The amount of vacuum is controlled by the cranking speed, throttle position, and condition of the engine.
3. Be sure to reset the idle speed or reconnect the solenoid before starting the engine.

If the vacuum reading has a slight pulsation or is steady, this is acceptable. You will normally see between 1 and 2 inches of swing to the needle as the engine cranks. If, however, the reading drops toward zero occasionally, it needs service. If the vacuum gauge has indicated a loss in compression in one or more cylinders due to mechanical problems, a compression test should be made to pinpoint the cylinder that has the problem and determine the cause.

PCV Test

This test checks the PCV (positive crankcase ventilation) system.

While cranking the engine, remove the PCV valve and close off the end or alternately pinch the PCV hose closed. Watch the vacuum gauge. It is acceptable if the vacuum increases slightly when the PCV hose or valve is closed off. If there is no change in vacuum, cleaning or replacing the PCV valve is necessary. Be sure to check PCV hoses for build-up of oil or dirt.

Idle Vacuum

This checks the engine condition and carburetor mixture at idle.

Reconnect the coil lead, start the engine, and allow it to warm up. Read the vacuum gauge while the engine is at specified idle rpm. The vacuum should be steady and should read: late model cars 15 to 22 inches; older models 18 to 22 inches. Long-duration, high-performance cams may cause lower, and less steady vacuum readings. If the reading is low or unsteady, one of the following is wrong and corrective action may be taken:

1. Lower than normal readings are caused by incorrect ignition timing, incorrect valve timing or adjustment, misadjusted idle mixture, worn piston rings or a leak in the intake manifold.
2. Readings that slowly change (3 to 5 inches) indicate incorrect idle-mixture adjustment.
3. Readings that oscillate rapidly are due to sticking valves, a leak in the head gasket, or worn valve guides. Increase the engine speed to 2000 rpm. If the gauge becomes steady, the problem is probably worn valve guides.

High Speed Vacuum

This test will detect a restriction in the exhaust system which may be the cause of a loss of high-speed performance or weak valve springs.

1. Note vacuum at idle.
2. Increase the engine speed to about 2000 rpm. Read vacuum. The vacuum should be steady and higher at 2000 rpm than at idle.

If the vacuum falls below the reading at idle or the vacuum oscillates, the engine needs service. The fall in vacuum is due to a restriction in the exhaust system. Check for a crushed tailpipe, a muffler that is choked up with rust, has loose baffles, or a collapsed header pipe. To isolate the problem, remove each section, starting with the rear-most one, and repeat the test. On some large displacement engines you may have to conduct this test while the car is on the road. To do this, connect the vacuum gauge (use a "tee" fitting so the accessory is also connected and will operate) and run the hose back through the window into the car. Drive the car through the speed range where performance starts to fall off while watching the gauge.

The oscillations at high speeds mentioned earlier are due to weak valve springs.

Carburetor Adjustment

The vacuum gauge may be used to set the idle mixture. Be sure the compression is good and the ignition system is in proper working order before attempting to set the carburetor. The engine must be at correct operation temperature.

1. Set idle speed to manufacturer's specifications.
2. Turn the idle mixture screw out (counterclockwise) until the vacuum starts to drop.
3. Turn the screw in (clockwise) slowly until maximum vacuum is seen without a loss in engine rpm.

On multiple-barrel carburetors, adjust each mixture screw separately. On some emission-controlled engines, the manufacturer specifies that you must turn the idle mixture screw in after reaching the best idle speed until the engine slows down a specified amount. Use an RAC idle tachometer for this final adjustment. During mixture adjustments maintain idle rpm within 50 rpm of the specified idle speed by adjusting the idle speed screw.

Measuring Vacuum and Detecting Vacuum Leaks

The vacuum gauge may be used to test the amount of vacuum used to operate accessories, headlight covers, or emission controls. It also will detect any vacuum leaks which reduce the effectiveness of the system. Some tests may require the use of a "tee" fitting so the circuit may be monitored while under normal operation.

1. Connect the vacuum gauge to the vacuum line; use a "tee" fitting if the system is to operate while you are making the test.
2. Operate the engine. Read the vacuum.

The vacuum should be within the manufacturer's specification, or if not specified: (1) headlight covers, air-conditioner controls and most vacuum-powered accessories have a modulated vacuum and normally will read about 4 to 8 inches; (2) power brakes and accessories with vacuum boosters and reservoirs will read close to full manifold vacuum.

If the vacuum is below the amount specified, inspect the hoses, especially at connection points, for cracks and splits and replace as necessary. A small amount of soap-and-water solution may be brushed on the hose in question to find the leak. When the solution is pulled into the hose the indicated vacuum will increase. You can also move the "tee" fitting to the other end of the hose and compare readings. If there is a leak, the vacuum will be considerably lower on the side of the leak away from the intake manifold. Be sure you reconnect all vacuum lines correctly. Incorrect connections may affect the performance, reliability, and safety of your vehicle.

Fuel Pump Tests

This is a simple way to determine the overall condition of the fuel pump and fuel lines. Use extreme care when making fuel pump tests. Keep fire and sparks away from the gasoline.

1. Disconnect the fuel line between the fuel pump and carburetor.
2. Connect the gauge's hose to the fuel pump.
3. Operate the engine at idle rpm. Read the 0–10 psi pressure scale.
4. Stop engine and note the pressure gauge for 15 seconds.

The pressure should be within manufacturer's specifications or between 2–5 psi if specifications are not known and pressure holds after engine is stopped.

If the pressure is too low, visually inspect for a crimped fuel line or leaks between the tank and fuel pump. If the line is not restricted or leaking, then the fuel pump's spring is weak. Repair or replace the pump. The vehicle may have an electric fuel pump and regulator; be sure pressure is not too high. Should this occur, check the fuel pressure regulator. You need to replace the pump as its check valves are leaking if the pressure drops to 1/2 of maximum reading or less within 15 seconds after stopping the engine.

Volume Test

This test does not require the use of the gauge; however, it's included as it is part of a complete fuel pump test.

1. Direct the flow of fuel from the pump into a graduated container. Place the hose at the bottom of the container.
2. Run the engine for 30 seconds and measure the amount of gas pumped.

At least one pint should be pumped in 30 seconds unless more is specified by the manufacturer. If less fuel than specified is pumped or a large amount of bubbles is seen coming out of the hose, check for a crimped, restricted, or leaking fuel line. If volume is low but pressure was okay, inspect the pump's operating cam or rod and cam lobe for wear. If bubbles are seen, check for a leak between the fuel tank and the fuel pump.

Fuel Pump Vacuum Test

This test determines how much vacuum the fuel pump can develop to pull the fuel from the tank. It is made to pinpoint the cause of failure noted in the above fuel pump test.

1. Disconnect the fuel line from the pump inlet.
2. Connect the vacuum hose to the inlet of the fuel pump.
3. Start the engine and run it at idle. Watch the vacuum gauge.

The pump will not produce any vacuum until the fuel level in the carburetor drops and the pump attempts to fill the carburetor bowl. On some engines this may require 2 to 3 minutes. There should be from 2 to 10 inches of vacuum. If little or no vacuum is produced, the pump has a leak, a ruptured diaphragm, or a leaking check valve. Repair or replace it. If this test is run at the end of the fuel line near the fuel tank, it will also check for fuel leaks in that line.

HANDLING TUBING AND FITTINGS

Kinks in the refrigerant tubing or sharp bends in the refrigerant hose lines will greatly reduce the capacity of the entire system. High pressures are produced in the system when it is operating. Extreme care must be exercised to make sure that all connections are pressure tight. The following precautions must be observed.

The system must be completely discharged before opening any fitting or connection in the refrigeration system. Open fittings with caution even after the system has been discharged. If any pressure is noticed as a fitting is loosened, allow trapped pressure to bleed off very slowly. Use a suitable tube-bender when bending the refrigerant lines to avoid kinking. Never attempt to rebend formed lines to fit, and use the correct line for the installation you are servicing.

A good rule for flexible hose lines is to keep the radius of all bends at least 10 times the diameter of the hose. Sharper bends will reduce the flow of refrigerant. The flexible hose lines should also be routed so that they are at least 3 inches from the exhaust manifold. In fact, it is a good idea to inspect all flexible hose lines at least once a year to make sure they are in good condition and properly routed.

"O" rings and fittings (Fig. 13-17) must be in good condition as the slightest burr or foreign material may cause a leak. "O" rings and fittings must be coated with refrigerant oil to allow the connections to seat squarely and to be tightened evenly to the proper torque. Fittings which are not oiled with refrigerant oil are almost sure to leak.

The use of proper wrenches when making connections is another very important consideration, as improper wrenches or improper use of wrenches can damage the fittings. Always use two wrenches when loosening or tightening tube fittings to prevent distorting lines and components.

The internal parts of the refrigeration system will remain in a state of chemical stability as long as pure, moisture-free R-12 and refrigerant oil is used. Dirt, moisture, or air can upset the chemical stability and cause operational troubles or even serious damage if present in more than minute quantities.

When it is necessary to open the refrigeration system, have everything ready to service the system so that it will not be left open

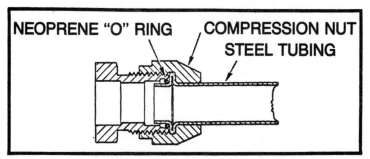

Fig. 13-17. Cross-section of refrigerant tubing joint. Refrigerant tubing joint. Refrigerant oil should be applied to "O" ring.

any longer than necessary. Cap or plug all lines and fittings as soon as they are opened to prevent the entrance of dirt and moisture. All lines and components in parts stock should be capped or sealed until they are ready to be used.

All tools, including the refrigerant dispensing manifold, the gauge set manifold, and the test hoses should be kept clean and dry.

The special refrigeration oil supplied for air-conditioning systems is manufactured as clean and dry as possible. Only refrigeration oil should be used in the system or on the fittings and lines. The oil container should be kept tightly capped until it is ready for use, and then tightly capped after use to prevent entrance of dirt and moisture. Refrigerant oil will quickly absorb any moisture with which it comes in contact.

Chapter 14

Heat Pumps
For Autos & RVs

Heat pumps have been in use for many years in homes and commercial buildings, but have only recently been introduced for automotive
use. Unlike most other air-conditioning units, the heat pump is
designed to provide both cooling and heating at the user's option. In
mild-weather areas, a heat pump can even eliminate the need for a
supplemental or separate heating unit. The reversible heat-pump
design is considered more efficient and yet costs less to operate than
conventional units.

Models are currently available with cooling capacity from
around 9,000 Btu to nearly 14,000 Btu; heating capacity is around
10,000 Btu to 12,000 Btu for all models. These units are made for
operation on 120-volt AC current so are presently limited to vans
and other RVs where power is available at campsites. Present
models could also be modified to be powered by the car's engine, the
same as conventional auto air conditioners.

HEAT PUMP OPERATION

The fundamentals of a refrigeration cycle were discussed previously along with the basic components of the system. The same
components of the fundamental system are shown somewhat dif-
ferently in Fig. 14-1.

The function of the conventional refrigeration system is to pick
up heat from a place where it is not wanted and pump it to some
waste point. Therefore, the basic function of an ordinary refrigeration system—like that used in autos—is to remove heat and hold, or

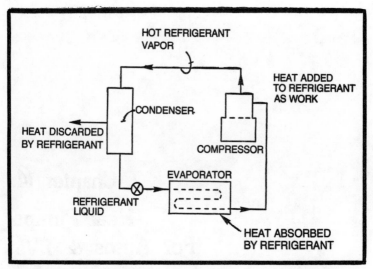

Fig. 14-1. Basic refrigeration cycle and heat pump on cooling cycle.

create, a lower temperature. Heat is absorbed by the refrigerant as it vaporizes from a liquid to a vapor in the evaporator (see Fig. 14-1). Then the vaporous refrigerant is pumped from the evaporator to the condenser by the compressor. Work is done on the refrigerant to accomplish this, and heat added as a result. In the condenser, the refrigerant releases its total heat as it changes from a vapor to a liquid. The rejection of heat from the condenser, in the usual refrigeration system, is just an incidental part of the cycle.

A heat pump differs from the normal refrigeration system in that the heat rejected from the compressor, in some cases, is as important as the refrigeration effect produced by the evaporator. This type of refrigeration system is commonly called a heat pump.

The heat pump operating on the cooling cycle is illustrated in Fig. 14-1. Note that the refrigerant absorbs heat in the evaporator. If the evaporator is maintained at 44°F as shown, air can flow over the outside of the evaporator and be cooled as the air gives up heat to the refrigerant. The refrigerant is then pumped to the condenser. The refrigerant gives up its heat of condensation to a cooling medium—like water or air—carrying heat from the condenser. Therefore, the operation of a heat pump operating on the cooling cycle is identical to a conventional air-conditioning unit.

At this point, the reader may wonder why a conventional air-conditioning unit is not called a heat pump since it does perform the operation of pumping heat from one place to another. Actually, the usual air conditioner could be called a heat pump since it does perform that function. However, it is customary to use the term heat pump only for those refrigeration systems having special provisions to utilize the heat rejected from the condenser.

A heat pump operating on the heating cycle is shown diagrammatically in Fig. 14-2. Note that in the evaporator heat is absorbed by the refrigerant, and that the refrigerant in the condenser discards heat. This procedure is repeated, with the same components functioning in the same manner as in the cooling cycle shown in Fig. 14-1. On the heating cycle, however, the emphasis is on the heat rejected from the condenser.

In the usual application of the heat pump, the heat available to vaporize the refrigerant in the evaporator is at a temperature much too low for heating. After the refrigerant is pumped to the higher temperature level of the condenser, however, the heating medium (water or air) absorbs heat from the condenser for space heating. The heat leaving the refrigerant in the condenser is the total of the heat pumped from the evaporator plus the heat equivalent of the work necessary to compress the refrigerant.

In order to perform its function, a heat pump must be capable of operating on either the cooling cycle or the heating cycle, and the methods of changing from one to the other must be relatively simple.

Changing from heating to cooling, or cooling to heating, is commonly called changeover. It can be accomplished either manually or automatically. Manual changeover is usually a matter of turning valves, setting dampers, or flipping switches. With automa-

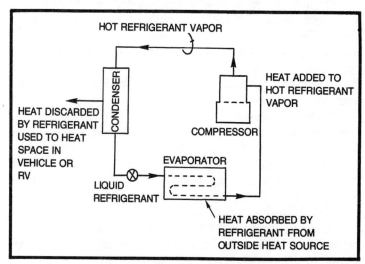

Fig. 14-2. Heat pump on heating cycle.

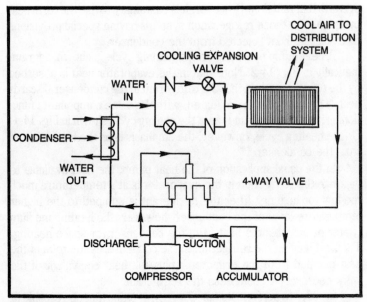

Fig. 14-3. Heat pump changeover by means of a 4-way valve used in conjunction with a variable refrigerant circuit. Here the heat pump is operating on a cooling cycle.

tic changeover, control devices alternate the heat pump between cooling and heating in response to demands from the conditioned space.

Changeover can be readily accomplished, whether the heat pump has a fixed refrigerant circuit or a variable refrigerant circuit. The evaporator, condenser and compressor do not change their relative positions or functions from the heating cycle to the cooling cycle. In both cases, the refrigerant flows in the same direction. If the refrigerant circuit is fixed, the air flow must be altered in order to facilitate changeover.

On the cooling cycle, dampers are opened so return air from the conditioned space passes over the evaporator and is cooled on its way back to the conditioned space. For operation on the heating cycle, dampers are opened to allow return air from the occupied space to pass over the condenser. This air picks up heat from the condenser and is then sent into the occupied space.

The refrigerant cycle remains exactly the same whether the heat pump is operating on the heating or cooling cycle. The dampers can be operated manually. Damper motors or solenoid valves can also be provided so that, in response to a controller, the dampers are automatically changed to the opposite cycle. For some cross-connected damper arrangements, only two damper motors are required; in other arrangements, four damper motors are used.

Changeover with the variable-refrigerant circuit is accomplished by a 4-way valve illustrated in Fig. 14-3 and 14-4. The heat pump is operating on the cooling cycle in Fig. 14-3. Hot refrigerant vapor from the compressor flows through the 4-way valve to the condenser. Here the refrigerant vapor condenses to a liquid, opens the check valve, and flows through the expansion valve to the evaporator. The refrigerant vaporizes and absorbs its latent heat of vaporization from the air passing over the evaporator coil. The low-pressure refrigerant vapor is then directed by the 4-way valve through the accumulator to the suction side of the compressor to complete the circuit.

In this cycle, the important end product is the cooled air that gave up its latent heat in vaporizing the refrigerant in the evaporator. This air is then sent to a distributing system for space cooling.

When the automatic changeover thermostat selects the heating cycle, the 4-way valve switches its position. As shown in Fig. 14-4, the flow of refrigerant reverses in all parts of the system except the accumulator and compressor. The hot vapor discharge from the compressor flows through the 4-way valve to the coil that was formerly the evaporator, but now functions as the condenser. Air

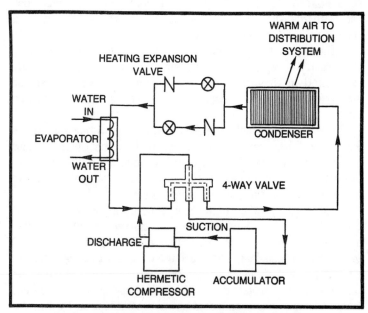

Fig. 14-4. Variable-refrigerant circuit with a 4-way valve.

from the space to be heated passes over the condenser tubes and absorbs heat from the refrigerant vapor to condense it. After the liquid refrigerant leaves the condenser, it lifts the lower check valve and flows through the expansion valve to the coil that was formerly the condenser, but now functions as the evaporator. After evaporation, the refrigerant flows through the 4-way valve to the accumulator on its way to the compressor to complete the circuit.

The important end product in this cycle is the warmed air that absorbed heat from the condensing refrigerant vapor. This air is then sent through the distribution system to warm the conditioned space.

The accumulator is placed in the suction line to trap any liquid going to the compressor. Under steady operation, the refrigerant picks up sufficient heat in the evaporator to vaporize any liquid in the suction line. However, in changing from the cooling cycle to the heating cycle, the coil, which has been functioning as a condenser, contains a certain amount of liquid refrigerant. This liquid refrigerant should be allowed time to drain from the coil into a holding receiver before the system operates on the heating cycle. However, since there is no interruption in compressor operation when the 4-way valve changes to the heating cycle, the accumulator must trap liquid refrigerant and prevent it from entering the compressor. The liquid refrigerant in the accumulator is then metered in small quantities back into the suction line where it is evaporated—usually by a suction-to-liquid-line heat exchanger.

The heat pump is definitely a fascinating device for producing comfort. It has captivated the interest of the press, so is frequently mentioned in magazines and newspapers. From a business standpoint, heat pumps might be the "sleeping giant" that some experts predict, not only for buildings, but cars also.

The most used fuel, at present, for heating with heat pumps is electricity. Whenever you convert electricity to heat with ordinary electric resistance heaters, you do this heating at a 100% efficiency. For every one cent of electricity that you buy, you get one cent of electricity back in the form of useable heat.

The great advantage of the heat pump is that for every one cent of electricity that you buy, you will get back considerably more than one cent's worth of electric heat. With a well-designed air-to-air heat pump, you will usually get back about 3 cents worth of electric heat for every 1 cent of electricity you buy to run the heat pump in 40° winter weather. The two cents of electric heat that you get for free, in this example, has been pulled out of the outdoor air by the heat pump.

The ratio between the heat output and the heat (or electric) input to the heat pump, is known as the COP, which stands for "coefficient of performance." One kilowatt of electricity contains 3,413 Btu. If the COP of a heat pump is 3.00, then, for every kilowatt hour that you spend to run it, you will get three times this, or 10,239 Btus of heat delivered from the machine. As the weather gets colder, the COP of the heat pump goes down so that you get less and less heat out of the air "for free."

The heat pump cuts the cost of electric heating substantially. It is impossible to predict accurately just what the cost comparison will be between straight electric resistance heating and heat pump heating, because this depends on your climate, the ratio of winter heat loss to summer heat gains, and the size of the equipment in comparison to the loads.

In the midwestern states (Illinois, Iowa, Nebraska) the overall coefficient of performance of heat pumps can average as much as 2.50 for an entire heating season. This, however, is a very approximate figure. In warmer climates, the average COP for the entire heating season can be considerably higher, approaching 3.00 in California, for example.

Therefore, if you compare straight electric heating with the other fuels, you have a mathematically accurate comparison. By installing a good heat pump, you may get somewhere between two and three times as many Btus per cent as with straight electric heating. Remember also that in the severest winter months, with a heat pump you will probably be using auxiliary electric resistance heating a good deal of the time. Therefore, the overall COP for the auxiliary heaters and the heat pump is low during the coldest winter months. You offset this, however, by a marked increase in the COP during the milder winter months.

In general, heat pumps are an excellent choice where there is a rather high cooling requirement as compared with the heating load, and where more than average air circulation is desirable. Automobiles could fall in this category, where there are high heat gains from the engine, manifold, etc.

When heating, a heat pump performs low temperature refrigeration. Any moisture in the system can freeze and plug the system. The reversing valve is delicate and cannot have a strainer on the suction line side. Therefore, you must clean and evacuate heat pump systems even more carefully than regular refrigeration systems. Plan on great installation care with a heat pump.

Although most heat pumps in use at the present time are electrically operated, there is no reason why other sources of power cannot be used to provide the necessary power. The car's engine can be used to drive the compressor—just as it is now used to operate conventional automotive air-conditioning systems. However, we feel that the most advantageous use of the heat pump will be in electrically powered vehicles where there is no water system or manifold with which to capture heat. In these vehicles, an electric motor of 1/2 to 1 hp (designed for use on DC current of the same voltage that powers the drive motor) could be used to power the heat pump used for heating and cooling the vehicle. Very little modification and few additional controls would be necessary for the installation.

RV AIR CONDITIONERS

Most RV owners have come to expect temperate conditions in homes as well as their autos, vans, trailers, and other RV vehicles, and accept air conditioners as fundamental equipment.

The operation of RV air-conditioning systems differs little from those explained earlier in this book, except that most RV models operate on 120 volts rather than the engine of the car. Like conventional automotive air-conditioning systems, RV air-conditioning systems can be rather complex to repair. However, there are several ways in which the TV owner can prolong the trouble-free life of an air conditioner. A basic understanding of how the system functions, coupled with recognizing distress symptoms, can help an owner detect what he can repair and better describe those problems beyond the owner's reach to a professional repairman.

There are two basic types of air-conditioning systems used in RVs besides the heat pump described previously. All of them share the same principle of operation; cooling the air by removing heat. This is accomplished in all types by taking advantage of a natural property of liquids; that is, whenever a liquid vaporizes, heat is absorbed.

Compressor-type air conditioners—like the ones used in automotive systems—are the most efficient as they use a refrigerant that boils at a low temperature, and reuse the refrigerant over and over again. When this type of air conditioner is not installed so that it can be driven by the car's engine, 120-volt current must be available to power them, either at a campsite with a 120-volt outlet or by use of a 120-volt AC generator.

Evaporative air conditioners use a water-saturated mat over which air is circulated so that normal evaporation is accelerated. Water changes into a vapor (evaporation) and some heat is absorbed in the process.

The evaporative air conditioner is not as efficient as the compressor type, but the former does have the advantage of using 12-volt DC power and thus can be operated in transit or when the RV is in its self-contained mode. High outside humidity can halt cooling in this type of system.

Now let's get down to the nitty-gritty of each type so that the owners and repairmen will have a basic understanding of the operation of each type.

COMPRESSOR-TYPE AIR CONDITIONER

The compressor air conditioner is similar to those used in homes and in factory-installed air-conditioning systems in cars. Basic refrigeration has been explained earlier, so we won't go into great detail at this time. However, a review is in order.

Refrigeration is a process which involves the transfer of heat from any given space. In the compressor-type system, this transfer of heat is accomplished by means of a refrigerant, which is placed in such a condition that it will abstract heat from the space to be conditioned, and after this absorption, is placed in such a condition that it will give up this heat to an outside air supply.

The basic law in the transfer of heat is that it can flow only from a body of a higher temperature to a body of a lower temperature; never in the reverse direction. Therefore, the immediate result of such a transfer is that the colder body gains heat and the warmer body loses heat. When the colder body receives heat, two changes can take place:

1. Its temperature may rise.
2. Its state may change from a solid to liquid or liquid to gas.

When a warmer body loses heat, two changes can also take place:

1. Its temperature may lower.
2. Its state may change, but since it has lost some heat, this change will be from a gas to a liquid or from a liquid to a solid.

In an RV air conditioner, the actual cooling begins in the evaporator section. Here, the cold refrigerant absorbs heat from the warmer interior air forced across the evaporator coils by a fan or blower. The resultant cooler air is then blown back into the RV space. This accomplishes cooling, but the cycle must continue in the system so that the refrigerant may be reused.

As the colder refrigerant draws heat from the warmer air of the RV, the refrigerant is heated and, due to its characteristics, begins to boil. The vapor which is created when refrigerant boils is sucked into the compressor to be pressurized and pumped out to the condenser.

When the refrigerant (under pressure) arrives at the condenser, it is still hot, but as it circulates through the coils of the condenser, much of this heat is transferred to the cooler outside air being blown across the condenser fins by a fan or blower motor. As the gas cools, the pressure drops and the gas once again turns into a liquid. However, this liquid is still too hot to do too much cooling of the RV space. So, at this point, the liquid enters a specially designed capillary tube which further cools the liquid and meters the flow so that when the refrigerant reaches the evaporator, it is a cold, low-pressure liquid and will readily boil in the larger diameter of the evaporator coils, which begins another cycle.

The basic components of an RV air conditioner consist of a compressor, condenser, expansion valve, and an evaporator. These components are connected by copper tubing and the refrigerant circulates in one direction within this system to accomplish the function of cooling the space within the RV.

The purpose of the compressor is threefold. First, it pumps or withdraws heat-laden gas from the cooling unit through the suction line; second, it compresses this gas to a high pressure and discharges it into the condenser; finally, its discharge valve acts as the dividing point between the low- and high-pressure sides of the refrigerating system.

The function of the condenser is to reject the heat in the refrigerant to the surrounding air or to a water supply to condense it to a liquid. One type of air-cooled condenser is the fin-and-tube or radiator type. With this type, comparatively cool air is passed through a compact, finned radiator by a fan on the compressor-motor pulley.

As the compressor pumps the refrigerant from the cooling unit, it must be replenished with low-pressure, low-temperature liquid capable of absorbing heat. This is accomplished by a liquid control valve, which is known as the expansion valve. This valve has three functions. First, it acts as a pressure-reducing valve—reducing the high-pressure liquid that was condensed by the condenser to a low-pressure, low-temperature liquid capable of absorbing heat; second, it maintains a constant pressure of refrigerant in the evaporator; and third, the valve acts as a dividing point between the high- and low-pressure sides of the refrigerating system.

The evaporator is that part of the refrigeration system directly connected with the refrigerating process. The refrigerant in the

214

cooling unit absorbs heat from the RV and thus cools it. As the evaporator absorbs heat from the space, the low-pressure, low-temperature liquid refrigerant in the vaporizing tubes or coils is vaporized.

Other components include an electric motor that drives both the evaporator blower and the condenser fan, a thermostat which senses the return-air temperature at the evaporator and activates a switch that turns the compressor on or off, and several electrical relays, switches, and other controls.

An air filter is located where the cool air is delivered to the RV interior to trap dust and pollen. A strainer is also included on many models to collect any foreign matter that may be accidentally introduced during repair.

EVAPORATIVE-TYPE AIR CONDITIONERS

Evaporative-type air conditioners absorb heat by the process of evaporation—using water as a means of heat exchange. Water evaporates—in most cases—when it is exposed to the air. During this evaporation process, some of the heat of the air is absorbed. When air is blown across the wet surface, evaporation is accelerated.

In the evaporative air conditioner, outside air is pulled through a wet mat by a 12-volt fan. Some moisture is picked up as the water evaporates, and the cooler and more humid air is circulated in the RV. Some means, however, must be provided for the warmer air to escape and to prevent the interior from becoming cold and damp. An exhaust fan will work best, but an open window will work in most cases.

From the above description, it can be seen that evaporative air conditioners will work best in dry climates where the air will readily absorb moisture.

A water reservoir must be provided to furnish water to the mat; this can be hand-filled or connected to the RV's water system to automatically maintain the desired level. A pump within the system circulates water in an action similar to a lawn sprinkler so that the entire mat surface is sprayed equally and thoroughly.

Of the two types of RV air conditioners described, the evaporative type is the simplest. It is so simple, in fact, that it is almost trouble-free, though difficulties can arise from mechanical defects (fan or pump motors) or owner neglect.

Sticky Float Valve

In the automatic type of evaporative air conditioners, the desired water level is maintained by a float valve similar to that used in

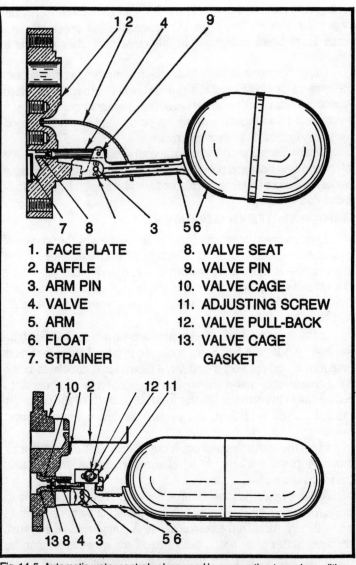

1. FACE PLATE
2. BAFFLE
3. ARM PIN
4. VALVE
5. ARM
6. FLOAT
7. STRAINER

8. VALVE SEAT
9. VALVE PIN
10. VALVE CAGE
11. ADJUSTING SCREW
12. VALVE PULL-BACK
13. VALVE CAGE
   GASKET

Fig. 14-5. Automatic water control valves used in evaporative-type air conditioners are usually controlled by a float similar to the one pictured here.

toilet storage tanks (Fig. 14-5). When the desired water level is reached, the float or bulb is raised which in turn closes the water inlet. Mineral deposits accumulate on this valve and make it function improperly. A thorough cleaning will usually take care of the problem, but often a complete overhaul requiring replacement of many of the parts will be necessary.

Restricted Air Flow

Mineral deposits can also seal the porous material of the mat so that it does not properly absorb water. The foam or wood fiber mats should be periodically cleaned by rinsing with a garden hose. Eventually, they will have to be replaced, but replacements are readily available from the manufacturer or through RV accessory stores.

Motor Failure

About the only other problem that will normally occur with the evaporative-type air conditioner is failure of the electric motors operating the fan and the pump. Check the voltage level at the motor terminals with a DC voltmeter. If no voltage is present, look for an open circuit like a blown fuse, broken wires, loose connection, etc. If the voltage is lower than 12 volts, this could be the problem. In most cases of low voltage (provided your battery is adequately charged), the wiring is not of sufficient size to carry the current so a voltage drop occurs. If this is the problem, the wires will have to be replaced with larger size conductors. If none of the above tests reveal the problem, chances are the motor is defective and should be replaced or repaired as necessary.

MAINTENANCE AND TROUBLESHOOTING: COMPRESSOR-TYPE CONDITIONERS

Just like conventional automobile air conditioners, special tools and skills are often required to service the compressor-type air conditioners. Refrigerant is used in compressor-type air conditioners and the serviceman must use precautions in handling this—refrigerant can freeze flesh and blind if any gets into the eyes. This imposes some stringent limitations on the do-it-yourselfer, but there are still things you can do to prolong the life of your RV air conditioner.

General maintenance of RV air conditioners includes frequent cleaning of the air filters—the frequency depending upon the amount the unit is used. Wash the filter with soap and water, rinse clean, and allow to dry thoroughly before placing it back into the unit. Completely new filters should be installed at least once each year; they can be obtained from the manufacturers or RV accessory stores.

Most RV air conditioners are roof-mounted and are therefore safe from ordinary road damage. However, when traveling the back roads, they are highly susceptible to impact from tree branches which can crack the cover, known as the shroud. It is best to replace the shroud should it become damaged, but often you may be on a trip and an immediate replacement may not be possible. In this case, remove the shroud from the unit and drill a small hole at the end of the crack. Apply a strip of wide tape on both sides of the crack to seal it. This will keep the crack from worsening until replacement becomes practical.

Dust and grime can settle on the evaporator and condenser coils, lessening operational efficiency. These items should be checked and cleaned if necessary. Also check the mounting bolts of the entire unit to ascertain that it is secure—road vibration will cause them to work loose.

Road vibration can also cause the condenser fan motor to work loose enough to obstruct the blades. Any clacking noise is an indication of this problem and such noise calls for a prompt investigation. To check for a fan obstruction, first turn off the air conditioner and remove the cover. Slowly rotate the fan blade by hand. If the blades strike any object, loosen the nuts securing the fan motor, and rotate the resilient rubber pads. Retighten the nuts and again test the blade motion with your hand. If the problem still exists, new mounting pads should be installed; they may be obtained from any repair center.

The RVer can save a great deal of time and money by doing his own troubleshooting and repairs when a problem occurs in a compressor-type air conditioner. Even if he finds that the repair is a little too complicated for him, he will still be money ahead by knowing the probable cause when a repairman takes a look at it.

Troubleshooting the RV air conditioner covers a wide range of electrical and mechanical problems from finding a short circuit in the power supply line through adjusting a pulley on a motor shaft, to tracing out loose connections in relatively complex control circuits. However, in nearly all cases, the owner can determine the cause of the trouble by using a systematic approach, checking one part of the system at a time—in the right order.

Always keep in mind that all of an air conditioner's problems can be solved, and it is the purpose of this chapter to show the reader exactly how to go about solving the more conventional ones in a safe and logical manner.

The following data is arranged so that the problem is listed first. Then the possible causes of this problem are listed in the order in which they should be checked. Finally, solutions to the various problems are given, including step-by-step procedures where it is felt that they are necessary.

TYPICAL COOLING PROBLEMS

Problem A: Compressor motor and condenser motor will not start, but fan-coil unit (blower motor) operates normally.

(1) Check the thermostat system switch setting to ascertain that it is set to cool.

(2) Check the thermostat temperature setting to make sure that it is set below room temperature.

(3) Check the thermostat to see if it is level. If not, the occupied area will be too hot or too cold and could prevent the compressor motor from operating. To correct, remove the cover plate, place a spirit level on top of the thermostat base, loosen the mounting screws, and adjust the base until it is level; then re-tighten the mounting screws.

(4) Check all connections for tightness.

(5) Make a voltage check with a voltmeter on the float switch, as the condensate may not be draining. The float switch is normally found in the fan-coil unit and typically consists of a normally closed mercury switch attached to a stainless steel arm and pin with a polystyrene float. The switch opens if the water level in the drain pan rises to approximately 1/2 inch. The water level in the drain pan should be between 1/4 and 3/8 inch when the unit is running.

In order to make the voltage check, set the thermostat on "cooling" and, with the fan running, check across the two lead wires at an accessible point—such as where they connect to a terminal block. If the float switch is broken, the mercury bulb loose, the contact does not open or close, or the float is loose, replace the float switch assembly.

If you find the float switch to be in good working order, clean out the condensate drain and trap; then check to see if the fan-coil unit is level. Continue by checking the pitch (1/4 inch for each foot of horizontal line) of the condensate drain line.

(6) Low air flow could be causing the trouble, so check the air filters; if dirty, clean or replace.

(7) Make a voltage check of the anti-frost control; replace if defective.

(8) Check all duct connections to the fan-coil unit; repair if necessary.

Problem B: Compressor, condenser, *and* fan-coil unit motors will not start.

(1) Check the thermostat system switch setting to ascertain that it is set to COOL.

(2) Check the thermostat temperature setting to make sure it is below room temperature.

(3) Check the thermostat to make sure it is level. If not, correct.

(4) Check all connections for tightness.

(5) Check for blown fuses or a tripped circuit breaker. Determine the cause of the open circuit and then replace the fuses or reset the circuit breaker.

(6) Check your electrical service against minimum requirements; that is, correct voltage, ampere rating, wire size, number of circuits, etc. Update your service if necessary.

Problem C: Condensing unit cycles, contactor opens and closes on each cycle and blower motor operates.

(1) The condensate drain may not be working properly. Run a check as described in No. 5 of Problem A. Then continue on to numbers 5, 6, 7, and 8 of the same problem.

(2) Check all wiring connections for tightness, and correct if necessary.

(3) The blower motor could be defective, so take an amperage reading on the motor while it is running. However, do not confuse the full load (starting) amps shown on the motor rating plate with the actual running amps. The latter should be about 25% less. If the amperage varies considerably from that on the nameplate, have the motor checked for bad bearings, defective winding insulation, etc. The problem could also be caused by low voltage on the circuit. Have the motor replaced or repaired if it's found to be defective.

Problem D: Inadequate cooling with condensing unit and blower running continuously.

(1) Check all connections against the wiring diagram furnished with the system. Correct if necessary. Then check for leaks in the refrigerant lines.

(2) The equipment could be undersized. Check heat gain calculations against the Btu output of your unit. Correct structural deficiencies with insulation, awnings, etc., or install proper size equipment.

Problem E: Condensing unit cycles but blower motor does not run.

(1) Check all connections against the wiring diagram furnished with the system. Correct if necessary.

(2) Check all connections for tightness.

(3) Make voltage check on blower relay and replace if necessary.

(4) Make electrical and mechanical checks on the blower motor. Check for correct voltage at the motor terminals. Mechanical problems could be bad bearings or a loose blower wheel. Bearing trouble can be detected by turning the blower wheel by hand (with current off), and checking for excessive wear, roughness, or seizure. Repair or replace the motor.

Problem F: Continuous short cycling of blower coil unit and insufficient cooling: thermostat is not satisfied.

(1) Make electrical and mechanical checks as described in No. 4 of Problem E. Repair or replace the motor if necessary.

Problem G: Sweating at blower coil outlet or at electric duct heater outlet.

(1) Check to see if proper insulation is installed and correct if necessary.

(2) Visually check to ascertain that shipping blocks and angles have been removed from the blower unit.

(3) Check the blower motor assembly suspensions and fasteners and tighten if necessary.

The old saying, "an ounce of prevention..." certainly holds true for cooling systems. A correctly installed system that is maintained according to the manufacturer's recommendations will give you years of trouble-free service with a minimum of cost to you.

Maintenance procedures and their frequency will depend a great deal on the type of system you have in your RV, but the information given herein is designed to cover most systems. For further information, consult your Owner's Handbook accompanying the equipment. If you don't have one, ask your supplier or write directly to the manufacturer to obtain a copy.

Chapter 15

Improving Efficiency
Of Cooling Systems

A number of methods discussed in this chapter will show you how to immediately reduce wasted energy and improve the efficiency of your car's cooling system without taking up too much of your time or requiring a large capital outlay.

SEALING CRACKS AND CREVICES

Cracks and crevices inevitably become a part of every car over a period of time. Rubber seals around doors and windows become brittle and crack or form gaps to let hot air in and conditioned air out; rust spots in the car's body eventually rust into holes; gaskets, grommets, and the like become worn. Besides allowing hot air to enter and conditioned air out, moisture, insects, dust and dirt are also allowed to enter the car. Therefore, the sealing of these cracks and crevices should be one of the first projects undertaken in preparing the car for a more efficient cooling system.

Olive oil rubbed on rubber seals around door and windows will make them pliable and in most cases cause them to seal properly. If this doesn't solve the problem, they should be replaced.

Kits are available from your local automotive supply house for replacing worn window channels and door gaskets. When properly installed, they will prevent leaks, drafts, and loss of conditioned air caused by worn original gaskets. Most are made from soft, molded, sponge rubber tailored to fit each make and model of the car perfectly. The kit will contain gaskets to fit the top and outer edge of one door, special weatherproof cement, and complete instructions.

You may want to consider inner and outer belt weather-stripping also. Flexible rubber and felt strips or formed rubber strips are available that fit between window glass and sill moulding or door. Besides serving as a weather seal, they also prevent rattles and cushion glass.

Remember that conditioned air also escapes through your trunk compartment, so don't overlook this when inspecting seals and gaskets. Specially molded sponge rubber trunk weatherstripping kits are available to fit practically any car. A proper installation will result in helping to keep conditioned air in and hot air out as well as sealing against rain, moisture and dust, keeping the trunk dry and clean. The installation will also prevent vibration of the trunk lid.

Tubes of caulking compound specially suited for automotive use are available from automotive accessory shops. Use the tubes in a regular caulking gun and you can quickly and easily stop all leaks anywhere on your car. It remains permanently elastic and is harmless to paint and rubber. Use this compound to caulk body cracks and around windshields.

To repair larger holes, cracks and rust spots, obtain one of the fiberglass repair kits—most are under $5. Such a kit will easily plug any hole or crack as the fiberglass will adhere to metal, wood, glass, ceramic, and other surfaces. It can be finished professionally to match the finish to which it is applied; most kits contain all items needed for a complete job, including: fiberglass body filler, hardener, sheet of fiberglass screen, sheets of sandpaper, spreader, and instructions.

INSULATION

Insulation is certainly not new. Natural substances were used by primitive man for centuries to keep heat in or out of his living quarters. The rough thatched huts of northern Europe and the British Isles had thick straw-covered roofs while huts in Africa and the South Seas were covered with hollow sea grass and reeds for natural insulation.

Due to their construction, it is extremely difficult to insulate automobiles adequately. However, there are some areas in which insulation should be provided. The roof (between the outer metal roof and the interior cloth or fiber finish) should have fiberglass insulation installed with aluminum backing facing the interior of the car. Insulation can also be provided under the floor carpet for some protection. In sedans, heavy insulation should be provided between the rear seat and the trunk compartment as well as between the passenger and engine compartment. Rigid sheets of insulation are available where rigidity is necessary.

HUMIDITY CONTROL

Now that your car is insulated and sealed up tight, your cooling system should operate at its greatest efficiency. However, you may have some problems with moisture control—especially on rainy days. The operating characteristics of the air-conditioning system will take care of most humidity problems while it is operating. But what about in winter months? All the cracks and leaks that allowed conditioned air to escape also carried away much of the excess moisture; with these cracks filled, the moisture has no place to go during the cold months when your heater is operating.

There are, however, several solutions to the problem of excessive moisture, the best being not to allow the moisture into your car in the first place. This is controlled by the use of vapor barriers which limit the moisture flow through body materials and prevent condensation on inner partitions. A 12-volt fan can be mounted on the car's dash so that air circulates across the windshield; this will keep your vision clear. You could even wire an automatic humidistat control to the fan to sense the moisture in the car's interior and automatically turn the fan on when it is needed.

MINIMIZING SOLAR LOADS

Minimizing solar loads in summer will reduce your car's cooling requirements tremendously. Large areas of glass let a lot of the sun's heat into your car. One quick solution to this problem is to install a reflective sun-control film over windows and other large areas of glass. With the kits available, you can do the job yourself in only minutes for about $0.80 per square foot of glass area. Such a shield also reduces heat loss through the glass during winter months.

Vans are constructed and used in a way that makes the use of awnings practical while the van is stopped. Several types are available for side and rear windows that quickly and easily unfold while camping and fold up compactly while traveling. One type that is designed to cover one whole side of your van is available complete with a high-impact case equipped with its own spring to make the awning retractable. The slide-on, slide-off feature makes it ideal for street vans as well as campers.

Awnings come in kits that are suited for the do-it-yourselfer. To install a folding side awning on your van, simply mount the slide rail and support-arm bracket permanently on your vehicle. Slide the awning case onto the rail, pull out the spring-loaded canopy, attach the support arms and braces, and you're in business. All this can be done from the ground—no ladder needed.

If you're camping, you can, of course, keep cooler if you park under shade trees. The color paint you choose also has an effect on the efficiency of your car's cooling system. Remember that a light color reflects the heat while a darker color absorbs it.

All of the items previously mentioned will help your auto air-conditioning unit function more efficiently and more economically. That's right, more economically! When your air-conditioning system is operating in your car, you will be getting fewer miles per gallon, as some of the engine's energy is needed to power the compressor. Therefore, with a more efficient system, the compressor will not have to operate as much, and will result in gas savings to you.

Of course, the system itself should be functioning properly also. If the system is low on refrigerant, you won't be getting top performance; if the compressor belt is too loose, you'll be losing out; clogged air vents will lower the efficiency of your system, as will bugs and other debris on your radiator.

The car's engine puts off a tremendous amount of heat as the explosions occur in the piston cyclinders—enough to heat a 1200-square foot residence the year round! Some of this heat is transferred to the passenger compartment which makes your air conditioner work harder. Insulation between the engine compartment and the passenger compartment will do wonders in helping to hold this heat transfer to a minimum, but you should also do everything possible to keep the temperature of your engine down; this means a properly-operating cooling system. Make sure it is operating as it should by following the procedures earlier in this book.

The additional hints to follow are most suited to RV air conditioners, but obviously, some will also apply to conventional automotive air-conditioning systems.

CLEANING

The cleaning of heating and cooling equipment should be done at regular intervals in order to maintain operating efficiency, lengthen the life of the equipment, and decrease energy consumption and operating cost.

Lint and dust should be removed from the air-conditioning evaporator and condenser air coils. Scrub the evaporator and condenser with a liquid solvent or detergent and then flush as applicable.

Air filters collect dust and although the frequency of cleaning will be determined by the air contamination, a periodic inspection should tell you how often this is necessary. Permanent metal-mesh filters should be washed and treated when needed, while throwaway filters should be replaced with the same size and type. Obtain them from your local hardware store or accessory supply house.

Vacuum or wipe off lint and dust from all supply and return air grilles, using a detergent solution if necessary. While you're doing this, also remove any dirt on the dampers at these outlets and check the levers for proper operation.

Motors should also be vacuumed to remove dust and lint, but it would be a good idea to disconnect the power supply before they are cleaned. Once free from dust and lint, wipe the exterior motor surfaces clean with a rag and reconnect the power.

Propeller fans and blower wheels are especially susceptible to dust deposits and should be cleaned often. Again, make certain that the power is turned off—to prevent losing a finger—and remove the dirt deposits with a liquid solvent.

Every periodic inspection of your RV cooling system should include a check on the condensate drain. Wash the drain pan with a mild detergent and flush out the drain line. All loose particles of dirt should be brushed from the evaporator coil and a fine comb should be used to open all clogged air passages in the coil. If the coil is extremely dirty, a small pressurized sprayer may be used with a strong dishwashing detergent to flush the coil. Always rinse with clean water after the use of detergent.

LUBRICATION

Adequately and properly administered lubrication insures efficient operation, long equipment life, and minimum maintenance cost, but never over-lubricate: Observe the manufacturer's instructions when lubricating all bearings, rotary seals, and movable linkages of:

1. Motors—Direct or belt-drive type
2. Shafts—Fans, blower wheel and damper
3. Pumps—Water circulation
4. Motor Controller—Sequential and damper operators

PERIODIC INSPECTION

The following checklist should be followed during periodic inspections of your cooling system in order to minimize maintenance expense and save as much fuel as possible.

1. DRIVE BELTS
   Examine for:
   Proper tension and alignment
   Sidewall wear

Deterioration cracks
Greasy surfaces
Safety guards in position and secure
2. "V" PULLEYS
Examine for:
Alignment
Wear of "V" wall
Tightness of pulley and set screws to shaft
3. FAN BLADE AND BLOWER WHEEL ASSEMBLIES
Examine for:
Metal fatigue cracks
Tightness of hubs and set screws to shaft
Balance
Safety guards in position and secure
4. ELECTRICAL COMPONENTS
Examine, clean, or replace electrical contacts of:
Magnetic contactors and relays
Thermal relays
Control switches, thermostats, timers, etc.
Examine wire and terminals for:
Corrosion and looseness at switches, relays, thermostats, controllers, fuse clips, capacitors, etc.
Examine motor capacitors for:
Case swelling
Electrolyte leakage

When checking over the electrical system, also examine all components for evidence of overheating and insulation deterioration.

Chapter 16
The RV Refrigerator

In automotive air-conditioning systems, refrigeration is used to cool the passenger compartment of the vehicle; a refrigerant is circulated within the system that extracts heat from the passenger compartment and then releases that heat to the outside air. This is accomplished by the familiar processes of evaporation and condensation; when the refrigerant evaporates it absorbs large quantities of heat and when the vapor turns back into a liquid it releases that heat to the outside air surrounding the vehicle.

The RV refrigerator—that little box that fits compactly in your van, camper, or travel trailer to keep foodstuffs from perishing quickly—works on the same basic principles as your automotive air-conditioning system.

Most refrigerators installed in RVs use the absorption system of refrigeration, which differs from that commonly used in home refrigerators in that it uses heat—rather than a compressor—to circulate the refrigerant. With this system, the lack of moving parts keeps repairs to a bare minimum, and since there is no compressor motor, the refrigerator does not have to depend on outside electric current for operation; it will operate on the RV's self-contained mode.

The absorption system permits the refrigerator to be operated on either LP gas or the RV's 12-volt electric system; this is especially convenient in states that do not allow LP gas operation on the road. The major drawback of these refrigerators is their dependence on gravity to circulate the refrigerant when it is a liquid. For this reason, the units must be level for proper operation.

The refrigeration cycle begins when heat, supplied by a gas burner or an electrical heating element, is applied to the refrigerant. This causes the ammonia solution (refrigerant normally used in absorption systems) to drip into an inner tube where it vaporizes;

the vapor bubbles through a strong solution and continues upward to the water separator. Here, circulating air around a tube causes any water in the ammonia to condense and return to the boiler while the ammonia vapor continues to the condenser.

Condensers in modern-day refrigeration systems are of the fin-and-tube type. The fins, which are placed around the refrigerant tubing, accelerate cooling and cause the ammonia vapor to liquefy.

The liquid ammonia travels on to the evaporator where it encounters hydrogen—a gas which lowers the surface pressure of the ammonia so that it evaporates at a lower temperature than elsewhere in the system. During this process, heat is extracted from the interior of the refrigerator and is carried off by the ammonia as it continues its cycle to the absorber.

While in the absorber, the mixture of hydrogen and ammonia gases is exposed to a dilute ammonia solution which separates the two gases. The ammonia goes into the solution and releases heat that is carried off by the circulating air while the freed hydrogen returns to the evaporator where it will again mix with recycled ammonia.

When the heat is released to the outside air, concentrated ammonia collects in the absorber vessel; when it reaches a certain level it flows into an exit tube and returns to the boiler for another cycle.

During the refrigeration cycle, note that the ammonia refrigerant travels in three different forms: (1) in solutions of varying strengths, (2) as a vapor, and (3) as a liquid. Figure 16-1 depicts this refrigeration cycle by tracing the refrigerant through the components just mentioned.

Just like conventional automotive air-conditioning systems, RV refrigerators have various controls to allow a range of operation as well as safety equipment to protect the system's components and to prevent accidents from the use of LP gas. Normally, those devices falling under the term "control" consist of ignition devices, thermostats, and cancel-out switches, while the safeguards will include thermocouplers, cutoff valves, and vents.

Ignition devices on RV refrigerators operate much the same as a cigarette lighter; that is, a flint or piezo electric device produces a spark. The thermostats, of course, regulate the amount of cooling by means of sensor tubes normally located in the freezer compartment. On gas/electric models, two sensor tubes are usually provided—one to operate the gas, the other to operate the electricity. A device should also be provided to eliminate the possibility of operating the refrigerator on gas and electricity at the same time.

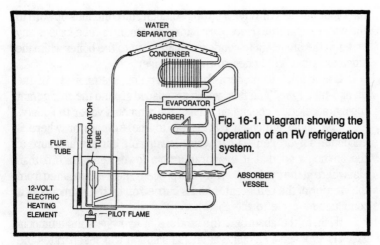

Fig. 16-1. Diagram showing the operation of an RV refrigeration system.

When one mode is in operation, the safety device automatically cancels out the other mode.

A thermocouple shuts off the gas supply if the pilot light should become extinguished. This device is positioned over the gas burner and, when warmed, the thermocouple opens a valve for the gas to flow. Should the pilot light go out, the thermocouple automatically shuts off the gas supply after it cools; this usually takes about 1 minute.

From the previous paragraph, the question may arise as to how the thermocouple allows gas to enter the pilot before it becomes warm. A push-button is usually provided to allow gas to feed the pilot until the thermocouple becomes warm; this allows the gas to bypass the thermocouple-control valve for the required amount of time.

Ventilation is also required to carry the products of combustion to the outside—away from the living space of the RV. One method is to provide a louvered access door which allows free air to circulate for the absorber, and a roof vent—positioned directly over the heat-generating portion of the refrigeration—to carry off the warm air.

MAINTENANCE AND TROUBLESHOOTING

The problems most commonly found in absorption refrigerators are due either to neglect, wear, or mechanical breakdown. Some of these will be discussed in the paragraphs that follow.

Obstructions

Insects and animals are attracted to burner ports, and can cause problems. For this reason, the burner port should be cleaned frequently. To do so, the burner tube should be disassembled and the parts soaked in an alcohol solvent. Then dry by blowing air through the tube with a hair dryer or similar device.

During the cleaning process, if the thermocouple or ignition device is disturbed, be certain that they are properly aligned over the burner port when you reconnect the tube. As mentioned previously, the thermocouple must be in the flame to function properly, and the igniter must be positioned over one of the burner holes.

The color of the gas flame is often a good indication of obstructions in the vent. A clean flame is blue; yellow occurs when the mixture of air and gas is impaired. Check the side louvers to make sure that they are not blocked and search the roof vent for bird nests, spider webs, and leaves. If these are clean and the flame is still yellow, the boiler flue may be the troublemaker.

The flue assembly should be cleaned at least once a year with an alcohol-based solution applied with the cleaning brush normally supplied with the refrigerator. If yours has become lost, new ones may be purchased from RV accessory dealers or you may use a 12-gauge shotgun cleaning brush—available at your local hardware or sporting goods store.

If you have any difficulty getting to the flue, contact the manufacturer for exact instructions. You may then want to take the refrigerator to a professional repair shop for the job.

GENERAL MAINTENANCE

The refrigerator door seals may become unseated with age—lowering the efficiency of the cooling. Check the seals periodically by opening the refrigerator door, inserting a piece of paper, and then closing the door on the paper. If you can pull the piece of paper out without tearing it, your seals need attention. You may be able to help the situation by coating the seal surfaces with olive oil; this will make them pliable and perhaps rejuvenate them. If this doesn't work, you'll have to buy replacements from the refrigerator manufacturer.

Have the gas regulator checked at least once a year as inadequate gas pressure can disturb the mixture of air and gas needed for clean burning. Any RV dealer or propane supplier will be able to perform the check for you.

Also check the thermostat annually; light the pilot and have someone watch the pilot flame while you warm the end of the thermostat feeler tube with your fingers. During this process, if the flame does not increase in size, the thermostat has lost its charge and must be replaced. Remember, there are usually two thermostats—one for the gas and one for the electric—so make certain you have the right one.

Table 16-1. Sulphur Dioxide Saturated Vapor (Temperature Table).

TEM.	PRESSURE		VOLUME		DENSITY		HEAT CONTENT ABOVE —40°			ENTROPY FROM —40°		
°F.	Abs. lb./in.²	Gage lb./in.²	Liquid ft.³/lb.	Vapor ft.³/lb.	Liquid lb./ft.³	Vapor lb./ft.³	Liquid Btu./lb.	Latent Btu./lb.	Vapor Btu./lb.	Liquid Btu./lb.°F.	Evap. Btu./lb.°F.	Vapor Btu./lb.°F.
—40	3.136	23.54*	0.010440	22.42	95.79	0.04460	0.00	178.61	178.61	0.00000	0.42562	0.42562
—35	3.693	22.41*	.010486	19.23	95.36	.05200	1.45	177.82	179.27	.00334	.41875	.42209
—30	4.331	21.10*	.010532	16.56	94.94	.06039	2.93	176.97	179.90	.00674	.41190	.41864
—25	5.058	19.63*	0.010580	14.31	94.52	0.06988	4.44	176.06	180.50	0.01016	0.40509	0.41525
—20	5.883	17.93*	.010627	12.42	94.10	.08119	5.98	175.09	181.07	.01366	.39826	.41192
—15	6.814	16.05*	.010674	10.81	93.68	.09250	7.56	174.06	181.62	.01719	.39146	.40865
—10	7.863	13.91*	.010721	9.44	93.27	.1025	9.16	172.98	182.13	.02075	.38469	.40544
— 5	9.038	11.52*	.010770	8.28	92.85	.1208	10.79	171.83	182.62	.02443	.37795	.40228
0	10.35	8.85*	0.010820	7.280	92.42	0.1374	12.44	170.63	183.07	0.02795	0.37122	0.39917
1	10.63	8.27*	.010830	7.099	92.33	.1408	12.79	170.38	183.17	.02869	.36987	.39856
2	10.91	7.70*	.010840	6.963	92.25	.1444	13.12	170.13	183.25	.02941	.36853	.39794
3	11.20	7.11*	.010850	6.751	92.16	.1481	13.45	169.88	183.33	.03013	.36719	.39732
4	11.50	6.50*	.010860	6.584	92.08	.1591	13.78	169.63	183.41	.03084	.36586	.39670
5	11.81	5.87*	0.010870	6.421	92.00	0.1558	14.11	169.38	183.49	0.03155	0.36454	0.39609
6	12.12	5.24*	.010880	6.266	91.91	.1596	14.45	169.12	183.57	.03228	.36319	.39547
7	12.43	4.61*	.010890	6.114	91.83	.1628	14.79	168.86	183.65	.03300	.36186	.39486
8	12.75	3.96*	.010900	5.967	91.74	.1676	15.13	168.60	183.73	.03373	.36053	.39426
9	13.08	3.29*	.010910	5.822	91.66	.1717	15.46	168.34	183.80	.03445	.35921	.39366
10	13.42	2.59*	0.010920	5.682	91.58	0.1760	15.80	168.07	183.87	0.03519	0.35787	0.39306
11	13.77	1.88*	.010930	5.548	91.49	.1803	16.14	167.80	183.94	.03592	.35654	.39246
12	14.12	1.17*	.010940	5.417	91.41	.1846	16.48	167.53	184.01	.03664	.35521	.39185
13	14.48	0.44*	.010950	5.289	91.33	.1890	16.81	167.26	184.07	.03737	.35388	.39125
14	14.84	.14	.010960	5.164	91.24	.1936	17.15	166.97	184.14	.03808	.35257	.39065
15	15.21	.51	0.010971	5.042	91.16	0.1983	17.49	166.72	184.21	0.03880	0.35125	0.39005
16	15.59	.89	.010981	4.926	91.07	.2030	17.84	166.44	184.28	.03953	.34993	.38946
17	15.98	1.28	.010992	4.812	90.98	.2078	18.18	166.16	184.34	.04026	.34861	.38887
18	16.37	1.67	.011003	4.701	90.89	.2127	18.52	165.88	184.40	.04098	.34729	.38827
19	16.77	2.07	.011014	4.593	90.80	.2177	18.86	165.60	184.46	.04169	.34598	.38767

20	17.18	2.48	0.011025	4.487	90.71	0.2228	19.20	165.32	184.52	0.04241	0.34466	0.38707
21	17.60	2.90	.011036	4.386	90.62	.2280	19.55	165.03	184.58	.04313	.34335	.38648
22	18.03	3.33	.011047	4.287	90.53	.2332	19.90	164.74	184.64	.04385	.34204	.38589
23	18.46	3.76	.011058	4.190	90.44	.2387	20.24	164.45	184.69	.04457	.34073	.38530
24	18.89	4.19	.011070	4.096	90.33	.2441	20.58	164.16	184.74	.04528	.33943	.38471
25	19.34	4.64	0.011082	3.994	90.24	0.2404	20.92	163.87	184.79	0.04600	0.33812	0.38412
26	19.80	5.10	.011093	3.915	90.15	.2559	21.26	163.58	184.84	.04671	.33683	.38354
27	20.26	5.56	.011104	3.829	90.06	.2611	21.61	163.28	184.89	.04743	.33553	.38296
28	20.73	6.03	.011116	3.744	89.96	.2671	21.96	162.98	184.94	.04814	.33422	.38237
29	21.21	6.51	.011128	3.662	89.86	.2731	22.30	162.68	184.98	.04886	.33292	.38178
30	21.70	7.00	0.011140	3.581	89.76	0.2800	22.64	162.38	185.02	0.04956	0.33163	0.38119
31	22.20	7.50	.011152	3.503	89.67	.2854	22.98	162.08	185.06	.05027	.33034	.38061
32	22.71	8.01	.011164	3.437	89.58	.2909	23.33	161.77	185.10	.05099	.32904	.38003
33	23.23	8.53	.011176	3.355	89.48	.2980	23.68	161.46	185.14	.05171	.32774	.37945
34	23.75	9.05	.011188	3.283	89.39	.3046	24.03	161.15	185.18	.05242	.32645	.37887
35	24.28	9.58	0.011200	3.212	89.29	0.3113	24.38	160.84	185.22	0.05312	0.32517	0.37829
36	24.82	10.12	.011212	3.144	89.18	.3181	24.72	160.53	185.25	.05384	.32388	.37772
37	25.39	10.69	.011224	3.078	89.09	.3249	25.07	160.21	185.28	.05456	.32259	.37715
38	25.95	11.25	.011236	3.013	89.00	.3319	25.42	159.89	185.31	.05527	.32130	.37657
39	26.52	11.82	.011248	2.949	88.90	.3391	25.77	159.57	185.34	.05598	.32001	.37599
40	27.10	12.40	0.011260	2.887	88.81	0.3464	26.12	159.25	185.37	0.05668	0.31873	0.37541
41	27.69	12.99	.011272	2.827	88.71	.3538	26.47	158.93	185.40	.05738	.31745	.37483
42	28.29	13.59	.011284	2.769	88.62	.3611	26.81	158.61	185.42	.05809	.31616	.37425
43	28.90	14.20	.011296	2.712	88.52	.3687	27.16	158.28	185.44	.05879	.31489	.37368
44	29.52	14.82	.011308	2.656	88.43	.3765	27.51	157.95	185.46	.05949	.31362	.37311
45	30.15	15.45	0.011320	2.601	88.34	0.3844	27.86	157.62	185.48	0.06020	0.31234	0.37254
46	30.79	16.09	.011332	2.548	88.24	.3925	28.21	157.29	185.50	.06090	.31107	.37197
47	31.44	16.74	.011344	2.497	88.15	.4005	28.56	156.96	185.52	.06161	.30979	.37140
48	32.10	17.40	.011356	2.446	88.05	.4088	28.92	156.62	185.54	.06231	.30852	.37083
49	32.77	18.07	.011368	2.397	87.96	.4172	29.27	156.28	185.55	.06301	.30725	.37026
50	33.45	18.75	0.011380	2.348	87.87	0.4259	29.61	155.95	185.56	0.06370	0.30599	0.36969
51	34.15	19.45	.011392	2.302	87.78	.4345	29.96	155.61	185.57	.06439	.30474	.36913
52	34.86	20.16	.011404	2.256	87.67	.4433	30.31	155.27	185.58	.06509	.30348	.36857
53	35.58	20.88	.011416	2.211	87.60	.4523	30.66	154.93	185.59	.06578	.30222	.36800
54	36.31	21.61	.011428	2.167	87.51	.4615	31.00	154.59	185.59	.06646	.30097	.36743

* Inches of Mercury

(Continued on page 234.)

(Continued from page 233.) Table 16-1. Sulphur Dioxide Saturated Vapor (Temperature Table).

TEM.	PRESSURE		VOLUME		DENSITY		HEAT CONTENT ABOVE −40°			ENTROPY FROM −40°		
°F.	Abs. lb./in.²	Gage lb./in.²	Liquid ft.³/lb.	Vapor ft.³/lb.	Liquid lb./ft.³	Vapor lb./ft.³	Liquid Btu./lb.	Latent Btu./lb.	Vapor Btu./lb.	Liquid Btu./lb.°F.	Evap. Btu./lb.°F.	Vapor Btu./lb.°F.
55	37.05	22.35	0.011440	2.124	87.41	0.4708	31.36	154.24	185.60	0.06715	0.29971	0.36686
56	37.80	23.10	.011452	2.083	87.31	.4801	31.72	153.89	185.61	.06785	.29844	.36629
57	38.56	23.86	.011464	2.043	87.22	.4894	32.08	153.54	185.62	.06854	.29719	.36573
58	39.33	24.63	.011476	2.003	87.13	.4992	32.42	153.19	185.61	.06923	.29549	.36517
59	40.12	25.42	.011488	1.964	87.04	.5092	32.76	152.84	185.60	.06992	.29469	.36461
60	40.93	26.23	.011500	1.926	86.95	.5194	33.10	152.49	185.59	.07060	.29345	.36405
61	41.75	27.05	.011512	1.889	86.86	.5294	33.44	152.14	185.58	.07128	.29221	.36349
62	42.58	27.88	.011524	1.853	86.77	.5396	33.79	151.78	185.57	.07196	.29097	.36293
63	43.42	28.72	.011536	1.816	86.68	.5507	34.14	151.42	185.56	.07265	.28972	.36237
64	44.27	29.57	.011548	1.783	86.59	.5609	34.49	151.06	185.55	.07333	.28848	.36181
65	45.13	30.43	0.011560	1.749	86.50	0.5717	34.84	150.70	185.54	0.07401	0.28724	0.36125
66	46.00	31.30	.011572	1.716	86.41	.5827	35.19	150.34	185.53	.07469	.28601	.36070
67	46.88	32.18	.011585	1.683	86.32	.5943	35.54	149.98	185.52	.07535	.28479	.36014
68	47.78	33.08	.011598	1.652	86.22	.6054	35.88	149.62	185.50	.07602	.28356	.35958
69	48.69	33.99	.011611	1.621	86.12	.6170	36.23	149.25	185.48	.07769	.28233	.35902
70	49.62	34.92	0.011626	1.590	86.02	0.6290	36.58	148.88	185.46	0.07736	0.28110	0.35846
71	50.57	35.87	.011639	1.557	85.92	.6423	36.93	148.51	185.44	.07804	.27987	.35791
72	51.54	36.84	.011652	1.532	85.82	.6527	37.28	148.14	185.42	.07871	.27865	.35736
73	52.51	37.81	.011666	1.503	85.72	.6657	37.63	147.77	185.40	.07937	.27743	.35680
74	53.48	38.78	.011680	1.476	85.62	.6777	37.97	147.40	185.37	.08003	.27621	.35624
75	54.47	39.77	0.011693	1.448	85.52	0.6907	38.32	147.02	185.34	0.08070	0.27498	0.35568
76	55.48	40.78	.011706	1.422	85.42	.7030	38.67	146.64	185.31	.08135	.27377	.35512
77	56.51	41.81	.011719	1.396	85.33	.7163	39.01	146.26	185.27	.08201	.27255	.35456
78	57.56	42.86	.011732	1.371	85.23	.7295	39.36	145.88	185.24	.08268	.27133	.35401
79	58.62	43.92	.011746	1.343	85.13	.7446	39.71	145.50	185.21	.08336	.27012	.35346
80	59.68	44.98	0.011760	1.321	85.03	0.7570	40.05	145.12	185.17	0.08399	0.26897	0.35291
81	60.77	46.07	.011773	1.297	84.93	.7720	40.39	144.74	185.13	.08462	.26772	.35234
82	61.88	47.18	.011786	1.274	84.84	.7850	40.75	144.36	185.09	.08525	.26652	.35177
83	63.01	48.31	.011800	1.253	84.74	.7980	41.08	143.97	185.05	.08589	.26532	.35121
84	64.14	49.44	.011814	1.229	84.64	.8140	41.43	143.58	185.01	.08653	.26412	.35065

(Temperature Table — continued)

Temp. °F.	Pressure lb./in.		Volume ft.³/lb.		Density lb./ft.³		Heat Content Btu./lb.			Entropy Btu./lb.°F.		
	Abs.	Gauge	Liquid	Vapor	Liquid	Vapor	Liquid	Latent	Vapor	Liquid	Latent	Vapor
85	65.28	50.58	0.011828	1.207	84.54	0.8285	41.78	143.19	184.97	0.08718	0.26291	0.35009
86	66.45	51.75	.011841	1.185	84.44	.8440	42.12	142.80	184.92	.08783	.26171	.34954
87	67.64	52.94	.011854	1.164	84.35	.8590	42.46	142.41	184.87	.08847	.26052	.34899
88	68.84	54.14	.011868	1.144	84.25	.8740	42.80	142.02	184.82	.08910	.25933	.34843
89	70.04	55.34	.011882	1.124	84.15	.8897	43.15	141.62	184.77	.08974	.25813	.34787
90	71.25	56.55	0.011896	1.104	84.05	0.9058	43.50	141.22	184.72	0.09038	0.25693	0.34731
91	72.46	57.76	.011909	1.084	83.96	.9225	43.85	140.82	184.67	.09102	.25574	.34676
92	73.70	59.00	.011923	1.065	83.86	.9390	44.19	140.42	184.61	.09165	.25455	.34620
93	74.98	60.18	.011937	1.047	83.77	.9551	44.53	140.02	184.55	.09227	.25337	.34564
94	76.30	61.60	.011951	1.028	83.67	.9730	44.86	139.62	184.49	.09289	.25219	.34508
95	77.60	62.90	0.011965	1.011	83.57	0.9890	45.20	139.23	184.43	0.09349	0.25103	0.34452
96	79.03	64.33	.011979	.9931	83.47	1.007	45.54	138.83	184.37	.09411	.24986	.34397
97	80.40	65.70	.011993	.9759	83.37	1.025	45.88	138.43	184.31	.09472	.24869	.34341
98	81.77	67.07	.012008	.9591	83.27	1.043	46.22	138.03	184.25	.09532	.24753	.34285
99	83.14	68.34	.012022	.9425	83.17	1.061	46.56	137.62	184.18	.09594	.24635	.34229
100	84.52	69.82	0.012038	0.9262	83.07	1.080	46.90	137.20	184.10	0.09657	0.24516	0.34173
105	91.85	77.15	.012110	.8498	82.57	1.176	48.58	135.14	183.72	.09958	.23934	.33892
110	99.76	85.06	.012190	.7804	82.03	1.281	50.26	133.05	183.31	.10254	.23357	.33611
115	108.02	93.32	.012275	.7174	81.46	1.394	51.93	130.92	182.85	.10546	.22783	.33329
120	116.54	101.80	.012360	.6598	80.90	1.515	53.58	128.78	182.36	.10829	.22217	.33046
125	126.43	111.73	0.012445	0.6079	80.35	1.645	55.31	126.51	181.82	0.11120	0.21639	0.32759
130	136.48	121.78	.012530	.5595	79.81	1.787	56.85	124.39	181.24	.11376	.21096	.32472
135	147.21	132.51	.012620	.5158	79.23	1.939	58.47	122.15	180.62	.11640	.20542	.32182
140	157.71	143.01	.012720	.4758	78.61	2.102	60.04	119.90	179.94	.11893	.19990	.31888

Table 16-2. Saturated Sulphur Dioxide (Pressure Table).

Press. Abs. lb./in.	Temp. °F.	Volume Vapor ft.³/lb.	Heat Content		Entropy	
			Liquid Btu./lb.	Vapor Btu./lb.	Liquid Btu./lb.°F.	Vapor Btu./lb.°F.
5	−25.40	14.47	4.32	180.45	0.00988	0.41552
10	−1.34	7.520	12.00	182.95	.02698	.40000
15	14.43	5.110	17.30	184.17	.03839	.39091
20	26.44	3.878	21.41	184.86	.04702	.38329
25	36.33	3.123	24.83	185.26	.05407	.37754
30	44.76	2.614	27.78	185.48	.06003	.37269
35	52.20	2.247	30.38	185.58	.06522	.36848
40	58.83	1.970	32.73	185.60	.06982	.36470
45	64.85	1.754	34.79	185.54	0.07390	0.36133
50	70.40	1.577	36.72	185.45	.07763	.35826
55	75.53	1.434	38.51	185.32	.08105	.35539
60	80.29	1.314	40.15	185.16	.08418	.35373
65	84.76	1.211	41.69	184.98	.08705	.35023
70	88.97	1.125	43.14	184.77	0.08975	0.34789
75	93.00	1.047	44.50	184.55	.09228	.34568
80	96.88	.9809	45.78	184.33	.09464	.34557

Table 16-3. Sulphur Dioxide Superheated Vapor (Temperature Table).

TEMP. °F.	Abs. Pressure 4 lb./in.² Gage Pressure 21.7 in. vac. (Sat'n Temp. — 32.60° F.)			Abs. Pressure 6 lb./in.² Gage Pressure 17.7 in. vac. (Sat'n Temp. — 19.37°F.)			Abs. Pressure 8 lb./in.² Gage Pressure 13.6 in. vac. (Sat'n Temp. — 8.99°F.)			Abs. Pressure 10 lb./in.² Gage Pressure 9.6 in. vac. (Sat'n Temp. — 1.34° F.)		
	Volume ft.³/lb.	Heat Content Btu./lb.	Entropy Btu./lb.°F.	Volume ft.³/lb.	Heat Content Btu./lb.	Entropy Btu./lb.°F.	Volume ft.³/lb.	Heat Content Btu./lb.	Entropy Btu./lb.°F.	Volume ft.³/lb.	Heat Content Btu./lb.	Entropy Btu./lb.°F.
(at sat'n)	(17.30)	(179.57)	(0.42043)	(12.22)	(181.14)	(0.41151)	(9.220)	(182.23)	(0.40482)	(7.520)	(182.95)	(0.40000)
−20	18.40	181.5	0.42487									
−10	18.83	183.0	.42836									
0	19.27	184.6	.43179	12.75	184.3	.41850	9.516	183.7	.40871	7.545	183.2	0.40046
10	19.70	186.1	.43516	13.04	185.9	.42198	9.751	185.4	.41230	7.744	185.0	.40432
20	20.14	187.7	.43847	13.34	187.5	.42538	9.983	187.1	.41579	7.939	186.7	.40802
30	20.57	189.3	.44161	13.63	189.1	.42869	10.21	188.8	.41922	8.030	188.4	.41159
40	21.00	190.9	.44491	13.93	190.7	.43196	10.44	190.5	.42256	8.316	190.1	.41505
50	21.42	192.5	.44806	14.23	192.3	.43517	10.66	192.2	.42582	8.500	191.8	.41837
60	21.85	194.1	.45116	14.52	193.9	.43833	10.88	193.8	.42903	8.681	193.5	.42161
70	22.27	195.7	.45421	14.71	195.6	.44140	11.10	195.5	.43216	8.860	195.2	.42480
80	22.70	197.3	.45722	15.11	197.2	.44443	11.32	197.1	.43524	9.038	196.9	.42795
90	23.12	198.9	.46018	15.40	198.8	.44741	11.54	198.8	.43825	9.214	198.6	.43104
100	23.54	200.5	.46311	15.69	200.5	.45035	11.75	200.4	.44123	9.389	200.3	.43407
110	23.96	202.1	.46600	15.97	202.2	.45326	11.97	202.1	.44416	9.563	202.0	.43705
120	24.39	203.8	.46885	16.26	203.8	.45613	12.18	203.7	.44705	9.736	203.7	.43997
130	24.81	205.2	.47167	16.54	205.3	.45890	12.39	205.4	.44990	9.908	205.4	.44283
140	25.23	207.1	.47445	16.82	207.1	.46176	12.61	207.0	.45271	10.08	207.1	.44565
150	25.65	208.8	.47720	17.09	208.8	.46451	12.82	208.8	.45543	10.25	208.8	.44842
160	26.08	210.4	.47991	17.35	210.4	.46722	13.03	210.3	.45820	10.42	210.5	.45116
170	26.50	212.1	.48259	17.62	212.1	.46990	13.24	212.0	.46089	10.59	212.2	.45296
180	26.92	213.8	.48523	17.88	213.7	.47254	13.46	213.6	.46353	10.76	213.8	.45651
190				18.13	215.4	.47514	13.66	215.3	.46614	10.93	215.4	.45913
200				18.38	217.0	.47769	13.88	216.9	.46871	11.10	217.0	.46171

TEMP. °F.	Abs. Pressure 15 lb./in.² Gage Pressure 0.30 lb./in.² (Sat'n. Temp. 14.43° F.)			Abs. Pressure 20 lb./in.² Gage Pressure 5.30 lb./in.² (Sat'n. Temp. 26.44° F.)			Abs. Pressure 25 lb./in.² Gage Pressure 10.30 lb./in.² (Sat'n. Temp. 36.33° F.)			Abs. Pressure 30 lb./in.² Gage Pressure 15.30 lb./in.² (Sat'n. Temp. 44.76° F.)		
(at sat'n)	(5.110)	(184.17)	(0.39091)	(3.878)	(184.86)	(0.38329)	(3.123)	(185.26)	(0.37754)	(2.614)	(185.48)	(0.37269)
20	5.192	185.4	0.39270	...	...	...	...	...	...	...	...	...
30	5.333	187.3	.39672	...	...	...	...	...	...	...	...	...
40	5.470	189.2	.40054	4.035	187.8	0.38959	3.181	186.1	0.37927	...	...	...
50	5.604	191.0	.40424	4.145	189.8	.39346	3.273	188.4	.38372	...	...	...
60	5.734	192.8	.40777	4.251	191.8	.39719	3.363	190.6	.38795	2.747	189.3	0.37969
70	5.862	195.6	0.41116	4.354	193.7	0.40080	3.451	192.7	0.39198	2.830	191.6	0.38428
80	5.988	196.4	.41443	4.454	195.6	.40429	3.536	194.7	.39582	2.907	193.8	.38848
90	6.112	198.2	.41765	4.552	197.5	.40758	3.618	196.7	.39945	2.980	195.9	.39236
100	6.233	199.9	.42076	4.648	199.3	.41093	3.696	198.6	.40291	3.052	197.9	.39603
110	6.353	201.6	.42383	4.742	201.1	.41415	3.772	200.5	.40625	3.122	199.9	.39955
120	6.471	203.3	0.42682	4.834	202.9	0.41726	3.848	202.4	0.40949	3.189	201.8	0.40293
130	6.588	205.6	.42976	4.925	204.7	.42027	3.923	204.2	.41261	3.254	203.7	.40619
140	6.705	206.7	.43264	5.015	206.5	.42322	3.998	206.0	.41568	3.318	205.6	.40935
150	6.821	208.4	.43548	5.104	208.2	.42613	4.073	207.8	.41866	3.381	207.5	.41241
160	6.937	210.1	.43825	5.193	209.9	.42898	4.145	209.6	.42156	3.443	209.3	.41539
170	7.052	211.8	0.44097	5.281	211.6	0.43176	4.216	211.4	0.42439	3.504	211.1	0.41829
180	7.167	213.5	.44366	5.369	213.3	.43449	4.287	213.2	.42717	3.565	212.9	.42112
190	7.282	215.2	.44630	5.456	215.0	.43716	4.358	215.0	.42988	3.625	214.7	.42387
200	7.396	216.9	.44889	5.542	216.7	.43977	4.428	216.7	.43253	3.685	216.5	.42657
210	...	...	...	5.629	218.4	.44234	4.498	218.4	.43413	3.744	218.3	.42921
220	...	...	...	5.715	220.1	0.44488	4.567	220.1	0.43769	3.803	220.1	0.43180
230	...	...	...	...	...	...	4.637	221.8	.44023	3.861	221.9	.43438
240	...	...	...	...	...	...	4.706	223.5	.44275	3.919	223.6	.43691
250	...	...	...	...	...	...	...	...	...	3.977	225.3	.43942
260	...	...	...	...	...	...	...	...	...	4.035	227.0	.44188

Table 16-4. Sulphur Dioxide Superheated Vapor (Temperature Table).

TEMP. °F.	Abs. Pressure 40 lb./in.² Gage Pressure 25.30 lb./in.² (Sat'n. Temp. 58.83° F.)			Abs. Pressure 50 lb./in.² Gage Pressure 35.30 lb./in.² (Sat'n. Temp. 70.40° F.)			Abs. Pressure 60 lb./in.² Gage Pressure 45.30 lb./in.² (Sat'n. Temp. 80.29° F.)			Abs. Pressure 70 lb./in.² Gage Pressure 55.30 lb./in.² (Sat'n. Temp. 88.97° F.)		
	Volume ft.³/lb.	Heat Content Btu./lb.	Entropy Btu./lb.°F.	Volume ft.³/lb.	Heat Content Btu./lb.	Entropy Btu./lb.°F.	Volume ft.³/lb.	Heat Content Btu./lb.	Entropy Btu./lb.°F.	Volume ft.³/lb.	Heat Content Btu./lb.	Entropy Btu./lb.°F.
(at sat'n)	(1.970)	(185.60)	(0.36470)	(1.577)	(185.45)	(0.35826)	(1.3142)	(185.16)	(0.35272)	(1.125)	(184.77)	(0.34789)
60	1.980	185.9	0.36544									
70	2.064	188.7	.37064									
80	2.121	191.3	.37544	1.668	188.4	.36366						
90	2.185	193.6	.37992	1.723	191.2	.36887						
100	2.246	196.1	.38415	1.775	193.9	.37369	1.288	191.4	.36403	1.181	187.6	.35443
110	2.304	198.3	.38810	1.825	196.4	.37815	1.346	194.3	.36906	1.228	191.6	.36020
120	2.360	200.4	.39183	1.872	198.8	.38234	1.403	197.0	.37375	1.272	194.8	.36545
130	2.413	202.5	.39541	1.917	201.1	.38627	1.459	199.5	.37810	1.313	197.6	.37028
140	2.465	204.6	.39881	1.961	203.3	.38998	1.514	201.9	.38217	1.352	200.3	.37478
150	2.515	206.5	.40209	2.003	205.4	.39353	1.563	204.2	.38603	1.389	202.9	.37897
160	2.565	208.5	.40525	2.044	207.5	.39691	1.608	206.5	.38963	1.424	205.3	.38291
170	2.614	210.4	.40831	2.084	209.6	.40015	1.650	208.6	.39310	1.457	207.6	.38662
180	2.662	212.3	.41127	2.123	211.6	.40327	1.689	210.7	.39639	1.489	209.9	.39014
190	2.709	214.2	.41416	2.161	213.4	.40628	1.726	212.8	.39956	1.521	212.0	.39348
200	2.755	216.0	.41694	2.199	215.4	.40919	1.751	214.8	.40260	1.551	214.1	.39670
210	2.800	217.9	.41966	2.237	217.3	.41200	1.785	216.8	.40554	1.580	216.1	.39978
220	2.845	219.7	.42233	2.274	219.2	.41477	1.819	218.7	.40839	1.608	218.1	.40275
230	2.889	221.5	.42494	2.311	221.1	.41748	1.853	220.7	.41118	1.636	220.1	.40564
240	2.933	223.3	.42751	2.347	223.0	.42015	1.885	222.6	.41391	1.664	222.1	.40845
250	2.977	225.1	.43007	2.383	224.9	.42275	1.917	224.5	.41657	1.691	224.1	.41120
260	3.021	227.0	.43262	2.418	226.7	.42535	1.948	226.4	.41917	1.718	226.0	.41389
270				2.454	228.5	.42791	1.979	228.2	.42175	1.745	227.9	.41653
280				2.489	230.3	.43045	2.010	230.1	.42431	1.771	229.8	.41912
290							2.040	232.0	.42685	1.798	231.7	.42167
300							2.070	233.8	.42935	1.824	233.5	.42418

TEMP. °F.	Abs. Pressure 80 lb./in.² Gage Pressure 65.30 lb./in.² (Sat'n. Temp. 96.88° F.)			Abs. Pressure 100 lb./in.² Gage Pressure 85.30 lb./in.² (Sat'n. Temp. 110.15° F.)			Abs. Pressure 120 lb./in.² Gage Pressure 105.30 lb./in.² (Sat'n. Temp. 121.52° F.)			Abs. Pressure 140 lb./in.² Gage Pressure 125.30 lb./in.² (Sat'n. Temp. 131.64° F.)		
(at sat'n)	(0.9809)	(184.33)	(0.34357)	(0.7786)	(183.30)	(0.33603)	(0.6430)	(182.19)	(0.33954)	(0.5451)	(181.04)	(0.32388)
100	0.993	185.6	0.34571	.....	.....	.....	.....	.....	.....	.....	.....	.....
110	1.040	189.1	35214	.....	.....	.....	.....	.....	.....	.....	.....	.....
120	1.084	192.5	35797	.8190	187.3	.34296	.....	.....	.....	.....	.....	.....
130	1.125	195.7	36330	.8575	191.0	.34942	.....	.....	.....	.....	.....	.....
140	1.163	198.6	36819	.8928	194.6	.35528	.7085	190.1	.34264	.5734	185.1	.33089
150	1.199	201.3	37270	.9255	197.9	.36061	.7403	193.9	.34904	.6055	189.7	.33777
160	1.232	203.9	37692	.9561	200.9	.36558	.7700	197.4	.35484	.6345	193.6	.34442
170	1.263	206.4	38093	.9848	203.7	.37009	.7972	200.6	.36012	.6613	196.3	.35041
180	1.292	208.7	38461	1.012	206.4	.37431	.8228	203.7	.36494	.6861	200.8	.35588
190	1.320	211.0	38813	1.038	209.0	.37829	.8470	206.7	.36936	.7092	204.0	.36088
200	1.347	213.3	39150	1.062	211.5	.38203	.8699	209.4	.37348	.7309	207.1	.36548
210	1.374	215.5	39471	1.086	213.8	.38556	.8916	212.0	.37737	.7513	210.0	.36976
220	1.400	217.5	39780	1.109	216.1	.38892	.9124	214.5	.38104	.7707	212.7	.37379
230	1.426	219.6	40079	1.131	218.4	.39214	.9324	217.0	.38451	.7892	215.4	.37758
240	1.451	221.6	40369	1.152	220.5	.39524	.9515	219.3	.38785	.8070	217.9	.38118
250	1.476	223.6	40651	1.173	222.6	.39824	.9700	221.5	.39106	.8241	220.3	.38461
260	1.500	225.6	40926	1.194	224.7	.40114	.9880	223.7	.39416	.8405	222.6	.38789
270	1.524	227.6	41195	1.213	226.8	.40397	1.006	225.9	.39713	.8564	224.9	.39105
280	1.547	229.5	41459	1.232	228.8	.40673	1.023	228.0	.40002	.8720	227.1	.39408
290	1.570	231.5	41719	1.251	230.8	.40944	1.040	230.1	.40284	.8970	229.3	.39701
300	1.593	233.4	41974	1.268	232.8	.41207	1.056	233.2	.40558	.9017	231.5	.39985
310	.....	.....	.....	1.284	234.8	.41464	1.072	234.3	.40825	.9161	233.6	.40261
320	.....	.....	.....	1.299	236.7	.41716	1.088	236.3	.41085	.9302	235.7	.40529
330	.....	.....	.....	.....	.....	.....	1.104	238.3	.41338	.9441	237.7	.40791
340	.....	.....	.....	.....	.....	.....	1.120	240.3	.41583	.9579	239.7	.41049

Table 16-5. Methyl Chloride Saturated Vapor (Temperature Table).

TEM.	PRESSURE		SPECIFIC VOLUME		DENSITY		HEAT CONTENT Above −40° F.			ENTROPY From − 40°		
°F.	lbs./sq. in. Abs.	Gage lbs./in.	Liquid ft.³/lb.	Vapor ft.³/lb.	Liquid lbs./ft.²	Vapor lbs./ft.²	Liquid Btu./lb.	Latent Btu./lb.	Vapor Btu./lb.	Liquid	Evap.	Vapor
−40	7.40	14.86*	0.01553	13.05	64.39	0.0766	.0	190.7	190.7	0	0.4540	0.4540
−38	7.80	14.03*	.01556	12.32	64.27	.0812	0.7	190.3	191.0	0.0016	.4509	.4525
−36	8.20	13.23*	.01558	11.68	64.18	.0860	1.4	189.9	191.3	.0032	.4479	.4511
−34	8.60	12.41*	.01561	11.10	64.06	.0900	2.0	189.4	191.4	.0048	.4446	.4494
−32	9.00	11.60*	.01564	10.61	63.94	.0940	2.7	189.0	191.7	.0064	.4416	.4480
−30	9.40	10.79*	.01567	10.14	63.82	.0990	3.4	188.6	192.0	.0080	.4386	.4466
−28	9.80	9.98*	.01570	9.67	63.69	.1030	4.0	188.2	192.2	.0096	.4357	.4453
−26	10.25	9.05*	.01573	9.25	63.57	.1080	4.7	187.8	192.5	.0112	.4327	.4439
−24	10.70	8.14*	.01576	8.86	63.45	.1130	5.4	187.4	192.8	.0128	.4298	.4426
−22	11.19	7.15*	.01579	8.46	63.33	.1182	6.1	186.8	192.9	.0144	.4266	.4410
−20	11.78	5.94*	.01582	8.06	63.21	.1240	6.9	186.4	193.3	.0160	.4237	.4397
−18	12.38	4.72*	.01585	7.70	63.09	.1299	7.6	186.0	193.6	.0175	.4208	.4383
−16	12.96	3.54*	.01588	7.38	62.97	.1356	8.3	185.5	193.8	.0192	.4179	.4371
−14	13.60	2.24*	.01591	7.05	62.85	.1420	9.0	185.1	194.1	.0208	.4150	.4358
−12	14.23	.96*	.01594	6.73	62.74	.1490	9.7	184.6	194.3	.0224	.4122	.4346
−10	14.90	0.20	.01597	6.46	62.62	.01550	10.4	184.2	194.6	.0240	.4093	.4333
−8	15.62	.92	.01601	6.20	62.46	.1610	11.1	183.7	194.8	.0256	.4065	.4321
−6	16.30	1.60	.01604	5.93	62.34	.1690	11.8	183.3	195.1	.0272	.4039	.4311
−4	17.07	2.37	.01607	5.67	62.23	.1764	12.62	182.9	195.5	.0288	.4011	.4299
−2	17.86	3.16	.01610	5.43	62.11	.1840	13.35	182.4	195.8	.0304	.3984	.4288

0	18.70	4.00	0.01613	5.19	61.99	0.1930	14.08	181.9	196.0	0.0320	0.3955	0.4275
+2	19.56	4.86	.01616	4.97	61.88	.2010	14.81	181.5	196.3	.0336	.3929	.4265
+4	20.43	5.73	.01620	4.76	61.73	.2100	15.54	181.0	196.6	.0352	.3902	.4254
+5	20.80	6.10	.01621	4.66	61.66	.2160	15.82	180.8	196.7	.0359	.3889	.4248
+6	21.34	6.64	.01623	4.55	61.61	.2200	16.27	180.6	196.9	.0368	.3876	.4244
+8	22.26	7.56	.01626	4.35	61.50	.2300	17.00	180.1	197.1	.0384	.3848	.4232
10	23.26	8.56	0.01630	4.18	61.35	0.2390	17.73	179.6	197.3	0.0400	0.3822	0.4222
12	24.26	9.56	.01633	4.01	61.24	.2490	18.46	179.2	197.7	.0416	.3797	.4213
14	25.37	10.67	.01637	3.86	61.09	.2591	19.22	178.7	198.0	.0432	.3771	.4203
16	26.48	11.78	.01640	3.72	60.98	.2690	19.96	178.2	198.2	.0448	.3745	.4193
18	27.62	12.92	.01644	3.58	60.83	.2800	20.70	177.8	198.5	.0464	.3720	.4184
20	28.76	14.06	0.01648	3.43	60.68	.2920	21.44	177.3	198.7	.0480	.3694	.4174
22	29.94	15.24	.01651	3.31	60.57	.3030	22.18	176.9	199.1	.0496	.3670	.4166
24	31.20	16.50	.01654	3.18	60.46	.3140	22.92	176.4	199.3	.0510	.3645	.4155
26	32.50	17.80	.01658	3.05	60.31	.3280	23.66	175.9	199.6	.0526	.3619	.4145
28	33.83	19.13	.01661	2.93	60.20	.3420	24.40	175.4	199.8	.0541	.3595	.4136
30	35.19	20.49	0.01665	2.81	60.06	0.3560	25.15	174.9	200.1	0.0556	0.3570	0.4126
32	36.57	21.87	.01669	2.69	59.92	.3716	25.90	174.5	200.4	.0570	.3546	.4116
34	37.99	23.29	.01672	2.59	59.81	.3870	26.65	174.0	200.6	.0585	.3522	.4107
36	39.47	24.79	.01676	2.50	59.67	.4010	27.40	173.5	200.9	.0600	.3498	.4098
38	41.01	26.31	.01680	2.41	59.52	.4160	28.15	173.0	201.1	.0615	.3474	.4089
40	42.61	27.91	0.01683	2.32	59.42	0.4320	28.90	172.4	201.3	0.0630	0.3449	0.4079
42	44.27	29.57	.01687	2.23	59.28	.4480	29.65	171.9	201.6	.0645	.3425	.4070
44	45.99	31.29	.01691	2.15	59.14	.4650	30.40	171.5	201.9	.0660	.3403	.4063
46	47.77	33.07	.01694	2.07	59.03	.4830	31.15	171.0	202.1	.0675	.3379	.4054
48	49.61	34.97	.01698	1.99	58.89	.5030	31.91	170.4	202.3	.0690	.3355	.4045

*Inches of mercury

(Continued on page 242.)

Table 16-5. Methyl Chloride Saturated Vapor (Temperature Table) (Continued).

(Continued from page 241.)

TEM.	PRESSURE		SPECIFIC VOLUME		DENSITY		HEAT CONTENT Above — 40° F.				ENTROPY From — 40°		
°F.	lbs./sq. in. Abs.	Gage lbs./in.²	Liquid ft.³/lb.	Vapor ft.³/lb.	Liquid lbs./ft.³	Vapor lbs./ft.³	Liquid Btu./lb.	Latent Btu./lb.	Vapor Btu./lb.	Liquid	Evap.	Vapor
50	51.52	36.82	0.01702	1.92	58.75	0.5203	32.67	169.9	202.6	0.0705	0.3332	0.4037
52	53.44	38.74	.01705	1.85	58.65	.5410	33.43	169.4	202.8	.0719	.3309	.4028
54	55.44	40.74	.01709	1.79	58.51	.5600	34.19	168.9	203.1	.0734	.3286	.4020
56	57.66	42.96	.01713	1.72	58.38	.5810	34.95	168.3	203.3	.0749	.3263	.4012
58	59.70	45.00	.01717	1.66	58.24	.6040	35.71	167.8	203.5	.0764	.3239	.4003
60	61.74	47.04	0.01721	1.59	58.11	0.6290	36.47	167.2	203.7	0.0779	0.3216	.3995
62	63.86	49.16	.01725	1.53	57.97	.6510	37.23	166.7	203.9	.0794	.3193	.3987
64	66.08	51.38	.01729	1.48	57.84	.6760	37.99	166.2	204.2	.0809	.3172	.3981
66	68.52	53.82	.01733	1.44	57.70	.6940	38.75	165.6	204.4	.0823	.3149	.3972
68	70.90	56.20	.01737	1.40	57.57	.7153	39.51	165.1	204.6	.0837	.3128	.3965
70	73.40	58.70	0.01741	1.35	57.44	0.7410	40.27	164.5	204.8	0.0852	0.3105	.03957
72	75.98	61.18	.01746	1.31	57.27	.7660	41.03	164.0	205.0	.0866	.3084	.3950
74	78.58	63.88	.01750	1.26	57.14	.7940	41.80	163.5	205.3	.0880	.3062	.3942
76	81.20	66.50	.01754	1.22	57.01	.8200	42.57	163.0	205.6	.0895	.3041	.3936
78	83.98	69.28	.01758	1.18	56.88	.8470	43.34	162.4	205.7	.0909	.3019	.3928
80	86.72	72.02	0.01763	1.14	56.72	0.8770	44.11	161.8	205.9	0.0924	0.2996	0.3920
82	89.50	74.80	.01767	1.11	56.59	.9050	44.88	161.3	206.2	.0938	.2976	.3914
84	92.50	77.88	.01772	1.07	56.43	.9350	45.65	160.7	206.3	.0952	.2954	.3906
86	95.52	80.82	.01776	1.04	56.31	.9590	46.42	160.2	206.6	.0966	.2934	.3900
88	98.73	84.03	.01780	1.013	56.18	.9870	47.19	159.6	206.8	.0980	.2912	.3892

242

90	101.99	87.29	0.01785	0.983	56.02	1.017	47.96	159.0	207.0	0.0994	0.2891	0.3885
92	105.30	90.69	.01789	.953	55.90	1.049	48.74	158.5	207.2	.1008	.2871	.3879
94	108.66	93.96	.01793	.923	55.77	1.083	49.52	157.9	207.4	.1022	.2850	.3872
96	112.07	97.37	.01798	.893	55.62	1.120	50.30	157.3	207.6	.1036	.2830	.3866
98	115.53	100.83	.01802	.868	55.49	1.152	51.08	156.8	207.9	.1050	.2810	.3860
100	119.04	104.34	0.01807	0.847	55.34	1.181	51.86	156.2	208.1	0.1064	0.2789	.03853
102	122.60	107.90	.01811	.830	55.22	1.205	52.64	155.6	208.2	.1078	.2769	.3847
104	126.22	111.52	.01816	.818	55.07	1.223	53.42	155.1	208.5	.1092	.2749	.3841
106	129.80	115.10	.01821	.798	54.91	1.253	54.11	154.4	208.5	.1106	.2728	.3834
108	133.60	118.90	.01827	.778	54.73	1.285	54.73	153.8	208.5	.1120	.2708	.3828
110	137.20	122.50	0.01832	0.758	54.59	1.319	55.35	153.2	208.5	0.1134	0.2688	0.3822
112	140.90	126.20	.01838	.738	54.41	1.355	55.96	152.6	208.6	.1148	.2668	.3816
114	144.60	129.90	.01844	.720	54.23	1.389	56.67	151.9	208.6	.1162	.2646	.3808
116	148.50	133.80	.01850	.703	54.05	1.422	57.28	151.3	208.6	.1176	.2627	.3803
118	152.20	137.50	.01856	.686	53.88	1.458	57.89	150.7	208.6	.1190	.2607	.3797
120	155.80	141.10	0.01862	0.669	53.71	1.495	58.60	150.0	208.6	0.1204	0.2586	0.3790
122	159.50	144.80	.01868	.653	53.53	1.531	59.30	149.3	208.6	.1218	.2565	.3783
124	163.50	148.80	.01874	.637	53.36	1.570	60.00	148.6	208.6	.1232	.2545	.3777
126	167.60	152.90	.01881	.621	53.16	1.610	60.70	147.9	208.6	.1246	.2524	.3770
128	171.80	157.10	.01888	.605	52.97	1.653	61.40	147.2	208.6	.1260	.2503	.3763
130	176.30	161.60	0.01894	0.590	52.80	1.695	62.20	146.4	208.6	0.1274	0.2481	0.3755
132	180.60	165.90	.01902	.575	52.58	1.739	63.10	145.5	208.6	.1288	.2458	.3746
134	185.00	170.80	.01908	.560	52.41	1.786	64.00	144.6	208.6	.1301	.2434	.3735
136	190.00	175.80	.01916	.547	52.19	1.828	64.90	143.7	208.6	.1313	.2411	.3724
138	194.70	180.00	.01923	.535	52.00	1.869	65.90	142.7	208.6	.1326	.2386	.3712
140	200.00	185.30	0.01930	0.525	51.81	1.905	66.90	141.7	208.6	.1336	.2362	.3698

Table 16-6. Properties of Superheated Methyl Chloride.

TEMP. °F.	10 lbs./sq. in. Abs. (—27.1° F.)			12 lbs./sq. in. Abs. (—19.2° F.)			14 lbs./sq. in. Abs. (—12.7° F.)			16 lbs./sq. in. Abs. (—6.8° F.)		
	Volume ft.³/lb.	Heat Content Btu./lb.	Entropy Btu./lb.°F.	Volume ft.³/lb.	Heat Content Btu./lb.	Entropy Btu./lb.°F.	Volume ft.³/lb.	Heat Content Btu./lb.	Entropy Btu./lb.°F.	Volume ft.³/lb.	Heat Content Btu./lb.	Entropy Btu./lb.°F.
SAT	9.48	192.3	0.4447	7.90	193.4	0.4392	6.84	194.3	0.4350	6.04	195.0	0.4314
—20	9.63	193.8	.4480									
—10	9.85	195.9	.4527	8.05	195.4	.4436	6.97	194.9	.4363			
0	10.07	198.0	.4573	8.23	197.6	.4484	7.13	197.1	.4411	6.12	196.3	.4342
10	10.29	200.2	.4621	8.41	199.8	.4531	7.28	199.3	.4458	6.25	198.4	.4389
20	10.51	202.3	0.4665	8.59	202.0	0.4577	7.44	201.4	0.4508	6.39	200.6	0.4434
30	10.72	204.4	.4708	8.77	204.1	.4622	7.60	203.6	.4550	6.52	202.8	.4479
40	10.94	206.6	.4753	8.95	206.3	.4666	7.75	205.8	.4594	6.65	205.0	.4523
50	11.17	208.7	.4794	9.13	208.5	.4709	7.90	208.0	.4637	6.79	207.2	.4566
60	11.38	210.8	.4835	9.21	210.7	.4751	8.16	210.2	.4680	6.92	209.3	.4611
70	11.60	212.9	0.4875	9.49	212.9	0.4793	8.22	212.3	0.4721	7.05	211.5	0.4652
80	11.82	214.1	.4914	9.67	215.0	.4834	8.37	214.5	.4762	7.19	213.7	.4693
90	12.04	216.2	.4953	9.85	217.2	.4874	8.53	216.7	.4802	7.32	215.9	.4733
100	12.25	218.3	.4991	10.03	219.4	.4913	8.68	218.9	.4841	7.45	218.1	.4772

Top section

TEMP. °F.	18 lbs./sq. in. Abs. (−1.5° F.)			20 lbs./sq. in. Abs. (2.9° F.)			22 lbs./sq. in. Abs. (7.5° F.)			24 lbs./sq. in. Abs. (11.7° F.)		
SAT	5.38	195.7	0.4284	4.86	196.4	0.4257	4.40	197.0	0.4234	4.10	197.5	0.4214
0	5.40	196.0	.4287									
10	5.52	198.2	.4334	4.93	197.9	.4290	4.43	197.5	.4246			
20	5.64	200.4	.4380	5.04	200.1	.4336	4.52	199.7	.4292	4.17	199.3	.4252
30	5.75	202.6	.4425	5.15	202.3	.4381	4.61	201.9	.4337	4.26	201.5	.4297
40	5.87	204.7	.4469	5.25	204.5	.4425	4.70	204.1	.4381	4.35	203.7	.4341
50	5.99	206.9	.4512	5.35	206.6	.4468	4.80	206.3	.4423	4.44	205.9	.4384
60	6.10	209.1	.4554	5.46	208.8	.4510	4.90	208.4	.4465	4.52	208.1	.4427
70	6.22	211.3	.4596	5.56	211.0	.4552	4.99	210.6	.4507	4.61	210.2	.4468
80	6.34	213.5	.4636	5.67	213.2	.4593	5.08	212.8	.4547	4.70	212.4	.4509
90	6.45	215.6	.4676	5.77	215.4	.4633	5.18	215.0	.4587	4.78	214.6	.4549
100	6.57	217.8	.4726	5.88	217.6	.4672	5.27	217.2	.4627	4.87	216.8	.4588
110	6.69	220.0	.4764	5.98	219.7	.4710	5.37	219.3	.4665	4.95	219.0	.4626
120	6.80	222.2	.4802	6.09	221.9	.4748	5.46	221.5	.4703	5.04	221.2	.4664

Bottom section

TEMP. °F.	27 lbs./sq. in. Abs. (16.9° F.)			30 lbs./sq. in. Abs. (22.1° F.)			35 lbs./sq. in. Abs. (29.7° F.)			40 lbs./sq. in. Abs. (36.9° F.)		
SAT	3.65	198.4	0.4189	3.30	199.0	0.4164	2.82	200.1	0.4128	2.46	201.0	0.4095
20	3.67	199.1	.4203									
30	3.75	201.2	.4248	3.36	200.7	.4200						
40	3.83	203.4	.4292	3.42	202.9	.4244	2.88	202.3	.4172	2.48	201.7	.4108
50	3.90	205.6	.4335	3.49	205.1	.4287	2.94	204.5	.4215	2.53	203.8	.4151
60	3.98	207.8	.4378	3.56	207.3	.4329	2.99	206.6	.4258	2.58	206.0	.4194
70	4.05	210.0	.4419	3.63	209.5	.4371	3.05	208.6	.4299	2.63	208.2	.4235
80	4.13	212.1	.4460	3.70	211.6	.4412	3.11	210.8	.4340	2.68	210.4	.4276
90	4.21	214.3	.4500	3.77	213.8	.4452	3.16	213.0	.4380	2.72	212.6	.4316
100	4.29	216.5	.4539	3.84	216.0	.4491	3.22	215.2	.4419	2.77	214.7	.4355
110	4.37	218.7	.4578	3.90	218.2	.4526	3.28	217.3	.4458	2.82	216.9	.4394
120	4.44	220.9	.4616	3.97	220.4	.4568	3.34	219.5	.4496	2.87	219.1	.4432

Appendix A
Reference Aids

The charts and tables presented here should be useful to those engaged in advanced automotive air-conditioning installations, repairs, and maintenance.

Table A-1. Refrigerant Pressure and Template Curves.

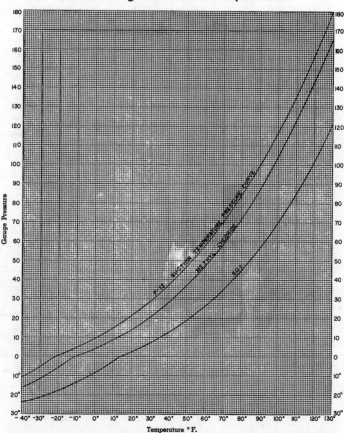

Table A-2. Refrigerant Temperature Pressure Conversion Tables.

REFRIGERANT TEMPERATURE PRESSURE CONVERSION TABLES							
CONVERSION TABLE "A" TEMPERATURE TO PRESSURE (Saturated Vapor)			CONVERSION TABLE "B" PRESSURE TO TEMPERATURE (Saturated Vapor)				
	Gauge Pressure (#/Sq. In.)				Temperature °F.		
Temperature °F.	Freon F-12	Methyl Chloride CH_3CL	Sulphur Dioxide SO_2	Gauge Pressure (#/Sq. In.)	Freon F-12	Methyl Chloride CH_3CL	Sulphur Dioxide SO_2
0	9.2	4.1	8.8*	0	—21.0	—11.0	13.8
1	9.7	4.5	8.3*	1	—18.8	— 8.1	16.3
2	10.2	4.9	7.3*	2	—16.1	— 5.3	18.9
3	10.7	5.3	7.1*	3	—13.7	— 2.8	21.3
4	11.3	5.8	6.5*	4	—11.2	— .3	23.7
5	11.8	6.2	5.9*	5	— 9.0	2.1	25.9
6	12.3	6.8	5.2*	6	— 6.7	4.4	28.0
7	12.8	7.2	4.6*	7	— 4.5	6.7	30.1
8	13.5	7.7	3.9*	8	— 2.3	8.9	32.2
9	13.9	8.1	3.3*	9	— .2	10.9	34.0
10	14.6	8.6	2.6*	10	1.8	12.9	35.9
11	15.2	9.1	1.9*	11	3.8	14.9	37.8
12	15.9	9.7	1.8*	12	5.6	16.7	39.5
13	16.4	10.1	.4*	13	7.2	18.4	41.2
14	17.1	10.6	.1	14	9.0	20.2	42.8
15	17.7	11.2	.5	15	10.8	21.9	44.5
16	18.4	11.8	.9	16	12.4	23.5	45.9
17	19.0	12.3	1.3	17	14.0	25.1	47.4
18	19.7	12.9	1.7	18	15.7	26.7	48.9
19	20.6	13.5	2.1	19	17.1	28.2	50.4
20	21.0	14.1	2.5	20	18.7	29.7	51.9
21	21.7	14.6	2.9	21	20.1	31.1	53.3
22	22.4	15.1	3.3	22	21.5	32.4	54.7
23	23.0	15.8	3.8	23	23.0	33.8	55.9
24	23.9	16.5	4.2	24	24.3	35.1	57.3
25	24.5	17.1	4.6	25	25.7	36.4	58.7
26	25.4	17.8	5.1	26	27.0	37.8	59.8
27	26.0	18.4	5.6	27	28.2	39.0	61.0
28	26.9	19.1	6.0	28	29.5	40.2	62.1
29	27.7	19.8	6.5	29	30.8	41.4	63.4
30	28.5	20.5	7.0	30	32.0	42.6	64.7
31	29.2	21.1	7.5	31	33.1	43.8	65.9
32	30.1	21.8	8.0	32	34.3	44.9	67.0
33	30.9	22.5	8.5	33	35.5	46.0	68.0
34	31.7	23.2	9.0	34	36.7	47.1	69.1
35	32.6	24.0	9.6	35	37.8	48.1	70.2
36	33.4	24.8	10.1	36	39.0	49.2	71.2
37	34.2	25.6	10.7	37	40.1	50.3	72.3
38	35.2	26.4	11.2	38	41.1	51.3	73.2
39	36.1	27.1	11.8	39	42.2	52.3	74.3
40	37.0	27.9	12.4	40	43.2	53.3	75.3
41	37.9	28.7	13.0	41	44.2	54.3	76.2
42	38.8	29.6	13.6	42	45.3	55.3	77.2
43	39.8	30.5	14.2	43	46.4	56.3	78.1
44	40.7	31.4	14.8	44	47.5	57.2	79.1
45	41.7	32.2	15.4	45	48.4	58.1	80.0
46	42.6	33.1	16.1	46	49.4	59.1	81.0
47	43.6	34.0	16.7	47	50.5	60.0	82.0
48	44.6	34.9	17.4	48	51.3	60.9	82.9
49	45.6	35.8	18.1	49	52.2	61.8	83.8
50	46.7	36.8	18.7	50	53.1	62.7	84.7
51	47.7	37.8	19.4	51	54.1	63.6	85.6
52	48.8	38.8	20.2	52	55.0	64.5	86.5
53	49.8	39.7	20.9	53	55.9	65.4	87.3
54	50.9	40.7	21.6	54	56.9	66.3	88.1
55	52.0	41.7	22.3	55	57.7	67.1	88.9
56	53.1	42.7	23.1	56	58.5	68.0	89.7
57	54.2	43.6	23.9	57	59.3	68.8	90.5
58	55.4	44.6	24.6	58	60.2	69.7	91.3
59	56.6	45.7	25.5	59	61.0	70.5	92.1
60	57.7	46.9	26.2	60	61.9	71.3	92.9
61	58.9	48.0	27.0	61	62.8	72.0	93.7
62	60.1	49.1	27.9	62	63.6	72.8	94.4
63	61.3	50.2	28.7	63	64.4	73.6	95.2
64	62.5	51.4	29.6	64	65.2	74.3	96.0
65	63.8	52.5	30.4	65	66.0	75.1	96.7
70	70.1	58.6	34.9	70	70.0	78.8	100.4
75	77.1	64.6	39.8	75	73.8	82.3	103.8
80	84.1	70.6	45.0	80	77.3	85.6	107.0
85	91.8	79.0	50.6	85	80.8	88.8	110.2
90	99.6	87.4	56.5	90	84.0	91.8	113.1
95	108.2	95.7	62.9	95	87.1	94.7	116.1
100	116.9	104.1	69.8	100	90.3	97.5	118.9

*Vacuum in inches of Mercury

Table A-3. Properties of Superheated Freon Vapor.

TEMP. °F.	Abs. Pressure 28 lb./in.² Gage Pressure 13.3 lb./in.² (Sat'n. Temp. 7.7° F.)			Abs. Pressure 30 lb./in.² Gage Pressure 15.3 lb./in.² (Sat'n. Temp. 11.1° F.)			Abs. Pressure 32 lb./in.² Gage Pressure 17.3 lb./in.² (Sat'n. Temp. 14.3° F.)			Abs. Pressure 34 lb./in.² Gage Pressure 19.3 lb./in.² (Sat'n. Temp. 17.4° F.)		
	Volume ft.³/lb.	Heat Content Btu./lb.	Entropy Btu./lb.°F.	Volume ft.³/lb.	Heat Content Btu./lb.	Entropy Btu./lb.°F.	Volume ft.³/lb.	Heat Content Btu./lb.	Entropy Btu./lb.°F.	Volume ft.³/lb.	Heat Content Btu./lb.	Entropy Btu./lb.°F.
(at sat'n)	(1.409)	(79.10)	(0.17032)	(1.323)	(79.47)	(0.17008)	(1.245)	(79.84)	(0.16985)	(1.175)	(80.20)	(0.16965)
10	1.415	79.41	0.17099									
20	1.450	80.81	.17393	1.350	80.73	0.17269	1.262	80.67	0.17152	1.183	80.58	0.17040
30	1.485	82.23	.17685	1.383	82.15	.17562	1.293	82.08	.17445	1.212	82.00	.17333
40	1.520	83.66	.17975	1.415	83.58	.17851	1.323	83.51	.17734	1.241	83.44	.17623
50	1.555	85.11	0.18261	1.448	85.03	0.18138	1.354	84.96	0.18022	1.270	84.88	0.17910
60	1.590	86.56	.18544	1.480	86.48	.18420	1.384	86.41	.18304	1.299	86.34	.18194
70	1.625	88.03	.18823	1.512	87.95	.18699	1.414	87.88	.18583	1.328	87.81	.18474
80	1.659	89.51	.19097	1.544	89.43	.18974	1.444	89.36	.18860	1.356	89.29	.18750
90	1.693	90.99	.19371	1.576	90.91	.19249	1.474	90.85	.19133	1.385	90.78	.19025
100	1.727	92.49	0.19642	1.608	92.41	0.19519	1.504	92.35	0.19404	1.413	92.29	0.19295
110	1.761	94.01	.19909	1.640	93.93	.19787	1.535	93.87	.19673	1.441	93.81	.19563
120	1.795	95.53	.20174	1.672	95.46	.20053	1.565	95.40	.19940	1.470	95.34	.19831
130	1.828	97.07	.20436	1.703	97.00	.20315	1.595	96.94	.20202	1.498	96.88	.20094
140	1.862	98.62	.20698	1.735	98.54	.20577	1.624	98.50	.20463	1.526	98.43	.20356
150	1.896	100.18	0.20956	1.767	100.11	0.20836	1.654	100.06	0.20721	1.554	100.00	0.20614
160	1.930	101.75	.21212	1.799	101.69	.21092	1.683	101.64	.20977	1.582	101.58	.20871
170	1.963	103.33	.21466	1.829	103.28	.21344	1.713	103.23	.21232	1.610	103.17	.21125
180	1.997	104.93	.21719	1.860	104.88	.21597	1.743	104.83	.21486	1.638	104.78	.21379
190	2.030	106.55	.21967	1.891	106.49	.21846	1.772	106.45	.21735	1.666	106.40	.21629
200	2.063	108.17	0.22216	1.923	108.12	0.22096	1.802	108.08	0.21985	1.693	108.03	0.21878
210	2.096	109.81	.22462	1.954	109.76	.22342	1.831	109.72	.22231	1.721	109.67	.22125
220	2.129	111.46	.22706	1.986	111.41	.22588	1.860	111.36	.22476	1.749	111.32	.22370
230	2.163	113.12	.22949	2.017	113.08	.22830	1.889	113.03	.22718	1.776	112.98	.22613
240	2.196	114.80	.23191	2.048	114.75	.23072	1.918	114.72	.22960	1.804	114.66	.22856
250	2.229	116.49	0.23430	2.079	116.44	0.23312	1.948	116.41	0.23200	1.833	116.35	0.23097
260	2.262	118.19	.23669	2.110	118.15	.23550	1.977	118.11	.23439	1.860	118.06	.23335
270	2.295	119.91	.23905	2.141	119.87	.23787	2.006	119.82	.23676	1.888	119.79	.23573
280	2.329	121.65	.24141	2.172	121.60	.24023	2.035	121.55	.23912	1.916	121.54	.23809
290							2.065	123.30	.24146	1.944	123.31	.24043

continued on page 249

248

continued from page 248

TEMP. °F.	Abs. Pressure 36 lb./in.² Gage Pressure 21.3 lb./in.² (Sat'n. Temp. 20.4° F.)			Abs. Pressure 38 lb./in.² Gage Pressure 23.3 lb./in.² (Sat'n. Temp. 23.2° F.)			Abs. Pressure 40 lb./in.² Gage Pressure 25.3 lb./in.² (Sat'n. Temp. 25.9° F.)			Abs. Pressure 42 lb./in.² Gage Pressure 27.3 lb./in.² (Sat'n. Temp. 28.5° F.)		
(at sat'n)	(1.113)	(80.54)	(0.16947)	(1.058)	(80.86)	(0.16931)	(1.009)	(81.16)	(0.16914)	(0.963)	(81.44)	(0.16897)
30	1.140	81.90	0.17227	1.076	81.82	0.17126	1.019	81.76	0.17030	0.967	81.65	0.16939
40	1.168	83.35	.17518	1.103	83.27	.17418	1.044	83.20	.17322	0.991	83.10	.17231
50	1.196	84.81	0.17806	1.129	84.72	0.17706	1.070	84.65	0.17612	1.016	84.56	0.17521
60	1.223	86.27	.18089	1.156	86.19	.17991	1.095	86.11	.17896	1.040	86.03	.17806
70	1.250	87.74	.18369	1.182	87.67	.18272	1.120	87.60	.18178	1.063	87.51	.18086
80	1.278	89.22	.18647	1.208	89.16	.18551	1.144	89.09	.18455	1.087	89.00	.18365
90	1.305	90.71	.18921	1.234	90.66	.18826	1.169	90.58	.18731	1.110	90.50	.18640
100	1.332	92.22	0.19193	1.260	92.17	0.19096	1.194	92.09	0.19004	1.134	92.01	0.18913
110	1.359	93.75	.19462	1.285	93.69	.19365	1.218	93.62	.19272	1.158	93.54	.19184
120	1.386	95.28	.19729	1.310	95.22	.19631	1.242	95.15	.19538	1.181	95.09	.19451
130	1.412	96.82	.19991	1.336	96.76	.19895	1.267	96.70	.19803	1.204	96.64	.19714
140	1.439	98.37	.20254	1.361	98.32	.20157	1.291	98.26	.20066	1.227	98.26	.19979
150	1.465	99.93	0.20512	1.387	99.89	0.20416	1.315	99.83	0.20325	1.250	99.77	0.20237
160	1.492	101.51	.20770	1.412	101.47	.20673	1.340	101.42	.20583	1.274	101.36	.20496
170	1.518	103.11	.21024	1.437	103.07	.20929	1.364	103.02	.20838	1.297	102.96	.20751
180	1.545	104.72	.21278	1.462	104.67	.21183	1.388	104.63	.21092	1.320	104.57	.21005
190	1.571	106.34	.21528	1.487	106.29	.21433	1.412	106.25	.21343	1.343	106.19	.21256
200	1.597	107.97	0.21778	1.512	107.93	0.21681	1.435	107.88	0.21592	1.365	107.82	0.21505
210	1.623	109.61	.22024	1.537	109.57	.21928	1.459	109.52	.21840	1.388	109.47	.21754
220	1.650	111.27	.22270	1.562	111.22	.22176	1.482	111.17	.22085	1.411	111.12	.22000
230	1.676	112.94	.22513	1.587	112.89	.22419	1.506	112.84	.22329	1.434	112.80	.22244
240	1.702	114.62	.22756	1.612	114.58	.22662	1.530	114.52	.22572	1.457	114.49	.22486
250	1.728	116.31	0.22996	1.637	116.28	0.22903	1.554	116.21	0.22813	1.480	116.19	0.22728
260	1.754	118.02	.23235	1.662	117.99	.23142	1.577	117.92	.23052	1.502	117.90	.22967
270	1.780	119.74	.23472	1.687	119.71	.23379	1.601	119.65	.23289	1.524	119.62	.23204
280	1.807	121.47	.23708	1.712	121.45	.23616	1.625	121.40	.23526	1.547	121.36	.23441
290	1.833	123.22	.23942	1.737	123.20	.23850	1.649	123.15	.23760	1.570	123.11	.23675
300	....	....	....	1.762	124.95	0.24083	1.673	124.92	0.23994	1.592	124.87	0.23909

Table A-4. Properties of Superheated Freon Vapor.

TEMP. °F.	Abs. Pressure 44 lb./in.² Gage Pressure 29.3 lb./in.² (Sat'n. Temp. 31.0° F.)			Abs. Pressure 46 lb./in.² Gage Pressure 31.3 lb./in.² (Sat'n. Temp. 33.5° F.)			Abs. Pressure 48 lb./in.² Gage Pressure 33.13 lb./in.² (Sat'n. Temp. 35.8° F.)			Abs. Pressure 50 lb./in.² Gage Pressure 35.3 lb./in.² (Sat'n. Temp. 38.3° F.)		
	Volume ft.²/lb.	Heat Content Btu./lb.	Entropy Btu./lb.°F.	Volume ft.²/lb.	Heat Content Btu./lb.	Entropy Btu./lb.°F.	Volume ft.²/lb.	Heat Content Btu./lb.	Entropy Btu./lb.°F.	Volume ft.²/lb.	Heat Content Btu./lb.	Entropy Btu./lb.°F.
(at sat'n)	(0.922)	(81.72)	(0.16882)	(0.885)	(82.00)	(0.16867)	(0.849)	(82.25)	(0.16855)	(0.817)	(82.52)	(0.16841)
40	0.943	83.03	0.17142	0.899	82.94	0.17057	0.858	82.85	0.16974	0.821	82.76	0.16895
50	0.966	84.48	0.17432	0.921	84.40	0.17347	0.880	84.32	0.17266	0.842	84.24	0.17187
60	0.989	85.96	.17717	0.943	85.88	.17633	0.902	85.80	.17554	0.863	85.72	.17475
70	1.012	87.45	.18000	0.965	87.37	.17916	0.923	87.29	.17837	0.884	87.22	.17760
80	1.035	88.94	.18279	0.988	88.88	.18198	0.944	88.79	.18117	0.904	88.72	.18040
90	1.058	90.44	.18556	1.010	90.39	.18474	0.965	90.30	.18394	0.924	90.23	.18317
100	1.080	91.95	.18828	1.031	91.90	.18746	0.986	91.82	.18668	0.944	91.75	.18591
110	1.103	93.48	.19099	1.053	93.43	.19016	1.007	93.35	.18939	0.964	93.29	.18862
120	1.125	95.02	.19367	1.074	94.96	.19285	1.028	94.89	.19208	0.984	94.83	.19132
130	1.147	96.57	.19630	1.096	96.51	.19551	1.048	96.44	.19472	1.004	96.39	.19397
140	1.170	98.14	.19895	1.117	98.08	.19814	1.069	98.01	.19737	1.024	97.96	.19662
150	1.192	99.72	0.20154	1.139	99.66	0.20075	1.089	99.59	0.19997	1.044	99.54	0.19923
160	1.214	101.31	20412	1.160	101.25	20333	1.110	101.18	20256	1.064	101.14	20182
170	1.236	102.91	20667	1.181	102.85	20588	1.130	102.79	20513	1.084	102.75	20439
180	1.258	104.52	20922	1.202	104.46	20843	1.150	104.40	20766	1.103	104.36	20694
190	1.280	106.14	21173	1.223	106.09	21094	1.170	106.02	21017	1.123	105.98	20946
200	1.302	107.78	0.21424	1.244	107.73	0.21344	1.191	107.66	0.21269	1.142	107.62	0.21196
210	1.324	109.42	21672	1.265	109.38	21592	1.211	109.31	21517	1.162	109.28	21444
220	1.346	111.08	21918	1.286	111.04	21839	1.231	110.98	21763	1.181	110.95	21691
230	1.367	112.75	22161	1.307	112.71	22083	1.251	112.66	22007	1.200	112.62	21935
240	1.389	114.44	22405	1.327	114.39	22326	1.271	114.35	22251	1.220	114.31	22179
250	1.411	116.14	0.22646	1.348	116.09	0.22567	1.291	116.05	0.22492	1.239	116.00	0.22419
260	1.432	117.85	22885	1.369	117.81	22806	1.311	117.77	22731	1.258	117.71	22660
270	1.454	119.57	23123	1.390	119.54	23044	1.331	119.49	22970	1.277	119.44	22898
280	1.475	121.31	23359	1.410	121.27	23281	1.351	121.23	23207	1.296	121.18	23134
290	1.496	123.06	23592	1.431	123.02	23515	1.370	122.98	23440	1.314	122.93	23367
300	1.518	124.82	23826	1.452	124.79	23749	1.390	124.75	23674	1.332	124.69	23600
310	1.539	126.59	24058	1.472	126.57	23981	1.410	126.53	23907	1.350	126.45	23831

continued on 251

continued from 250

TEMP. °F.	Abs. Pressure 52 lb./in.² Gage Pressure 37.3 lb./in.² (Sat'n. Temp. 40.4° F.)			Abs. Pressure 54 lb./in.² Gage Pressure 39.3 lb./in.² (Sat'n. Temp. 42.5° F.)			Abs. Pressure 56 lb./in.² Gage Pressure 41.3 lb./in.² (Sat'n. Temp. 44.6° F.)			Abs. Pressure 58 lb./in.² Gage Pressure 43.3 lb./in.² (Sat'n. Temp. 46.7° F.)		
(at sat'n)	(0.788)	(82.75)	(0.16831)	(0.759)	(82.98)	(0.16820)	(0.734)	(83.22)	(0.16810)	(0.710)	(83.44)	(0.16800)
50	0.808	84.17	0.17114	0.774	84.07	0.17036	0.744	83.99	0.16965	0.716	83.91	0.16896
60	0.827	85.65	.17400	0.794	85.56	.17326	0.763	85.48	.17255	0.734	85.40	.17185
70	0.847	87.14	.17684	0.814	87.06	.17612	0.782	86.98	.17541	0.752	86.90	.17471
80	0.867	88.64	.17966	0.833	88.57	.17894	0.801	88.49	.17824	0.770	88.41	.17753
90	0.886	90.15	.18244	0.852	90.08	.18172	0.819	90.01	.18102	0.788	89.93	.18033
100	0.906	91.68	0.18518	0.871	91.61	0.18446	0.837	91.54	0.18377	0.806	91.46	0.18309
110	0.925	93.22	.18789	0.890	93.16	.18718	0.856	93.08	.18651	0.824	93.00	.18583
120	0.945	94.77	.19059	0.908	94.71	.18989	0.874	94.63	.18921	0.842	94.55	.18854
130	0.964	96.33	.19325	0.927	96.27	.19255	0.892	96.19	.19188	0.860	96.11	.19122
140	0.983	97.90	.19590	0.945	97.84	.19520	0.910	97.77	.19453	0.877	97.68	.19387
150	1.002	99.48	0.19850	0.964	99.43	0.19782	0.928	99.36	0.19715	0.894	99.26	0.19648
160	1.021	101.07	.20109	0.982	101.03	.20043	0.946	100.96	.19975	0.912	100.86	.19908
170	1.040	102.68	.20365	1.001	102.64	.20299	0.964	102.57	.20232	0.929	102.47	.20166
180	1.059	104.30	.20621	1.019	104.25	.20554	0.981	104.19	.20487	0.946	104.09	.20423
190	1.078	105.93	.20873	1.037	105.88	.20806	0.999	105.83	.20739	0.963	105.72	.20676
200	1.097	107.58	0.21125	1.055	107.52	0.21057	1.016	107.48	0.20991	0.980	107.36	0.20927
210	1.116	109.23	.21374	1.073	109.17	.21305	1.034	109.14	.21241	0.997	109.02	.21177
220	1.134	110.89	.21620	1.091	110.84	.21553	1.051	110.81	.21487	1.014	110.70	.21424
230	1.153	112.56	.21865	1.109	112.51	.21797	1.068	112.49	.21731	1.031	112.39	.21669
240	1.172	114.26	.22110	1.127	114.20	.22042	1.086	114.18	.21977	1.048	114.10	.21914
250	1.190	115.96	0.22352	1.145	115.91	0.22283	1.103	115.88	0.22218	1.064	115.82	0.22155
260	1.208	117.67	.22591	1.163	117.63	.22523	1.120	117.59	.22458	1.081	117.55	.22396
270	1.227	119.40	.22829	1.181	119.37	.22762	1.138	119.31	.22698	1.098	119.29	.22635
280	1.245	121.14	.23065	1.199	121.11	.22999	1.155	121.05	.22934	1.114	121.04	.22871
290	1.263	122.90	.23299	1.216	122.86	.23233	1.172	122.80	.23169	1.130	122.80	.23105
300	1.281	124.66	0.23532	1.234	124.63	0.23467	1.189	124.57	0.23403	1.147	124.57	0.23340
310	1.298	126.42	.23763	1.251	126.40	.23699	1.206	126.36	.23635	1.164	126.35	.23574
320	.....	.....	.....	.....	.....	.....	1.223	128.17	.23867	1.180	128.14	.23806

Table A-5. Properties of Saturated Freon Vapor.

continued on 253

TEMP.	PRESSURE		VOLUME		DENSITY		HEAT CONTENT from −40°			ENTROPY from −40°		TEMP.
°F.	Abs. lb./in.²	Gage lb./in.²	Liquid ft.³/lb.	Vapor ft.³/lb.	Liquid lb./ft.³	Vapor lb./ft.³	Liquid Btu./lb.	Latent Btu./lb.	Vapor Btu./lb.	Liquid Btu./lb./°F.	Vapor Btu./lb./°F.	°F.
10	29.35	14.65	0.0112	1.351	89.45	0.7402	10.39	68.97	79.36	0.02328	0.17015	10
12	30.56	15.86	.0112	1.301	89.24	.7687	10.82	68.77	79.59	.02419	.17001	12
14	31.80	17.10	.0112	1.253	89.03	.7981	11.26	68.56	79.82	.02510	.16987	14
16	33.08	18.38	.0112	1.207	88.81	.8288	11.70	68.35	80.05	.02601	.16974	16
18	34.40	19.70	.0113	1.163	88.58	.8598	12.12	68.15	80.27	.02692	.16961	18
20	35.75	21.05	0.0113	1.121	88.37	0.8921	12.55	67.94	80.49	0.02783	0.16949	20
22	37.15	22.45	.0113	1.081	88.13	.9251	13.00	67.72	80.72	.02873	.16938	22
24	38.58	23.88	.0113	1.043	87.91	.9588	13.44	67.51	80.95	.02963	.16926	24
26	40.07	25.37	.0114	1.007	87.68	.9930	13.88	67.29	81.17	.03053	.16913	26
28	41.59	26.89	.014	.973	87.47	1.028	14.32	67.07	81.39	.03143	.16900	28
30	43.16	28.46	0.0115	.939	87.24	1.065	14.76	66.85	81.61	0.03233	0.16887	30
32	44.77	30.07	.0115	.908	87.02	1.102	15.21	66.62	81.83	.03323	.16876	32
34	46.42	31.72	.0115	.877	86.78	1.140	15.65	66.40	82.05	.03413	.16865	34
36	48.13	33.43	.0116	.848	86.55	1.180	16.10	66.17	82.27	.03502	.16854	36
38	49.88	35.18	.0116	.819	86.33	1.221	16.55	65.94	82.49	.03591	.16843	38
40	51.68	36.98	0.0116	.792	86.10	1.263	17.00	65.71	82.71	0.03680	·0.16833	40
42	53.51	38.81	.0116	.767	85.86	1.304	17.46	65.47	82.93	.03770	.16823	42
44	55.40	40.70	.0117	.742	85.66	1.349	17.91	65.24	83.15	.03859	.16813	44
46	57.35	42.65	.0117	.718	85.43	1.393	18.36	65.00	83.36	.03948	.16803	46
48	59.35	44.65	.0117	.695	85.19	1.438	18.82	64.74	83.57	.04037	.16794	48
50	61.39	46.69	0.0118	.673	84.94	1.485	19.27	64.51	83.78	0.04126	0.16785	50
52	63.49	48.79	.0118	.652	84.71	1.534	19.72	64.27	83.99	.04215	.16776	52
54	65.63	50.93	.0118	.632	84.50	1.583	20.18	64.02	84.20	.04304	.16767	54
56	67.84	53.14	.0119	.612	84.28	1.633	20.64	63.77	84.41	.04392	.16758	56
58	70.10	55.40	.0119	.593	84.04	1.686	21.11	63.51	84.62	.04480	.16749	58
60	72.41	57.71	0.0119	.575	83.78	1.740	21.57	63.25	84.82	0.04568	0.16741	60
62	74.77	60.07	.0120	.557	83.57	1.795	22.03	62.99	85.02	.04657	.16733	62
64	77.20	62.50	.0120	.540	83.34	1.851	22.49	62.73	85.22	.04745	.16725	64
66	79.67	64.97	.0120	.524	83.10	1.909	22.95	62.47	85.42	.04833	.16717	66
68	82.24	67.54	.0121	.508	82.86	1.968	23.42	62.20	85.62	.04921	.16709	68

70	0.16701	0.05009	85.82	61.92	23.90	2.028	82.60	0.493	0.0121	70.12	84.82	**70**
72	.16693	.05097	86.02	61.65	24.37	2.090	82.37	.479	.0121	72.80	87.50	72
74	.16685	.05185	86.22	61.38	24.84	2.153	82.12	.464	.0122	75.50	90.20	74
76	.16677	.05272	86.42	61.10	25.32	2.218	81.87	.451	.0122	78.30	93.00	76
78	.16669	.05359	86.61	60.81	25.80	2.284	81.62	.438	.0123	81.15	95.85	78
80	0.16662	0.05446	86.80	60.52	26.28	2.353	81.39	0.425	0.0123	84.06	98.76	**80**
82	.16655	.05534	86.99	60.23	26.76	2.423	81.12	.413	.0123	87.00	101.7	82
84	.16648	.05621	87.18	59.94	27.24	2.495	80.87	.401	.0124	90.1	104.8	84
86	.16640	.05708	87.37	59.65	27.72	2.569	80.63	.389	.0124	93.2	107.9	86
88	.16632	.05795	87.56	59.35	28.21	2.645	80.37	.378	.0124	96.4	111.1	88
90	0.16624	0.05882	87.74	59.04	28.70	2.721	80.11	0.368	0.0125	99.6	114.3	**90**
92	.16616	.05969	87.92	58.73	29.19	2.799	79.86	.357	.0125	103.0	117.7	92
94	.16608	.06056	88.10	58.42	29.68	2.880	79.60	.347	.0126	106.3	121.0	94
96	.16600	.06143	88.28	58.10	30.18	2.963	79.32	.338	.0126	109.8	124.5	96
98	.16592	.06230	88.45	57.78	30.67	3.048	79.06	.328	.0126	113.3	128.0	98
100	0.16584	0.06316	88.62	57.46	31.16	3.135	78.80	0.319	0.0127	116.9	131.6	**100**
102	.16576	.06403	88.79	57.14	31.65	3.224	78.54	.310	.0127	120.6	135.3	102
104	.16568	.06490	88.95	56.80	32.15	3.316	78.27	.302	.0128	124.3	139.0	104
106	.16560	.06577	89.11	56.46	32.65	3.411	78.00	.293	.0128	128.1	142.8	106
108	.16551	.06663	89.27	56.12	33.15	3.509	77.73	.285	.0129	132.1	146.8	108
110	0.16542	0.06749	89.43	55.78	33.65	3.610	77.46	0.277	0.0129	136.0	150.7	**110**
112	.16533	.06836	89.58	55.43	34.15	3.714	77.18	.269	.0130	140.1	154.8	112
114	.16524	.06922	89.73	55.08	34.65	3.823	76.89	.262	.0130	144.2	158.9	114
116	.16515	.07008	89.87	54.72	35.15	3.934	76.60	.254	.0131	148.4	163.1	116
118	.16505	.07094	90.01	54.36	35.65	4.049	76.32	.247	.0131	152.7	167.4	118
120	0.16495	0.07180	90.15	53.99	36.16	4.167	76.02	0.240	0.0132	157.1	171.8	**120**
122	.16484	.07266	90.28	53.62	36.66	4.288	75.72	.233	.0132	161.5	176.2	122
124	.16473	.07352	90.40	53.24	37.16	4.413	75.40	.227	.0132	166.1	180.8	124
126	.16462	.07437	90.52	52.85	37.67	4.541	75.10	.220	.0133	170.7	185.4	126
128	.16450	.07522	90.64	52.46	38.18	4.673	74.78	.214	.0134	175.4	190.1	128
130	0.16438	0.07607	90.76	52.07	38.69	4.808	74.46	0.208	0.0134	180.2	194.9	**130**
132	.16425	.07691	90.86	51.67	39.19	4.948	74.13	.202	.0135	185.1	199.8	132
134	.16411	.07775	90.96	51.26	39.70	5.094	73.81	.196	.0135	190.1	204.9	134
136	.16396	.07858	91.06	50.85	40.21	5.247	73.46	.191	.0136	195.2	209.9	136
138	.16380	.07941	91.15	50.43	40.72	5.405	73.10	.185	.0137	200.3	215.0	138
140	0.16363	0.08024	91.24	50.00	41.24	5.571	72.73	0.180	0.0138	205.5	220.2	**140**

Table A-6. Air Conditioning Performance Chart.

DRY BULB TEMP	WET BULB AIR																		
	52	53	54	55	56	57	58	59	60	61	62	63	64	65	66	67	68	69	70
75	50	50	50	50	50	50	50	50	51	51	51	52	52	53	53	54	55	55	56
76	50	50	50	50	50	50	51	51	51	51	51	52	52	53	53	54	55	55	56
77	50	50	50	50	51	51	51	51	51	51	52	52	52	53	53	54	55	55	56
78	50	50	51	51	51	51	51	51	52	52	52	52	53	53	54	54	55	56	56
79	51	51	51	51	51	51	51	52	52	52	52	52	53	53	54	54	55	56	56
80	51	51	51	51	51	52	52	52	52	52	52	52	53	53	54	54	55	56	56
81	51	51	51	52	52	52	52	52	52	52	53	53	53	54	54	55	55	56	57
82	52	52	52	52	52	52	52	52	53	53	53	53	54	54	55	55	56	56	57
83	52	52	52	53	53	53	53	53	53	53	54	54	54	55	55	56	56	57	57
•84	53	53	53	53	53	53	54	54	54	54	54	54	55	55	55	56	56	57	58
85	53	53	53	53	54	54	54	54	54	54	54	55	55	55	56	56	57	57	58
86	54	54	54	54	54	54	54	54	55	55	55	55	55	55	56	56	57	57	58
87	54	54	54	54	55	55	55	55	55	55	56	56	56	56	56	57	57	58	58
88	55	55	55	55	55	56	56	56	56	56	56	56	56	56	57	57	57	58	59
89	56	56	56	56	56	56	56	56	56	56	57	57	57	57	57	57	58	58	59
90			56	56	56	56	57	57	57	57	57	57	57	57	57	58	58	58	59
91					57	57	57	57	57	57	57	57	57	57	58	58	58	59	59
92					57	57	57	57	58	58	58	58	58	58	58	58	59	59	60
93						58	58	58	58	58	58	58	58	58	59	59	59	60	60
94						59	59	59	59	59	59	59	59	59	59	59	59	60	60
95						59	59	59	59	59	59	59	59	59	59	60	60	60	61
96							60	60	60	60	60	60	60	60	60	60	60	61	61
97							60	60	60	60	60	60	60	61	61	61	61	62	62
98								61	61	61	61	61	61	61	61	61	62	62	63
99								62	62	62	62	62	62	62	62	62	62	63	63
100								62	62	62	62	62	62	62	62	63	63	63	63
101															63	63	63	63	64
102															63	63	64	64	64
103															64	64	64	64	64
104					MAXIMUM DISCHARGE										64	64	64	64	65
105					AIR TEMPERATURE										64	64	64	65	65
106															65	65	65	65	65
107															65	66	66	66	66
108															66	66	66	66	66
109															66	66	66	67	67
110			NY283B												67	67	67	67	67

Performance Temperature

TEMPERATURE

71	72	73	74	75	76	77	78	79	80	81	82	83	84	85	86	87	88	89	90
57	57	58	59																
57	58	58	59	59															
57	58	59	59	59	61														
57	58	59	59	60	61	62													
57	58	59	60	60	61	62	63												
57	58	59	60	61	61	62	63	64											
57	58	59	60	61	62	63	64	65	65										
58	58	59	60	61	62	63	64	65	66	66									
58	59	60	60	61	62	63	64	65	66	67	68								
58	59	60	61	61	62	63	64	65	66	67	68	69							
59	59	60	61	62	62	63	64	65	66	67	68	69	70						
59	59	60	61	62	63	63	64	65	66	67	68	69	70	70					
59	60	60	61	62	63	64	65	65	66	67	68	69	70	70	71				
59	60	61	61	62	63	64	65	66	66	67	68	69	70	70	71	72			
59	60	61	62	62	63	64	65	66	66	67	68	69	70	70	71	72	73		
60	60	61	62	63	63	64	65	66	67	67	68	69	70	71	71	72	73	74	
60	60	61	62	63	63	64	65	66	67	68	68	69	70	71	72	72	73	74	75
60	61	61	62	63	64	64	65	66	67	68	68	69	70	70	72	72	73	74	75
61	61	62	63	63	64	65	65	66	67	68	68	69	70	71	72	72	73	74	75
61	62	62	63	63	64	65	65	66	67	68	68	69	70	71	72	72	73	74	75
61	62	62	63	64	64	65	65	66	67	68	68	69	70	71	72	72	73	74	75
61	62	63	63	64	64	65	66	66	67	68	69	69	70	71	72	73	73	74	75
62	63	63	64	64	65	65	66	67	67	68	69	70	70	71	72	73	74	74	75
63	63	64	64	65	65	66	66	67	68	69	69	70	71	71	72	73	74	74	75
63	64	64	65	65	65	66	67	67	68	69	69	70	71	72	72	73	74	74	75
64	64	64	65	65	65	66	67	67	68	69	69	70	71	72	72	73	74	74	75
64	64	65	65	65	66	66	67	68	68	69	70	70	71	72	73	73	74	75	76
64	64	65	65	66	66	67	67	68	68	69	70	71	71	72	73	73	74	75	76
65	65	65	66	66	66	67	67	68	69	69	70	71	72	72	73	74	75	76	76
65	65	65	66	66	67	67	68	68	69	69	70	71	72	72	73	74	75	76	77
65	65	66	66	66	67	67	68	68	69	69	70	71	72	72	73	74	75	76	77
65	66	66	66	67	67	67	68	68	69	70	70	71	72	73	73	74	75	76	77
66	66	66	67	67	67	68	68	69	69	70	71	71	72	73	74	74	75	76	77
66	67	67	67	67	68	68	69	69	70	70	71	71	72	73	74	75	76	77	78
67	67	67	67	68	68	68	69	69	70	70	71	72	72	73	74	75	76	77	78
67	67	67	67	68	68	68	69	69	70	70	71	72	72	73	74	75	76	77	78

Chart—Front Unit of Dual System

(Continued on page 256.)

Table A-7. Air Conditioning Performance Chart.
(Continued from page 255.)

DRY BULB TEMP.	52	53	54	55	56	57	58	59	60	61	62	63	64	65	66	67	68	69	70
75	48	48	48	48	48	48	48	48	49	49	49	50	50	51	51	52	53	53	54
76	48	48	48	48	48	48	49	49	49	49	49	50	50	51	51	52	53	53	54
77	48	48	48	48	49	49	49	49	49	49	50	50	50	51	51	52	53	53	54
78	48	48	49	49	49	49	49	49	50	50	50	50	51	51	52	52	53	54	54
79	49	49	49	49	49	49	49	50	50	50	50	50	51	51	52	52	53	54	54
80	49	49	49	49	49	50	50	50	50	50	50	50	51	51	52	52	53	54	54
81	49	49	49	50	50	50	50	50	50	50	51	51	51	52	52	53	53	54	55
82	50	50	50	50	50	50	50	50	51	51	51	51	52	52	53	53	54	54	55
83	50	50	50	51	51	51	51	51	51	51	52	52	52	53	53	54	54	55	55
84	51	51	51	51	51	51	52	52	52	52	52	52	53	53	53	54	54	55	56
85	51	51	51	51	52	52	52	52	52	52	52	53	53	53	54	54	55	55	56
86	52	52	52	52	52	52	52	52	53	53	53	53	53	53	54	54	55	55	56
87	52	52	52	52	53	53	53	53	53	53	54	54	54	54	54	55	55	56	56
88	53	53	53	53	53	54	54	54	54	54	54	54	54	54	55	55	55	56	57
89	54	54	54	54	54	54	54	54	54	54	55	55	55	55	55	55	56	56	57
90			54	54	54	54	55	55	55	55	55	55	55	55	56	56	56	56	57
91						55	55	55	55	55	55	55	55	55	56	56	56	57	57
92						55	55	55	55	56	56	56	56	56	56	56	57	57	58
93					56	56	56	56	56	56	56	56	56	56	57	57	57	58	58
94						57	57	57	57	57	57	57	57	57	57	57	57	58	58
95						57	57	57	57	57	57	57	57	57	57	58	58	58	59
96							58	58	58	58	58	58	58	58	58	58	58	58	59
97							58	58	58	58	58	58	58	58	59	59	59	59	60
98							59	59	59	59	59	59	59	59	59	59	60	60	61
99							60	60	60	60	60	60	60	60	60	60	60	61	61
100							60	60	60	60	60	60	60	60	60	61	61	61	61
101															61	61	61	61	62
102															61	61	62	62	62
103															62	62	62	62	62
104				MAXIMUM DISCHARGE AIR TEMPERATURE											62	62	62	62	63
105															62	62	62	63	63
106															63	63	63	63	63
107															63	64	64	64	64
108															64	64	64	64	64
109															64	64	64	65	65
110			NY282B												65	65	65	65	65

WET BULB AIR

Performance Temperature

71	72	73	74	75	76	77	78	79	80	81	82	83	84	85	86	87	88	89	90
55	55	56	57																
55	56	56	57	57															
55	56	57	57	57	59														
55	56	57	57	58	59	60													
55	56	57	58	58	59	60	61												
55	56	57	58	59	59	60	61	62											
55	56	57	58	59	60	61	62	63	63										
56	56	57	58	59	60	61	62	63	64	64									
56	57	58	58	59	60	61	62	63	64	65	66								
56	57	58	59	59	60	61	62	63	64	65	66	67							
57	57	58	59	60	60	61	62	63	64	65	66	67	68						
57	57	58	59	60	61	61	62	63	64	65	66	67	68	68					
57	58	58	59	60	61	62	63	63	64	65	66	67	68	68	69				
57	58	59	59	60	61	62	63	64	64	65	66	67	68	68	69	70			
57	58	59	60	60	61	62	63	64	64	65	66	67	68	68	69	70	71		
58	58	59	60	61	61	62	63	64	65	65	66	67	68	69	69	70	71	72	
58	58	59	60	61	61	62	63	64	65	66	66	67	68	69	70	70	71	72	73
58	59	59	60	61	62	62	63	64	65	66	66	67	68	69	70	71	72	72	73
59	59	60	61	61	62	63	63	64	65	66	66	67	68	69	70	70	71	72	73
59	60	60	61	61	62	63	63	64	65	66	66	67	68	69	70	70	71	72	73
59	60	60	61	62	62	63	63	64	65	66	66	67	68	69	70	70	71	72	73
59	60	61	61	62	62	63	64	64	65	66	67	67	68	69	70	71	71	72	73
60	61	61	62	62	63	63	64	65	65	66	67	68	68	69	70	71	72	72	73
61	61	62	62	63	63	64	64	65	66	67	67	68	69	69	70	71	72	72	73
61	62	62	63	63	63	64	65	65	66	67	67	68	69	70	70	71	72	72	73
62	62	62	63	63	63	64	65	65	66	67	67	68	69	70	70	71	72	72	73
62	62	63	63	63	64	64	65	66	66	67	68	68	69	70	71	71	72	73	74
62	62	63	63	64	64	65	65	66	66	67	68	69	69	70	71	71	72	73	74
63	63	63	64	64	64	65	65	66	67	67	68	69	70	70	71	72	73	74	74
63	63	63	64	64	65	65	66	66	67	67	68	69	70	70	71	72	73	74	75
63	63	64	64	64	65	65	66	66	67	67	68	69	70	70	71	72	73	74	75
63	64	64	64	65	65	65	66	66	67	68	68	69	70	71	71	72	73	74	75
64	64	64	65	65	65	66	66	67	67	68	69	69	70	71	72	72	73	74	75
64	65	65	65	65	66	66	67	67	68	68	69	69	70	71	72	73	74	75	76
65	65	65	65	66	66	66	67	67	68	68	69	70	70	71	72	73	74	75	76
65	65	65	65	66	66	66	67	67	68	68	69	70	70	71	72	73	74	75	76

Chart—Front Unit Only

Table A-8. Air Conditioning Performance Chart.

DRY BULB TEMP	52	53	54	55	56	57	58	59	60	61	62	63	64	65	66	67	68	69	70
75	45	45	45	45	45	45	45	45	46	46	46	46	47	48	48	49	50	50	51
76	45	45	45	45	45	45	46	46	46	46	46	47	47	48	48	49	50	50	51
77	45	45	45	45	46	46	46	46	46	46	47	47	47	48	48	49	50	50	51
78	45	45	46	46	46	46	46	46	47	47	47	47	48	48	49	49	50	51	51
79	46	46	46	46	46	46	46	47	47	47	47	47	48	48	49	49	50	51	51
80	46	46	46	46	46	47	47	47	47	47	47	47	48	48	49	49	50	51	51
81	46	46	46	47	47	47	47	47	47	47	48	48	48	49	49	50	50	51	52
82	47	47	47	47	47	47	47	47	48	48	48	48	49	49	50	50	51	51	52
83	47	47	47	48	48	48	48	48	48	48	49	49	49	50	50	51	51	52	52
84	48	48	48	48	48	48	49	49	49	49	49	49	50	50	50	51	51	52	53
85	48	48	48	48	49	49	49	49	49	49	49	50	50	50	51	51	52	52	53
86	49	49	49	49	49	49	49	49	50	50	50	50	50	50	51	51	52	52	53
87	49	49	49	49	50	50	50	50	50	50	51	51	51	51	51	52	52	53	53
88	50	50	50	50	50	51	51	51	51	51	51	51	51	51	52	52	52	53	54
89	51	51	51	51	51	51	51	51	51	51	52	52	52	52	52	52	53	53	54
90				51	51	51	51	52	52	52	52	52	52	52	52	53	53	53	54
91				52	52	52	52	52	52	52	52	52	52	52	53	53	53	54	54
92				52	52	52	52	52	53	53	53	53	53	53	53	53	54	54	55
93						53	53	53	53	53	53	53	53	53	54	54	54	55	55
94						54	54	54	54	54	54	54	54	54	54	54	54	55	55
95						54	54	54	54	54	54	54	54	54	54	55	55	55	56
96					55	55	55	55	55	55	55	55	55	55	55	55	55	56	56
97					55	55	55	55	55	55	55	55	55	56	56	56	56	57	57
98							56	56	56	56	56	56	56	56	56	56	57	57	58
99							57	57	57	57	57	57	57	57	57	57	57	58	58
100							57	57	57	57	57	57	57	57	57	58	58	58	58
101															58	58	58	58	59
102															58	58	59	59	59
103															59	59	59	59	59
104															59	59	59	59	60
105					MAXIMUM DISCHARGE										59	59	59	60	60
106					AIR TEMPERATURE										60	60	60	60	60
107															60	61	61	61	61
108															61	61	61	61	61
109															61	61	61	62	62
110			NY285B												62	62	62	62	62

Performance Temperature

PERFORMANCE CHART

TEMPERATURE

71	72	73	74	75	76	77	78	79	80	81	82	83	84	85	86	87	88	89	90
52	52	53	54																
52	53	53	54	54															
52	53	54	54	54	56														
52	53	54	54	55	56	57													
52	53	54	55	55	56	57	58												
52	53	54	55	56	56	57	58	59											
52	53	54	55	56	57	58	59	60	60										
53	53	54	55	56	57	58	59	60	61	61									
53	54	55	55	56	57	58	59	60	61	62	63								
53	54	55	56	56	57	58	59	60	61	62	63	64							
54	54	55	56	57	57	58	59	60	61	62	63	64	65						
54	54	55	56	57	58	58	59	60	61	62	63	64	65	65					
54	55	55	56	57	58	59	60	60	61	62	63	64	65	65	66				
54	55	56	56	57	58	59	60	61	61	62	63	64	65	65	66	67			
54	55	56	57	57	58	59	60	61	61	62	63	64	65	65	66	67	68		
55	55	56	57	58	58	59	60	61	62	62	63	64	65	66	66	67	68	69	
55	55	56	57	58	58	59	60	61	62	63	63	64	65	66	67	67	68	69	70
55	56	56	57	58	59	59	60	61	62	63	63	64	65	66	67	67	68	69	70
56	56	57	58	58	59	60	60	61	62	63	63	64	65	66	67	67	68	69	70
56	57	57	58	58	59	60	60	61	62	63	63	64	65	66	67	67	68	69	70
56	57	57	58	59	59	60	60	61	62	63	63	64	65	66	67	67	68	69	70
56	57	58	58	59	59	60	61	61	62	63	64	64	65	66	67	68	68	69	70
57	58	58	59	59	60	60	61	62	62	63	64	65	65	66	67	68	69	69	70
58	58	59	59	60	60	61	61	62	63	64	64	65	66	66	67	68	69	69	70
58	59	59	60	60	60	61	62	62	63	64	64	65	66	67	67	68	69	69	70
59	59	59	60	60	60	61	62	62	63	64	64	65	66	67	67	68	69	69	70
59	59	60	60	60	61	61	62	63	63	64	65	65	66	67	68	68	69	70	71
59	59	60	60	61	61	62	62	63	63	64	65	66	66	67	68	68	69	70	71
60	60	60	61	61	61	62	62	63	64	64	65	66	67	67	68	69	70	71	71
60	60	60	61	61	62	62	63	63	64	64	65	66	67	67	68	69	70	71	72
60	60	61	61	61	62	62	63	63	64	64	65	66	67	67	68	69	70	71	72
60	61	61	61	62	62	62	63	63	64	65	65	66	67	68	68	69	70	71	72
61	61	61	62	62	62	63	63	64	64	65	66	66	67	68	69	69	70	71	72
61	62	62	62	62	63	63	64	64	65	65	66	66	67	68	69	70	71	72	73
62	62	62	62	63	63	63	64	64	65	65	66	67	67	68	69	70	71	72	73
62	62	62	62	63	63	63	64	64	65	65	66	67	67	68	69	70	71	72	73

Chart—Trunk Unit of Dual System

Table A-9. Performance Temperature Chart—Front Unit Only.

SINGLE UNIT

INLET AIR WET BULB TEMPERATURE

55	56	57	58	59	60	61	62	63	64	65	66	67	68	69	70	71	72	73	74	75	76	77	78	79	80	81	82	83	84	85	86	87	88	89	90
41	42	43	44	45	46	47	48	49	50	50	51	51	52	52	53	53	53	54	54,	55	56	57	58	59	59	60	62	64	66	67	68	69	70	71

DISCHARGE AIR DRY BULB TEMPERATURE

INLET AIR DRY BULB TEMPERATURE MUST BE BETWEEN 75° AND 110°F

NK1342A

Table A-10. Performance Temperature Chart—Front Unit of Dual System.

FRONT UNIT OF DUAL

INLET AIR WET BULB TEMPERATURE

55	56	57	58	59	60	61	62	63	64	65	66	67	68	69	70	71	72	73	74	75	76	77	78	79	80	81	82	83	84	85	86	87	88	89	90
43	44	45	46	47	48	49	50	51	52	52	52	53	54	54	54	55	55	55	56	56	57	58	59	60	61	61	62	64	66	68	69	70	71	72	73

DISCHARGE AIR DRY BULB TEMPERATURE

INLET AIR DRY BULB TEMPERATURE MUST BE BETWEEN 75° AND 110°F

NK1343A

261

Table A-11. Performance Temperature Chart—Roof Unit of Dual System.

ROOF UNIT OF DUAL

INLET AIR WET BULB TEMPERATURE																																			
55	56	57	58	59	60	61	62	63	64	65	66	67	68	69	70	71	72	73	74	75	76	77	78	79	80	81	82	83	84	85	86	87	88	89	90
52	53	54	55	56	57	58	59	60	61	61	61	62	63	63	64	64	65	66	67	68	69	70	71	71	72	74	76	78	79	79	80	80	81		

DISCHARGE AIR DRY BULB TEMPERATURE

INLET AIR DRY BULB TEMPERATURE MUST BE BETWEEN 75° AND 110°F

NK1344A

Table A-12. Dimensions and Physical Data for Copper Tubing.

Size Inches O.D.	Type	Internal Dia. Inches	Thickness of Metal Inches	Transverse Area Square Inches Internal	Length of Pipe in Ft. Containing 1-Cu. Foot	Weight Per Foot Pounds
1/4	—	.190	.030**	.028	5090.0	.080
3/8	K	.311	.032**	.076	1895.0	.134
1/2	K	.402	.049	.127	1135.0	.269
	L	.430	.035	.144	1001.0	.198
5/8	K	.527	.049	.218	660.5	.344
	L	.545	.040	.232	621.0	.284
3/4	K	.652	.049	.333	432.5	.418
	L	.660	.042	.341	422.0	.362
7/8	K	.745	.065	.435	331.0	.641
	L	.785	.045	.482	299.0	.454
1-1/8	K	.995	.065	.775	186.0	.839
	L	1.025	.050	.825	174.7	.653
1-3/8	K	1.245	.065	1.215	118.9	1.04
	L	1.265	.055	1.255	115.0	.882
1-5/8	K	1.481	.072	1.725	83.5	1.36
	L	1.505	.060	1.771	81.4	1.14
2-1/8	K	1.959	.083	3.000	48.0	2.06
	L	1.985	.070	3.090	46.6	1.75

Appendix B
Glossary

absolute humidity: Amount of moisture in the air, indicated in grains of moisture per cubic foot.

absolute pressure: Pressure that is measured from absolute zero instead of normal atmospheric pressure.

absolute temperature: Temperature measured from absolute zero.

absolute zero temperature: Temperature at which all molecular motion ceases. (−460°F and −273°C)

air conditioner: A device used to control temperature, humidity, and air movement.

air conditioning: The control of temperature, humidity, and movement of air.

air inlet valve: An adjustable door in the plenum blower assembly that permits selection of outside and inside air for heating and cooling systems.

ambient air temperature: Temperature of air surrounding an air-conditioned unit such as a vehicle, measured 2 inches in front of the condenser.

ambient switch: An outside air-sensing switch used to control compressor clutch operation and prevent compressor operation at low temperatures when air conditioning is not required.

atmospheric pressure: Air pressure at a given altitude above sea level. Atmospheric pressure at sea level is 14.696 psi.

back pressure: Pressure in low side of refrigerating system; also called suction pressure or low side pressure.

back seat: Refers to turning the service valve stem all the way to the left and "back seating" the valve. In this position the valve outlet to the system is open and the service port in the valve is closed. This is the normal operating position.

baffle: Plate or vane used to direct or control movement of fluid or air within a confined area.

battery: Electricity-producing cells which use interaction of metals and chemicals to create electrical current flow.

bellows: A sealed accordion-type chamber (gas-filled or evacuated) which expands and contracts in accordance with temperature changes. Used as a control device in air-conditioning systems.

bimetal: An arm made of two dissimilar metals (with different rates of expansion) which flexes in accordance with temperature changes. Used as a control device in air-conditioning systems.

blower fan: A motor-driven fan used to force air through the evaporator and circulate this cooled air through the passenger compartment of the automobile.

boiling point: The temperature at which a liquid changes to a vapor.

bowden cable: A cable or wire inside a metal or rubber housing used to actuate a valve or control from a distance.

British thermal unit (But): Used in measuring the quantity of heat. One Btu is the amount of heat necessary to raise one pound of water one degree Fahrenheit.

calibrate: To position instrument indicators as required to obtain accurate measurements.

calorie: Heat required to raise temperature of one gram of water one degree Celsius.

can valve: A mechanical device used to pierce, dispense, and seal small cans of refrigerant.

capillary tube: A tube with calibrated inside diameter and length (usually gas-filled), used to control the flow of refrigerant. In automotive air conditioning, the tube connecting the remote bulb or coil to the expansion valve or to the thermostat is called the capillary tube.

capacity: Refrigeration produced, measured in tons or Btus per hour.

Celsius: A thermometer scale using the freezing point of water as zero. The boiling point of water is 100°C.

change of state: Rearrangement of the molecular structure of matter as it changes between any two of the three physical states; solid, liquid, or gas.

charge: A specific amount of refrigerant or oil volume or weight.

charging: The act of placing a charge of refrigerant or oil into the air-conditioning system.

charging station: A unit containing a manifold gauge set, charging cylinder, vacuum pump, and leak detector, for servicing air conditioners.

charging hose: A small-diameter hose constructed to withstand high pressures between the unit and manifold set.

chemical instability: An undesirable condition caused by the presence of contaminants in the refrigeration system.

circuit breaker: A bimetal device used instead of a fuse to protect a circuit.

clutch: A coupling device which transfers torque from a driving to a driven member when desired.

clutch armature: That part of the clutch that is pulled in when engaged.

clutch field: Consists of many windings of wire and is fastened to the front of the compressor. Current applied sets up a magnetic field that pulls the armature in to engage the clutch.

clutch rotor: That portion of the clutch that the belt rides in, and is free-wheeling until engaged. On some clutches the field is found in the rotor, the electrical connection being made by the use of brushes.

cold: The absence of heat.

compound gauge: A gauge that will register both pressure and vacuum, used on the low side of the systems.

compressor: A component of the refrigeration system that pumps refrigerant and increases the pressure of refrigerant vapor.

compressor displacement: A figure obtained by multiplying displacement of compressor cylinder or cylinders by a given rpm.

compressor shaft seal: An assembly consisting of springs, snap rings, O-rings, shaft seal, seal seat, and gaskets, mounted on the compressor crankshaft permitting the shaft to be turned without loss of refrigerant or oil.

condensate: Water taken from the air which forms on the exterior surface of the evaporator.

condensation: The act of changing a vapor to a liquid.

condenser: The component of a refrigeration system in which refrigerant vapor is changed to a liquid by the removal of heat.

condensing pressure: Head pressure as read from the gauge at the high-side service valve; pressure from the discharge side of the compressor into the condenser.

conduction of heat: The ability of a substance to conduct heat or the passage of heat through such a substance.

contaminants: Anything other than refrigerant and refrigeration oil in the system.

convection: The transfer of heat by the circulation of a vapor or liquid.

cycling clutch system: Referring to a system which uses a clutch, thermostatically controlled, as a means of temperature control.

cylinder: A circular drum used to store refrigerant.

cylinder head: Part which encloses compression end of compressor cylinder.

cylinder, refrigerant: Cylinder in which refrigerant is purchased and dispensed. Color code painted on cylinder indicates kind of refrigerant cylinder contains.

damper: Valve for controlling airflow.

declutching fan: An engine cooling fan mounted on the water pump with a temperature-sensitive device to govern or limit terminal speed.

defrost cycle: Refrigerating cycle in which evaporator frost and ice accumulation is melted.

defrosting: Process of removing frost accumulation from evaporators.

degreasing: Solution or solvent used to remove oil or grease from refrigerator parts.

dehydrated oil: Lubricant which has had most of its water content removed (a dry oil).

dehydrator-receiver: A small tank which serves as liquid refrigerant reservoir and which also contains a desiccant to remove moisture. Used on most automobile air-conditioning installations.

density: Closeness of texture or consistency.

desiccant: A drying agent used in refrigeration systems to remove excess moisture. Common desiccants are activated alumina, silica gel.

design working pressure: The maximum allowable working pressure for which a specific system component is designed to work safely.

diagnosis: The procedure followed to locate the cause of a malfunction.

diaphragm: A rubber-like piston or bellows assembly dividing the inner and outer chambers of back-pressure-regulated air-conditioning control devices.

dichlorodifluoromethane: Refrigerant commonly known as R-12.

discharge: To bleed some or all of the refrigerant from a system by opening a valve or connection and permitting the refrigerant to escape slowly.

discharge air: Conditioned air as it passes through the outlets and enters the passenger compartment.

discharge valve: A device located on the discharge side of the compressor to allow the serviceman to check high-side pressures and perform other necessary operations.

displacement: In automotive air conditioning this refers to the length of compressor piston stroke multiplied by the area of the cylinder bore.

drier: A device containing desiccant placed in the liquid line to absorb moisture in the system. Ordinarily combined with the receiver.

drying agent: A substance used to remove moisture from a refrigeration system.

effective temperature: Overall effect on a human of air temperature, humidity, and air movement.

electromagnet: Made by winding a coil of wire around a soft iron core. When electric current is run through the wire, the coil becomes a magnet.

electronic leak detector: Electronic instrument which measures electronic flow across a gas gap. Electronic flow changes indicate presence of refrigerant gas molecules.

end play: Slight movement of shaft along center line.

equalizer line: A line or connection used specifically for obtaining required operation from certain control valves. Very little, if any, refrigerant flows through this line.

evacuate: To create a vacuum within a system to remove all trace of air and moisture.

evaporation: A change of state from a liquid to a vapor.

evaporator: The component of an air-conditioning system in which refrigerant liquid is changed into a vapor when removing heat from the air discharged into the passenger compartment.

evaporator pressure regulator (EPR valve): A back-pressure-regulated temperature-control device used on the evaporator.

evaporator temperature regulator (ETR valve): A temperature-regulated evaporator temperature-control device.

expansion valve: A device in a refrigerating system which maintains a pressure difference between the high side and low side and is operated by pressure.

external equalizer: Tube connected to low-pressure side of an expansion valve diaphragm and to the exit of the evaporator.

Fahrenheit: A thermometer scale using 32° as the freezing point of water and 212° as the boiling point of water.

fan: A device having two or more blades attached to the shaft of a motor, mounted in the evaporator, which causes air to pass over the evaporator.

field: A coil with many turns of wire located behind the clutch rotor. Current passing through this coil sets up a magnetic field and causes the clutch to engage.

filter: A device used with the drier or as a separate unit to remove foreign material from the refrigerant.

flame test for leaks: Tool which is principally a torch; when an air-refrigerant mixture is fed to flame, this flame will change color in presence of heated copper.

flare: Copper tubing is often connected to parts of refrigerating system by use of flared fittings. These fittings require that the end of tube be expanded at about a 45 degree angle. This flare is firmly gripped by fittings to make a strong leakproof seal.

flare nut: Fitting used to clamp tubing flare against another fitting.

flooding: A condition caused by too much liquid refrigerant being metered into the evaporator.

fluid: A liquid, gas, or vapor.

flush: To remove solid particles such as metal flakes or dirt. Refrigerant passages are purged with refrigerant.

foaming: The formation of a froth of oil and refrigerant due to rapid boiling of the refrigerant dissolved in the oil when the pressure is suddenly reduced. Foam in the sight glass is an indication of a very low refrigerant level.

foot-pound: Unit of energy required to raise one pound one foot. A tightening torque equal to one pound of force applied at the outer end of a one-foot wrench.

freeze protection: Controlling evaporator temperature so moisture on its surface will not freeze and block the air flow.

freeze-up: Failure of a unit to operate properly due to the formation of ice at the expansion valve orifice or on the evaporator coils or fins.

freezing point: The temperature at which a given liquid will solidify. Water will freeze at 32°F.

Freon 12: Another name for R-12.

front seat: Closing of the compressor service valves by turning them all the way in, clockwise. This position is used only to "isolate" the compressor and the compressor is never operated with valves in this position.

fuse: An electrical device used to protect a circuit against accidental overload or unit malfunction.

gas: Vapor phase or state of a substance.

gauge, high-pressure: Instrument for measuring pressures in the range of 0 psi to 500 psi.

gauge, low-pressure: Instrument for measuring pressures in the range of 0 psi to 50 psi.

gauge, manifold: A device constructed to hold compound and high-pressure gauges, valved to control the flow of fluids through it.

gauge, vacuum: Instrument used to measure pressures below atmospheric pressure.

grommet: A plastic, metal, or rubber doughnut-shaped protector for wires or tubing as they pass through a hole.

ground, short circuit: A fault in an electrical circuit allowing electricity to flow into the metal parts of the structure.

head pressure: Pressure which exists in condensing side of refrigerating system.

heat: Form of energy, the addition of which causes substances to rise in temperature; energy associated with random motion of molecules.

heat exchanger: An apparatus in which heat is transferred from one fluid to another, on the principle that heat will move to an object with less heat.

heat intensity: The measurement of heat concentration with a thermometer.

heat transfer: Movement of heat from one body or substance to another. Heat may be transferred by radiation, conduction, convection, or a combination of these three methods.

heat transmission: Any flow of heat.

heating control: Device which controls the temperature of a heat transfer unit which releases heat.

Hg: Chemical symbol for mercury. Used in reference to vacuum (inches of Hg).

high head: A term used when the head, or high-side, pressure of the system is excessive.

high load condition: Refers to times when the air conditioner must operate continuously at maximum capacity to provide the cool air required.

high pressure cut-out: Electrical control switch-operated by the high-side pressure, which automatically opens the electrical circuit if excessive head pressure or condensing pressure is reached.

high-pressure lines: The lines from the compressor outlet to the expansion valve inlet that carry high pressure liquid and gas.

high suction: Low-side pressure higher than normal due to a malfunction of the system.

high-vacuum pump: A two-state vacuum pump that has the capability of pulling below 500 microns. Many vacuum pumps will pull to 25 microns of mercury.

horsepower: A unit of power equal to 33,000 foot-pounds of work per minute. One electrical horsepower equals 746 watts.

hot gas: The condition of the refrigerant as it leaves the compressor until it gives up its heat and condenses.

humidity: Moisture; dampness. Relative humidity is the ratio of the quantity of vapor present in air to the greatest amount possible at given temperature.

hydrolizing action: The corrosive action within the air-conditioning system induced by a weak solution of hydrochloric acid formed by excessive moisture reacting with the refrigerant chemically.

hydrometer: Floating instrument used to measure specific gravity of a liquid. Specific gravity is the ratio of weight of equal volume of substance used as a standard.

idler: A pulley used on some belt-drives to provide the proper belt tension and to eliminate belt vibration.

inches of mercury: A unit of measurement in reference to a vacuum (inches of Hg).

inch-pound: Unit of energy required to raise one pound one inch. A tightening torque equal to one pound of force applied at the outer end of a one-inch wrench.

insulation, thermal: Substance used to retard or slow flow of heat through a wall or partition.

intermittent cycle: A cycle which repeats itself at different intervals.

Kelvin scale (K): Thermometer scale on which a unit of measurement equals the Celsius degree and uses absolute zero ($-273°C$) as $0°$. Water freezes at $273°K$ and boils at $373°K$.

kilowatt: Unit of electrical power, equal to 1000 watts.

latent heat: Heat energy absorbed or released while changing state (melting, vaporization, fusion) without change in temperature or pressure.

latent heat of condensation: The quantity of heat given off while changing a substance from vapor to a liquid at the same temperature.

latent heat of evaporation: The quantity of heat required to change a liquid into a vapor without raising the temperature of the vapor above that of the original liquid.

leak detector: Device or instrument such as a halide torch, an electronic sniffer, or soap solution used to detect leaks.

limit control: Control used to open or close electrical circuits as temperature or pressure limits are reached.

liquid line: Line connecting the drier outlet with the expansion valve inlet. The line from the condenser outlet to the drier inlet is sometimes referred to as a liquid line also.

load: The required rate of heat removal in a given time.

low head pressure: High-side pressure lower than normal due to a malfulction of the system.

low side: That portion of a refrigerating system which is under the lowest evaporating pressure.

low-side service valve: A device located on the suction side of the compressor to allow the serviceman to check low-side pressures or perform other necessary service operations.

low-side pressure: Pressure in cooling side of refrigerating cycle.

low-side pressure control: Device used to keep the low-side evaporating pressure from dropping below a certain pressure.

low suction pressure: Pressure lower than normal in the suction side of the system due to a malfunction of the unit.

lubricant: Highly refined oil free from all contaminants, such as sulfur, moisture, and tars.

magnetic clutch: A device operated by magnetism to connect or disconnect a power drive.

manifold gauge: A calibrated instrument used for measuring pressures of the system.

manifold gauge set: A manifold complete with gauges and charging hoses.

melting point: The temperature and pressure above which a solid changes to a liquid.

methyl chloride (R-40): A chemical once commonly used as a refrigerant. Cylinder color code is orange. The boiling point at atmospheric pressure is $-10.4°F$.

metric system: A decimal system of measures and weights, based on the meter and gram. The length of one meter is 39.38 inches.

micron: A unit of measure: 1,000 microns equal 1 millimeter.

modulating: A type of device or control which tends to adjust by increments (minute changes) rather than by either full-on or full-off operation.

monochlorodifluoromethane: A refrigerant used in some early automotive applications. Not used today because of high pressure.

muffler, compressor: Sound absorber chamber in a refrigeration system used to reduce the sound of gas pulsations.

natural convection: Movement of a fluid caused by temperature differences.

neoprene: A synthetic rubber which is resistant to deterioration by hydrocarbon oil and gas.

neutralizer: Substance used to counteract acids in a refrigeration system.

nonferrous: Group of metals and metal alloys which contain no iron.

normal charge: The thermal element charge which is part liquid and part gas under all operating conditions.

oil bleed line: An external line bypassing the evaporator pressure regulator or bypass valve to insure positive oil return to the compressor at high speeds and under a low charge or clogged system condition.

oil bleed passage: Internal orifice bypassing an expansion valve, evaporator pressure regulator, or bypass valve to insure positive oil return to the compressor.

overcharge: Too much refrigerant or refrigeration oil in the refrigeration system.

performance test: The taking of temperature and pressure readings under controlled conditions to determine if an air-conditioning system is operating at full efficiency.

POA value: Pilot Operated Absolute valve. A suction throttling valve used on some types of air-conditioning systems.

power servo: A vacuum or electrically operated servo unit used to operate duct doors and switches on air-conditioning systems with automatic temperature control.

pressure: Force per unit of area. Pressure of refrigerant, for example. is measured in pounds per square inch (psi).

propane: A flammable gas used in the torch-type leak detectors.

psi: Abbreviation for pounds per square inch.

pulley: A flat wheel with a V-groove machined around its outer edge and attached to the driveshaft and driven members to enable the compressor to be driven by a V-belt.

pump: The compressor (and also a vacuum pump) when related to automotive air conditioning.

purge: To remove moisture and air from a system or a component by flushing with a dry gas refrigerant.

radiation: The passage of heat through air or space without heating of this intervening substance.

Rankine: A thermometer using a scale for the freezing point of water.

ram air: Air that is forced through the condenser coils by the movement of the vehicle or action of the fan.

receiver-drier: A combination container for the storage of liquid refrigerant and a drying agent.

reciprocating compressor: A positive-displacement compressor with pistons that travel back and forth in a cylinder.

reed valves: Thin leaves of steel located in the valve plate of automotive compressors to act as suction and discharge valves. The suction valve is located on the bottom of the valve plate and the discharge on top.

refrigerant: The chemical compound used in a refrigeration system to produce the desired cooling.

refrigerant-12: The refrigerant used in automotive air conditioners.

refrigerant-22: A refrigerant used in some early automotive applications, but rarely used today due to high pressures.

refrigeration cycle: The complete circulation of refrigerant through an air-conditioning system accompanied by changes in temperature and pressure.

refrigeration oil: Highly refined oil free from all contaminants, such as sulfur, moisture, and tars.

relative humidity: The actual moisture content of the air in relation to the total moisture that the air can hold at a given temperature.

remote bulb: A sensing device connected to the expansion valve by a capillary tube to sense tailpipe temperature and transmit pressure to the expansion valve for its operation.

resistor: A voltage-dropping device, usually wire-wound to provide a means of controlling fan speeds.

saturated vapor: Saturation indicates that the space holds just as much vapor as it possibly can. No further vaporization is possible at this particular temperature.

Schrader valve: A spring-loaded valve similar to a tire valve located inside the service valve fitting and used on some control devices to hold refrigerant in the system. Special adapters must be used with the gauge hose to allow access to the system.

screen: A metal mesh located in the receiver, expansion valve, and compressor inlet to prevent particles of dirt from being circulated through the system.

sensible heat: Heat that causes a change in temperature of a substance but not a change of state.

sensors: Temperature-sensitive units used to sense air temperatures and provide a control voltage for operation of automatic-temperature-control-type air-conditioning systems.

service port: A fitting on the service valves and some control devices to allow manifold set charging hoses to be connected.

short cycling: A condition caused by poor air circulation or a thermostat out of adjustment, causing the air-conditioning unit to run for very short periods.

sight glass: A window in the liquid line or on top of the drier used to observe the liquid refrigerant flow.

silica gel: A drying agent used in air-conditioning systems to remove moisture from the refrigerant. It is usually located in the receiver-drier.

specifications: Information provided by the manufacturer that describes an air-conditioning system and its function.

specific heat: The quantity of heat required to change one pound of a substance one degree Fahrenheit.

suction line: The line connecting the evaporator outlet to the compressor inlet.

suction side: That portion of the refrigeration system under low pressure, extending from the expansion valve to the compressor inlet.

suction throttling valve: A back-pressure-regulated device that prevents evaporator core freezing.

suction pressure: Compressor inlet pressure; that is, the pressure on the low side.

superheat: Adding heat to a gas after complete evaporation of a liquid.

system: All of the components and lines which together make up a complete air-conditioning system.

tailpipe: The outlet pipe from the evaporator to the compressor.

temperature: Heat intensity measured on a thermometer.

thermistor: A temperature-sensitive unit.

thermostatic switch: A temperature-sensitive switch used to control the compressor clutch and cycle the compressor as a means of temperature control in an air-conditioning system.

thermostatic expansion valve: A component of a refrigeration system that regulates the rate of flow of refrigerant into the evaporator as governed by action of the remote bulb sensing tailpipe temperatures.

total heat load: The human heat load, plus heat entering through the floor, glass, roof, and sides.

torque: A turning force, such as that required to seal a connection, measured in foot-pounds or inch-pounds.

transducer: An electrically controlled vacuum valve used to transform the sensor control voltage into a regulated vacuum for operation of the vacuum-type power servo in an automatic-temperature-control-type air-conditioning system.

undercharge: A system short of refrigerant which will result in improper cooling.

vacuum: Referring to less than atmospheric pressure, usually expressed in inches of mercury (Hg).

vacuum power unit: A device for operating doors and valves of an air conditioner using vacuum as a source of power.

vacuum pump: A mechanical device used to evacuate the refrigeration system to rid it of excess moisture and air.

vapor: A gas, specifically, the gaseous state of refrigerant.

vapor lines: Lines in an air-conditioning system in which the refrigerant is normally in a gaseous or vapor state.

viscosity: The thickness of a liquid or its resistance to flow.

volatile liquid: One that evaporates readily to become a vapor.

water valve: A shutoff valve, mechanically or vacuum operated, for stopping the flow of hot water to the automotive heater.

Woodruff key: An index key used to prevent a pulley from turning on a shaft.

Index